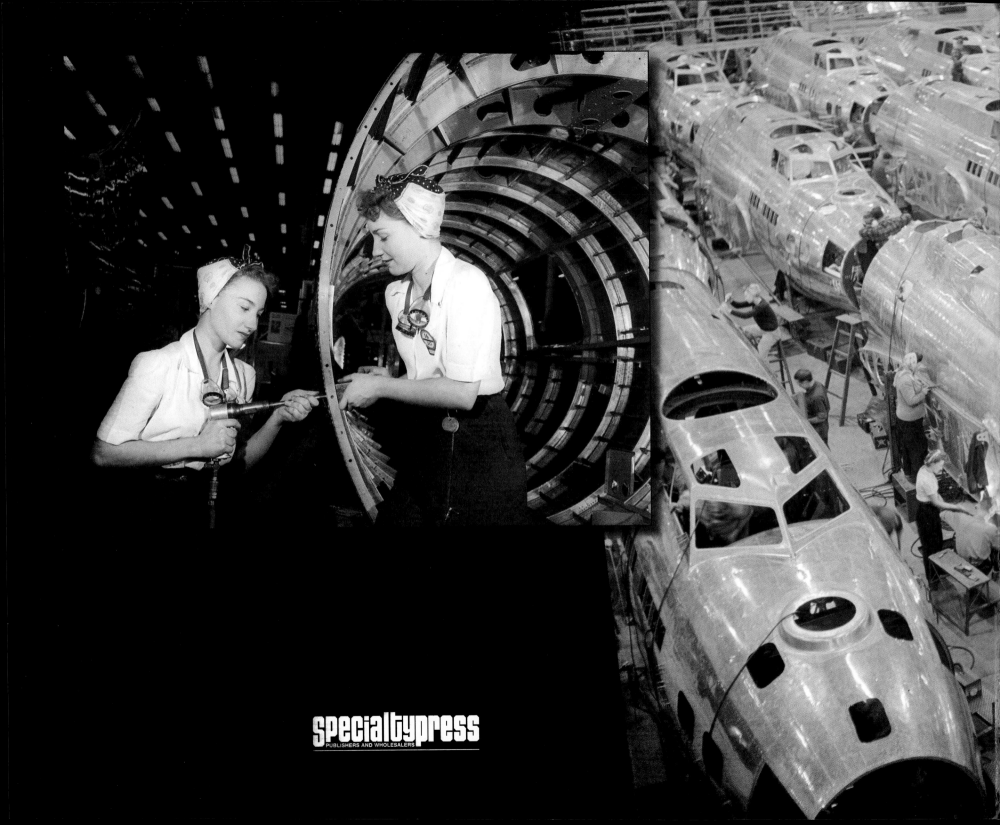

BUILDING THE B-17
FLYING FORTRESS

Bill Yenne

A Detailed Look at Manufacturing Boeing's Legendary World War II Bomber in Original Photos

Specialty Press
6118 Main Street
North Branch, MN 55056
Phone: 651-277-1400 or 800-895-4585
Fax: 651-277-1203
www.specialtypress.com

The information in this work is true and complete to the best of our knowledge. However, all information is presented without any guarantee on the part of the Author or Publisher, who also disclaim any liability incurred in connection with the use of the information and any implied warranties of merchantability or fitness for a particular purpose. Readers are responsible for taking suitable and appropriate safety measures when performing any of the operations or activities described in this work.

All trademarks, trade names, model names and numbers, and other product designations referred to herein are the property of their respective owners and are used solely for identification purposes. This work is a publication of Specialty Press, and has not been licensed, approved, sponsored, or endorsed by any other person or entity. The publisher is not associated with any product, service, or vendor mentioned in this book, and does not endorse the products or services of any vendor mentioned in this book.

Publisher's Note: In reporting history, the images required to tell the tale will vary greatly in quality, especially by modern photographic standards. While some images in this volume are not up to those digital standards, we have included them, as we feel they are an important element in telling the story.

Edit by Mike Machat
Layout by Monica Seiberlich

ISBN 978-1-58007-271-7
Item No. SP271

Library of Congress Cataloging-in-Publication Data Available

Written, edited, and designed in the U.S.A.
Printed in China
10 9 8 7 6 5 4 3 2

Frontispiece: *Betty McDonald performs electrical work at the bombardier's station inside the nose of B-17F on the ramp at the Vega Aircraft Company plant in Burbank, California.*

Title page: *Work is in progress on fuselage sections for B-17F Flying Fortresses on the factory floor at Boeing's Plant 2 at Boeing Field in Seattle. US Office of War Information photographer Andreas Feininger took this photo in December 1942 as the production line was changing over from the Block 50 B-17Fs to the Block 55 series of aircraft. Boeing production of this variant continued through Block 85 and included 2,300 B-17Fs. (Photo by Andreas Feininger, Library of Congress)*

Title page (inset left): *Sisters at work in the Vega Aircraft plant in Burbank, California, in 1942. Jean and Joan Wickmire rivet the aluminum skin of a B-17F from the inside out.*

Title page (inset right): *Edward Curtiss Wells, project engineer for the Flying Fortress program, studies the first installation of a Sperry Ball Turret in February 1941. (Boeing Photo Courtesy Mike Lombardi)*

Table of contents: *Inside the flight deck of a restored B-17G-85-DL Flying Fortress. (Photo by Bill Yenne)*

DISTRIBUTION BY:
Europe
PGUK
63 Hatton Garden
London EC1N 8LE, England
Phone: 020 7061 1980 • Fax: 020 7242 3725
www.pguk.co.uk

Australia
Renniks Publications Ltd.
3/37-39 Green Street
Banksmeadow, NSW 2109, Australia
Phone: 2 9695 7055 • Fax: 2 9695 7355
www.renniks.com

Canada
Login Canada
300 Saulteaux Crescent
Winnipeg, MB, R3J 3T2 Canada
Phone: 800 665 1148 • Fax: 800 665 0103
www.lb.ca

TABLE OF CONTENTS

NOTES ON FLYING FORTRESS DESIGNATIONS

The basic military designation of the Flying Fortress was "B-17," which originated in the US Army Air Corps sequence of bomber designations. Although, Boeing assigned it unofficially for its own first XB-17 prototype. The designation thereafter became official and continued to be used through the production run of the aircraft.

The "X" prefix designates an experimental aircraft. In this case, there was a single XB-17, which was owned and unofficially designated by the manufacturer. The "Y" prefix designated a service test aircraft, and a "Y1" prefix designated a service test aircraft acquired with supplemental fiscal year funding.

Suffixes, beginning with "A," identify each variant of the aircraft. In the case of the Flying Fortress, they were manufactured in variants up through B-17G. No Flying Fortresses were manufactured with higher letter designations, although some B-17G and earlier aircraft were redesignated by the United States Army Air Forces (USAAF) and United States Air Force (USAF) with higher letters. (Those are discussed at the end of Chapter 8.)

Except for the lone XB-17, all Flying Fortresses were ordered under US Army contracts and given US Army serial numbers. Some were transferred to Britain's Royal Air Force and redesignated as Fortress Mk. I through Fortress Mk. IIIA, and those are discussed herein. Some were transferred to the US Navy and redesignated as "PB" for Patrol, Boeing. (Those are discussed at the end of Chapter 8.)

Probably the most complicated designations came within the production blocks for the B-17F and B-17G. These were manufactured by three separate manufacturers and delivered in 104 separate blocks, which are listed in detail in Appendix II. Some blocks contained a handful of individual aircraft, while others contained more—as many as 100 or 200.

The designation for each of these 104 blocks was specific to that block. For example, Boeing blocks for the B-17F ran from 1 to 130 and from 1 to 110 for the B-17G. A Boeing Block 40 B-17F carried the full designation B-17F-40-BO. This includes "B-17F" for the basic type, "40" for Block 40, and "BO," which was the manufacturer's code for "Boeing, Seattle."

Meanwhile, a Block 40 B-17F from Vega was designated as B-17F-40-VE. Obviously, the "VE" is Vega's manufacturer's code. For a Douglas Block 40 B-17F, it would be B-17F-40-DL because they were manufactured by Douglas in Long Beach, California. Vega had one factory and one manufacturer's code, while Douglas had a code for each of its factories: "DA" for Chicago, "SE" for El Segundo, "DK" for Oklahoma City, "DO" for Santa Monica, and "DT" for Tulsa. B-17s were made by Douglas only in Long Beach.

In turn, B-17G blocks followed the same pattern as the B-17F: B-17G-1-BO through B-17G-110-BO for Boeing; B-17G-1-VE through B-17G-110-VE for Vega; and B-17G-5-DL through B-17G-95-DL for Douglas.

NOTES ON NOMENCLATURE OF US MILITARY ORGANIZATIONS

(1) The organization operating the B-17 Flying Fortress went through several name changes during the period covered by this book:

Service Name	Date Formed
US Army Air Service	May 24, 1918
US Army Air Corps	July 2, 1926
US Army Air Forces	June 20, 1941
US Air Force	September 18, 1947

(2) The organization within (1) above that participated in development of the B-17 Flying Fortress went through several name changes during the period covered by this book:

Organization Name	Date Formed
Engineering Division (HQ McCook Field, Ohio)	Circa 1919
Materiel Division (HQ Wright Field, Ohio)	October 15, 1926
Chief of Materiel Division to Washington	October 1939
Materiel Command (HQ Washington, DC) [Wright Field then became Materiel Center of Materiel Command]	March 9, 1942
Materiel Command (HQ Wright Field) [Materiel Command's Washington Office became "Assistant Chief of Air Staff, Materiel, Maintenance, & Distribution" (AC/AS MM&D) [on this date.]	March 29, 1943
Technical Service Command (HQ Wright Field)	August 31, 1944
Materiel Command and Air Service Command were merged	September 1, 1944
Air Technical Service Command (HQ Wright Field)	July 1, 1945
Air Materiel Command (HQ Wright Field, Wright-Patterson AFB from 1947)	March 9, 1946
Air Force Logistics Command (HQ Wright Patterson AFB)	April 1, 1961

The center of activity for the Materiel Command, its predecessor and successor organizations, was at Wright Field, near Dayton, Ohio. The term "Wright Field" was often used informally as a synonym for the formal name of the organization.

BOEING AIRCRAFT COMPANY OR BOEING AIRPLANE COMPANY?

These two names for what would seem to be the same thing are often used interchangeably, and this requires clarification. The entity that we know as Boeing was born in 1916 as the Pacific Aero Products Company and became the Boeing Airplane Company in 1917.

In 1927, company founder William Edward Boeing started the airline Boeing Air Transport (BAT). A year later, he acquired Pacific Air Transport (PAT), and created the Boeing Airplane & Transport Corporation (BATC) as a holding company for BAT and PAT, as well as the Boeing Airplane Company. Through 1931, he acquired several new manufacturing and airline subsidiaries and merged all of his airlines into an entity called United Air Lines. He created the United Aircraft & Transport Corporation (UATC) as a holding company for everything.

In 1934, when companies were forbidden to own both airlines and planemakers, UATC was broken up. The Boeing Airplane Company was then reorganized as a corporate holding company to hold the manufacturing subsidiaries of UATC that included Boeing Airplane Company, Stearman Aircraft, and Boeing Aircraft of Canada.

As Boeing historian Michael Lombardi said, "The original manufacturing company known as the Boeing Airplane Company was renamed the Boeing Aircraft Company on August 28, 1934. Eventually those manufacturing companies were reorganized as divisions of the Boeing Airplane Company . . . the Boeing Aircraft Company was the manufacturing subsidiary of the Boeing Airplane Company from 1934 to 1947. The Boeing Airplane Company became The Boeing Company in May 21, 1961."

ACKNOWLEDGMENTS

The author wishes to thank all of the people who contributed to his interest in the B-17 Flying Fortress through the years and to those who contributed to the completion of this book. It all begins with the author's father, W. J. Yenne, who was working in the parts department on the B-17 program at the Boeing Airplane Company at the time he learned of the attack on Pearl Harbor in 1941 and whose stories about those times lent fire to a passion. Since the author has pursued a career as an aviation writer, many people have assisted on projects related to this subject and related aircraft. They are too many to mention them all, but they certainly include Marilyn Phipps, Tom Lubbesmeyer, Eric Schulzinger, Erik Simonsen, Richard Wolf of the Air Force Historical Support Division, and Patricia McGinnis of Boeing in Long Beach.

Those deserving of the biggest thanks include Mike Machat, the editor who commissioned this book; Boeing Historian Mike Lombardi, whose kindness, patience, and assistance through many years is vastly appreciated; and finally, J. A. (Bill) Saavedra of the Air Force Historical Support Division, whose tireless and enthusiastic support across a multitude of projects through the years cannot be measured. It is with great sadness that I commemorate the passing of Bill Saavedra at the midpoint of this project.

ABOUT THE AUTHOR

Bill Yenne is the San Francisco–based author of more than two dozen books on military and historical topics. He is also a member of the American Aviation Historical Society, and he has contributed to encyclopedias of World War I and World War II. His work has been selected for the official Chief of Staff of the Air Force Reading List, and he is the recipient of the Air Force Association's Gill Robb Wilson Award for his "most outstanding contribution in the field of arts and letters, [and for his] work of over two dozen airpower-themed books, and for years of effort shaping how many people understand and appreciate airpower."

The *Wall Street Journal* observed that Yenne writes with "cinematic vividness" and described his historical writing as having "the rare quality of being both an excellent reference work and a pleasure to read."

Walter J. Boyne, the former head of the Smithsonian National Air and Space Museum, recommended Mr. Yenne's work. He wrote, "I can guarantee that you will be engaged by his master storytelling from his opening words to the very last page."

Mr. Yenne's extensive writings about aviation and aerospace history include several distinct corporate histories of the Boeing Company that have been published over many years as well as corporate histories of Convair, Lockheed, McDonnell Douglas, North American, and Rockwell International.

Aviation biographies penned by Mr. Yenne include *Hap Arnold: The General Who Invented the US Air Force*, a book that General Craig McKinley, president of the Air Force Association, described as doing "a superior job helping the reader better understand General Arnold," and his dual biography of Dick Bong and Tommy McGuire titled *Aces High: The Heroic Story of the Two Top-Scoring American Aces of World War II*, which was described by pilot and best-selling author Dan Roam as "The greatest flying story of all time."

Mr. Yenne has appeared in documentaries airing on the History Channel, the National Geographic Channel, the Smithsonian Channel, ARD German Television, and NHK Japanese Television. His book signings have been covered by C-SPAN.

Visit him on the web at BillYenne.com.

Rosie the Riveter (or in this case, Rosie the skilled electrician) is at work inside the blown-Plexiglas nose of a B-17F. With the exception of the flat bomb aiming panel on the bottom, the B-17F nose was a single piece of Plexiglas. This feature distinguished this variant from the B-17E nose with its multiple Plexiglas panels. (Photo by Alfred Palmer, Library of Congress)

INTRODUCTION

The Boeing B-17 Flying Fortress is well remembered as one of the greatest aircraft in aviation history, rating a place at or near the top of almost any aviation historian's short list of the best of the best. It certainly ranks high in the pantheon of the greats from World War II.

William Green, perhaps the foremost aviation historian of the early postwar generation, wrote that "few other aircraft of the Second World War gained the universal affection of their aircrew over so long an operational period as did the Boeing B-17 Fortress, which formed the spearhead of the American bombing offensive in Europe from beginning to end, as well as serving in every other theater of war. No single aircraft type contributed more to the defeat of the Luftwaffe, both in the air and on the ground."

It was, at least in the European Theater of World War II, the preeminent symbol of the doctrine of strategic airpower. It led the way in the strategic air offensive, which reached into the heart of the Third Reich to systematically disassemble its war economy and ability to feed weapons and equipment into its once-invincible war machine.

The production of 12,731 B-17 Flying Fortresses, most of them in a span of three and a half years, was itself the product of an immense war economy that mushroomed from modest beginnings to become part of a broad-ranging industrial phenomena the likes of which the world had never seen.

As an author, I have written extensively about American military aviation in World War II and beyond. I have written at least a half dozen books that focus on the combat career of the B-17 Flying Fortress, and I have written about the staggering scale of the growth and accomplishments of the American aircraft industry during this greatest of global wars.

I have found my focusing upon the Flying Fortress to be an amazing experience. Looking at the combat history of the Flying Fortress and the individual stories of those 12,731 distinct airplanes is truly breathtaking. Likewise was the experience of looking at the production history of those aircraft. The scope is hard to grasp. It is like trying to wrap your mind around counting stars in the sky or grains of sand at the beach. Yet, they were not grains of sand.

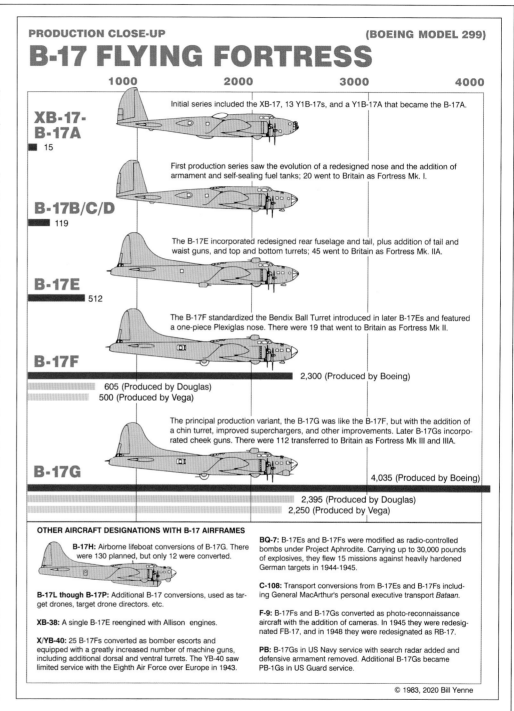

PRODUCTION CLOSE-UP (BOEING MODEL 299)

B-17 FLYING FORTRESS

1000   2000   3000   4000

XB-17-B-17A — ■ 15
Initial series included the XB-17, 13 Y1B-17s, and a Y1B-17A that became the B-17A.

B-17B/C/D — 119
First production series saw the evolution of a redesigned nose and the addition of armament and self-sealing fuel tanks; 20 went to Britain as Fortress Mk. I.

B-17E — 512
The B-17E incorporated redesigned rear fuselage and tail, plus addition of tail and waist guns, and top and bottom turrets; 45 went to Britain as Fortress Mk. IIA.

B-17F
The B-17F standardized the Bendix Ball Turret introduced in later B-17Es and featured a one-piece Plexiglas nose. There were 19 that went to Britain as Fortress Mk II.

2,300 (Produced by Boeing)
605 (Produced by Douglas)
500 (Produced by Vega)

B-17G
The principal production variant, the B-17G was like the B-17F, but with the addition of a chin turret, improved superchargers, and other improvements. Later B-17Gs incorporated cheek guns. There were 112 transferred to Britain as Fortress Mk III and IIIA.

4,035 (Produced by Boeing)
2,395 (Produced by Douglas)
2,250 (Produced by Vega)

OTHER AIRCRAFT DESIGNATIONS WITH B-17 AIRFRAMES

B-17H: Airborne lifeboat conversions of B-17G. There were 130 planned, but only 12 were converted.

B-17L though B-17P: Additional B-17 conversions, used as target drones, target drone directors. etc.

XB-38: A single B-17E reengined with Allison engines.

X/YB-40: 25 B-17Fs converted as bomber escorts and equipped with a greatly increased number of machine guns, including additional dorsal and ventral turrets. The YB-40 saw limited service with the Eighth Air Force over Europe in 1943.

BQ-7: B-17Es and B-17Fs were modified as radio-controlled bombs under Project Aphrodite. Carrying up to 30,000 pounds of explosives, they flew 15 missions against heavily hardened German targets in 1944-1945.

C-108: Transport conversions from B-17Es and B-17Fs including General MacArthur's personal executive transport *Bataan*.

F-9: B-17Fs and B-17Gs converted as photo-reconnaissance aircraft with the addition of cameras. In 1945 they were redesignated FB-17, and in 1948 they were redesignated as RB-17.

PB: B-17Gs in US Navy service with search radar added and defensive armament removed. Additional B-17Gs became PB-1Gs in US Guard service.

© 1983, 2020 Bill Yenne

They were complex mechanisms containing numerous complex submechanisms—and they were a moving target because they and their subcomponents were constantly and quickly changing and evolving.

The Flying Fortress was not the most-produced airplane of World War II—not even in the top ten. Nor was it even the most produced four-engine American bomber, a distinction that belonged to the B-24 Liberator. Nevertheless, the fact that this is an amazing story among amazing stories (from an era in aviation manufacturing that had never been seen before and will never be seen again) only underscores the importance of this narrative.

The Flying Fortress story is a production story tempered by both speed and complexity. The swiftness of production during World War II is hard to comprehend. In looking at the most-produced aircraft in the world today, the Cessna 172 tops the list. More than 44,000 have been built and production is still going strong, but it has been spread out over more than 60 years. Boeing itself has produced more than 10,000 variations on its 737 jetliner, but they have come off the assembly lines over more than half a century.

The building of the Flying Fortress was in a completely distinct realm of scheduling. There were 512 B-17Es built in 8 months, 3,405 B-17Fs produced in 12 months, and 8,680 B-17Gs rolled out in 26 months. By 1944, Boeing had achieved a monthly total in excess of 360 aircraft and actually had days when its vast Plant 2 complex rolled out as many as 16 in a single day.

This incredible production accomplishment was not achieved on one endless assembly line spinning out identical machines, one after another. In fact, there were three assembly lines, owned and operated by three rival companies (Boeing, Douglas Aircraft in Santa Monica, and the Vega Aircraft division of Lockheed in Burbank, California) that comprised the BDV Committee, an amazing entity in itself.

Nor was the design of these aircraft static. The B-17F was produced in 56 individual and distinct production blocks, and the B-17G in 48. Each block incorporated many changes that had to be standardized across three companies. Often, the changes appeared mid-block and almost always on different assembly lines at different times—yet, it worked.

It was not just the coordination of the building of the airplanes themselves, components and subassemblies came from countless subcontractors and suppliers throughout the country. Keeping track of such esoteric components as Type B-2 landing light relays, AiResearch 2R6697 engine oil coolers, Type AN5735 directional gyro indicators, and thousands of others was a monumental challenge, especially in an era without the sort of computing power we now take for granted.

Of course, all of the components and subassemblies, such as the overall aircraft—never mind the Wright Cyclone engines—went through numerous changes, dozens at every block turn, boggling the mind in a "grains of sand" way.

Of course, these components themselves often came from multiple suppliers. For instance, the AN/APT-2 L-Band transmitter was delivered by both Delco Electronics and Hudson American, and components went through multiple changes themselves, often being eliminated or superseded by entirely different equipment. All of this required minute coordination.

Meanwhile, every iota of work on the airplanes and the subassemblies, as well as the vast progression of necessary machine tools that made them, originated with people exhaustively executing drawings with India ink

Workers inside the nose section of a B-17F-50-BO attach components just behind Bulkhead 2, which separated this area from the flight deck. (Photo by Andreas Feininger, Library of Congress)

on drafting vellum. In turn, all the work through the entire process had to be done without access to the simplest electronic computer or even something as elementary as a handheld pocket calculator. In turn, it had to be coordinated on a daily (often minute by minute) basis without access to email or text massaging.

In the context of how well the finished Flying Fortresses cared for their crews and executed their missions, it is easy to overlook all the underlying nuances—all the minute grains of sand. When one really pauses to consider all of this and how hard it would ever be to replicate, even with 21st-century technology, it is easy to think of building the B-17 being nothing short of miraculous.

The four Wright R-1840 Cyclone engines come to life as this B-17F-50-BO prepares to depart Boeing Field on its delivery flight. (Photo by Andreas Feininger, Library of Congress)

Chapter 1

SETTING THE STAGE FOR THE FLYING FORTRESS

The Boeing B-17 Flying Fortress would not have existed without the doctrine of strategic airpower, a precept that began to evolve in the early days of the use of aircraft in warfare. Aviation technology grew gradually in the first years of the 20th century, but the pace of the development of aircraft as war machines quickened as World War I started. Air-to-air combat began with men in observation planes taking potshots at one another and quickly evolved into aircraft armed with synchronized machine guns. Aerial bombardment, meanwhile, started before the war. In 1911, Italy was at war with the Ottoman Empire over Libya when Italian pilot Giulio Gavotti dropped a few hand grenade–sized bombs on Turkish positions, thus beginning the use of aircraft as offensive weapons on the battlefield.

Nevertheless, as World War I unfolded, the men who wrote the overarching strategic doctrine still considered aircraft to be novelties when it came to the serious business of military operations. Apropos the attacking of an enemy on the ground, the prevailing school of thought is perhaps best summarized by an article that appeared in *Scientific American* in October 1910. It was concluded that "outside of scouting duties, we are inclined to think that the field of usefulness of the aeroplane will be rather limited. Because of its small carrying capacity and the necessity for its operating at great altitude, if it is to escape hostile fire, the amount of damage it will do by dropping explosives upon cities, forts, hostile camps, or bodies of troops in the field to say nothing of battleships at sea, will be so limited as to have no material effects on the issues of a campaign."

Gradually, though, bomber aircraft began to demonstrate their usefulness, producing small but measurable results against forts, hostile camps, and bodies of troops in the field. This was the birth of "tactical" airpower, the use of bombers as part of an integrated air-land battlefield action at or near the front and in direct support of friendly ground troops in the field. The prevailing view at the time among senior military leadership was that airpower was simply another means of accomplishing the land army mission, tasks for which commanders had long used artillery.

However, at the middle levels of military establishments around the world, there were eager young airpower advocates who did not hold themselves bound to the established strategic doctrine of the past. They started to imagine a doctrine in which aircraft could reach beyond the front lines and deep into an enemy's heartland, striking his factories and transportation network, thus compromising his ability to wage war. This was "strategic" airpower.

General William Lendrum "Billy" Mitchell, an airpower visionary, was one of the early advocates of the doctrine of using strategic airpower to defeat an enemy's war economy from the inside by striking its ability to produce war machines. He started the US Army Air Service on the technological development road that led to the B-17 Flying Fortress. (Photo Courtesy USAF)

Sikorsky's Ilya Muromets was the world's first operational four-engine bomber. Built in St. Petersburg by the Russo-Baltic Wagon Factory, it was flying operational long-range strategic missions in the first year of World War I.

As the war began, most heavier-than-air aircraft did not have the range to do this, but Britain and Germany used enormous airships to conduct raids against one another. These operations continued throughout the war, and the Germans also attacked targets in Belgium, France, and elsewhere.

It was Igor Sikorsky, the Russian aviation pioneer who later became an icon of American aviation, who designed the first long-range bomber with four engines. Built

Igor Ivanovich Sikorsky was a Russian aviation pioneer who created a four-engine airplane in 1913 and the first operational four-engine bomber a year later. Having immigrated to the USA after World War I, he became a pioneer in helicopter development.

under his direction at the Russo-Baltic Carriage Factory in St. Petersburg, this aircraft made its debut flight in 1913. It was named Ilya Muromets (after a heroic knight from Russian folklore) and was built under a series of designations ranging from S-22 through S-27.

Sikorsky's big ship was 57 feet 5 inches long and had a wingspan of 97 feet 9 inches, making it a giant for its era. Foreshadowing future heavy bombers, it had several machine gun turrets, including one in the tail. By the end of 1914, the Imperial Russian Air Service had a 10-ship squadron that began operations in February 1915. The bomb load of each bomber exceeded half a ton, and with a range of nearly 400 miles, they were able to hit targets well behind German lines. The Russians conducted over 400 raids, but in the end, other factors intervened. After initial victories, the Russian army was defeated on the ground by 1917, the Tsar had abdicated, and the events leading to the Russian Revolution were rapidly underway.

The largest of German strategic bombers was the Gothaer Waggonfabrik Gotha G.IV, a twin-engine bomber. It had its debut in 1916, and 230 were built. They each had a wingspan of 77 feet 9 inches and were 40 feet long. With a range of 500 miles and a bomb load of 1,100 pounds, the G.IV fleet was used extensively for raids on the United Kingdom, especially in 1917.

Britain's own reciprocal strategic air operations against Germany hit their stride in 1918, with ambitions to strike deep into enemy territory. The largest of the British heavy bombers was the Handley Page Type O, a twin-engine aircraft that entered service in 1916. It was nearly 63 feet long and had a wingspan of 100 feet. It carried 2,000 pounds of bombs and had a range of 700 miles. In April 1918, shortly after being established as an independent service, Britain's Royal Air Force (RAF) conducted a series of raids on German cities in the Ruhr. They even ranged as far south as Frankfurt, though the raids were more of a strategic bombing experiment than a strategic bombing offensive.

The larger, four-engine Handley Page V/1500 carried 7,500 pounds of bombs and had a range sufficient to reach Berlin, but it was not yet in service when the war ended in November 1918. The V/1500 does, however, illustrate how rapidly the technology was evolving.

Watching all of this was Colonel William Lendrum "Billy" Mitchell. He commanded the Air Service of the American Expeditionary Force (AEF), which was in turn commanded by General John J. "Blackjack" Pershing, one of the stellar figures in American military history. Pershing, who graduated from West Point in 1886 and who had fought against the Lakota in the Indian Wars, was a soldier of an earlier generation. Like members of that earlier generation, Pershing saw airpower strictly as tactical ground support, while Mitchell saw the future of airpower as a strategic weapon.

"Aircraft move hundreds of miles in an incredibly short space of time, so that even if they are reported as coming into a country, across its frontiers, there is no telling where they are going to go to strike," Mitchell wrote, describing a method of warfare that was still many years in the future. "Wherever an object can be seen from the air, aircraft are able to hit it with their guns, bombs, and other weapons. Cities and towns, railway lines and canals cannot be hidden. Not only is this the case on land, it is even more the case on the water because on the water no object can be concealed unless it dives beneath the surface."

After the war, Mitchell, now a brigadier general, became the central figure in the crusade for strategic airpower within an American military establishment dominated by men who had entered the service in the 19th century. Most important was that within the Air Service there was a growing number of junior officers who had adopted Mitchell's theories as dogma.

Indeed, within military establishments elsewhere, the doctrine of strategic airpower (like a genie freed from its bottle) had taken on a life of its own. From Giulio Douhet in Italy to Hugh Trenchard in the United Kingdom, Mitchell was not alone in his outspoken advocacy. Among the others was Brigadier General Benjamin Delahauf Foulois, who had served in France

In September 1921, Billy Mitchell's Air Service bombers engaged in a demonstration in Chesapeake Bay in which they successfully attacked US Navy warships. Here, a Martin MB-2 attacks the decommissioned battleship USS Alabama. *The USS* Indiana *is in the background. (Photo Courtesy US Navy)*

First flown in 1923, the Wittemann-Lewis NBL-1 "Barling Bomber" was a huge airplane that turned out to be an underpowered white elephant. Although, it was a step on the path to the Flying Fortress.

with the Air Service and who would command the US Army Air Corps in the early 1930s.

Although Foulois did not often see eye to eye with Mitchell, he nevertheless was a strong advocate of Army airpower. In 1919, Foulois told the Congressional Military Affairs Committee that "the General Staff of the Army is the policy-making body of the Army and, through lack of vision, lack of practical knowledge, or deliberate intention to subordinate the Air Service needs to the needs of the other combat arms, it has utterly failed to appreciate the full military value of this military weapon and, in my opinion, has utterly failed to accord it its just place in our military family."

In the days when battleships were seen as America's first line of defense, Mitchell argued that strategic bombers were cheaper to build and operate than battleships, and they could be used faster and more easily to project American power wherever it might be needed around the world. The US Navy and its admirals were none too pleased.

Mitchell especially angered them in 1921 when he told Congress that his bombers could sink any ship afloat. To prove him wrong, the Navy agreed to let him try out his theories on some captured German warships they had inherited at the end of the war that needed to be disposed of. The rules of engagement were written by the Navy's Atlantic Fleet commander. The Navy would regulate the weight of the bombs and the number of planes, and it reserved the right to call off the engagement at any time. Obviously, these were not restraints that could be imposed upon an enemy in wartime.

In a series of demonstrations held in July 1921, Mitchell's US Army Air Service Martin MB-2 (NBS-1) bombers attacked the German ships anchored in Chesapeake Bay. A destroyer went down, followed by the light cruiser *Frankfurt*, and ultimately the heavily armored battleship *Ostfriesland*. Mitchell had dramatically proven his point. Although certainly surprised, both the US Army and US Navy still remained officially unconvinced of the potential of airpower.

"Aircraft possess the most powerful weapons ever devised by man," Mitchell cautioned. "They carry not only guns and cannon but heavy missiles that utilize the force of gravity for their propulsion and which can cause more destruction than any other weapon. One of these great bombs hitting a battleship will completely destroy it. Consider what this means to the future systems of national defense. As battleships are relatively difficult to destroy, imagine how much easier it is to sink all other vessels and merchant craft."

A formation of US Army Air Corps bombers enter San Francisco Bay over the Golden Gate in April 1930, seven years before the completion of the bridge of the same name. The twin-engine Keystone LB-6 and LB-7 aircraft were standard equipment for Air Corps bomber squadrons in that era.

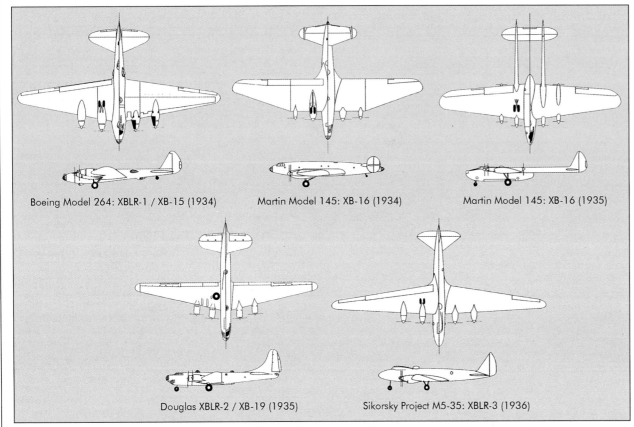

Boeing Model 264: XBLR-1 / XB-15 (1934)   Martin Model 145: XB-16 (1934)   Martin Model 145: XB-16 (1935)

Douglas XBLR-2 / XB-19 (1935)   Sikorsky Project M5-35: XBLR-3 (1936)

The US Army Air Corps Project A program led to the creation of a group of very large aircraft that pushed the limits of creativity at four planemakers. Only the Boeing and Douglas concepts reached the prototype stage.

restrained with airplane design, as Mitchell had been ambitious with his theories. However, one really big aircraft was brought forth to buck the trend.

The Experimental Night Bombardment Long Distance (XNBL-1) was a triplane designed by Walter Barling and built by the firm of Witteman-Lewis Company (also seen as Wittemann-Lewis). Weighing more than 16 tons, the "Barling Bomber" was 65 feet long with a wingspan of 120 feet. As the great aviation historian Ray Wagner wrote, "Three wings, four rudders, six engines, and ten landing wheels gave this behemoth a configuration more likely to antagonize the air than to pass through it."

It was assembled at Wright Field, near Dayton, Ohio, and made its first flight in 1923. It managed a cruising speed of barely 65 mph and had a range of only 170 miles when carrying a bomb load. A demonstration flight to Washington, DC, had to be canceled because the Barling could not get over the Appalachians!

This one really big bomber became a really big failure that hung over the Air Service like a shadow.

Meanwhile, as Mitchell became more

Far from being willing to accord airpower its "just place" in our military family, the US Army establishment seemed reticent to the point of being fearful. In a speech before the National Aeronautical Association in October 1923, Assistant Secretary of War (and later Secretary of War) Dwight Filley Davis portrayed the results of Mitchell's demonstration as having reduced a battleship to a "helpless ruin of tangled iron and steel by a single bomb." He went on to decry the damage to life and property that such a bomb would create if dropped upon a crowded city. Fearing an aerial arms race, he stated that he personally opposed strong offensive airpower, especially in rivalry with other nations.

Against this backdrop, as the US Army Air Service was pushing the prevailing dogma of the War Department, it also pushed the edges of the envelope of technology. When it came to aircraft development, the service had been as

and more outspoken, the Army transferred him from Langley Field in Virginia (too close to Washington for their comfort) to Kelly Field near San Antonio, Texas. In 1925, after the loss of life from the crash of the Navy dirigible *Shenandoah*, Mitchell called the management of national defense by the War and Navy departments "incompetent" and "treasonable." The Army had had enough. Mitchell was court-martialed for insubordination, convicted, reduced to colonel, and drummed out of the service on half pension. He died in 1936, just a few years short of seeing strategic airpower play a key role in the Allied victory in World War II.

Many voices were raised in Mitchell's support. South Carolina Congressman John Jackson McSwain charged the General Staff with "intolerance toward," and "persecution of," officers who dared to side with Mitchell's point of view, adding that the airmen were being "repressed and discouraged,"

The Boeing Model 294 in flight. The Army Air Corps designation was originally XBLR-1, but it was later redesignated as XB-15. The two designations were used interchangeably.

The Boeing Model 294 on the factory floor at Boeing Field in July 1936. At the time, the XBLR-1 designation was in use.

The gun blister on the side of the Boeing Model 294, seen here in March 1937, was similar to that being used on the Model 299, which became the B-17 Flying Fortress.

This detail of the nose turret of the Boeing Model 294, seen here in April 1937, shows a great deal of similarity to that of the Model 299, which made its debut nearly two years earlier.

The Boeing XB-15 makes its first flight over Seattle's Lake Union on October 15, 1937.

Building the B-17 Flying Fortress: A Detailed Look at Manufacturing Boeing's Legendary World War II Bomber in Original Photos

and that officers were being "muzzled and that every one from the grade of Major General to Second Lieutenant, including reserve officers, were subjected either to expulsion from the Army or to the consequences of an 'official frown' for their temerity in disagreeing with the General Staff."

At least one good thing for the airpower advocates came out of the Mitchell court martial. Reacting to pro-Mitchell popular opinion, Congress passed the Air Corps Act of July 1926, which elevated the status of the Air Service through its transformation into the US Army Air Corps. The Act called for a five-year plan to bring the total number of aircraft from 1,450 to an inventory "not to exceed" 1,800, with acquisitions to replace obsolete equipment "not to exceed" 400 annually. As older aircraft were scrapped, the number dipped to 1,000 in 1928 and was still 300 aircraft short of the goal of 1,800 when the plan terminated in 1931. Of the aircraft in service, most were fighters and observation types. There were fewer than 40 bombardment types. The official view of the War Department was that observation planes could be used to drop bombs.

As far as a strategic mission for bombers, that of striking deep into an enemy's war economy, there was still a great deal of opposition. Tactically,

the US Army establishment still saw the mission of its air arm as supporting ground forces. Writing in their 1951 Air Force historical document, *The Development of the Heavy Bomber*, Jean H. DuBuque and Robert Gleckner observed that "the concept that bombardment aviation, acting independently, could control the sea lanes, or defend the coasts, or produce decisive results in any general mission contemplated under the national defense policy, was labeled as 'visionary.'"

In 1934, Secretary of War George Henry Dern (grandfather of actor Bruce Dern) went so far as to declare that "the destruction of armies or populations by aerial bombardment" was the "phantasy [sic] of a dreamer." DuBuque and Robert Gleckner recalled that Dern went on to say that "the procurement of great numbers of airplanes would never protect the American people from a determined foe." Dern asserted that the best protection was to accept and build upon American tradition and not to "purchase freedom with gadgets."

Nevertheless, the gadgets continued to evolve, and the idea of large aircraft dedicated to the long-range bombing mission (in hibernation since the

The spacious flight deck of the Boeing XB-15 provided plenty of elbow room for the flight crew. This was vastly different from that of the B-17.

The Martin Model 145 went through a number of design changes before engineers settled on the twin boom configuration seen here. Designated as XB-16 by the Air Corps, it was never built.

Barling Bomber debacle) had not gone away. By 1933, a decade after the Barling, technology had evolved considerably, and the Air Corps was ready to go big again. At Wright Field, which has been (under various names) the center of aviation engineering and technology for the Army and Air Force from the time of the Wright brothers to today, an idea was born. Approved by the US Army General Staff in April 1934 and formalized under the name Project A, this top-secret initiative called for an aircraft with a range of 5,000 miles and a 1-ton payload capacity.

By this time, the junior officers of the 1920s, who had been Billy Mitchell's most ardent acolytes, had risen through the Air Corps chain of command, graduating from bars to oak leaves. Among them were the future generals who would define strategic airpower in World War II. In 1935, Ira Eaker became a major, Carl "Tooey" Spaatz became a lieutenant colonel, and Henry Harley "Hap" Arnold—who would command the US Army Air Forces, the largest air force in world history—became a brevet brigadier general and assistant chief of the Air Corps.

On their way up, these men and others were leaving their fingerprints not only on strategic theory but also on hardware development as well.

Under Project A, requests for proposals for a "Long Range Airplane Suitable for Military Purposes" went out to major planemakers. From Seattle, Boeing submitted its Model 294, while the Glenn L. Martin Company in Baltimore proposed its Model 145. Igor Sikorsky (now based in Stratford, Connecticut, after he escaped the Bolshevik takeover of his native Russia) presented what would be his final large bomber proposal.

In Santa Monica, California, the Douglas Aircraft Company was also among those responding. Coincidentally, Donald Douglas, the company's founder, had served as Glenn Martin's chief engineer in 1915 and 1916 and had been instrumental in the design of the Martin NBS-1, the bomber used by Billy Mitchell in his famous 1921 demonstrations.

Initially, the Air Corps assigned XBLR (Experimental Bomber, Long Range) designations to the Project A aircraft, with Boeing's being the XBLR-1, Sikorsky's the XBLR-2, and the Douglas bomber being the XBLR-3. The Martin entry was not designated. In the middle of 1935, Project A was merged with the parallel Project D, which had called for an aircraft with the "maximum feasible range into the future."

In July 1936, the aircraft in development received B-for-bomber designations. Sikorsky's XBLR-2 was not redesignated, but the others became the Boeing XB-15, Martin XB-16, and Douglas XB-19. Meanwhile, as the program evolved, the two designation series were often used interchangeably.

Only one each of two of the Project A/Project D aircraft were actually completed. The other two were canceled.

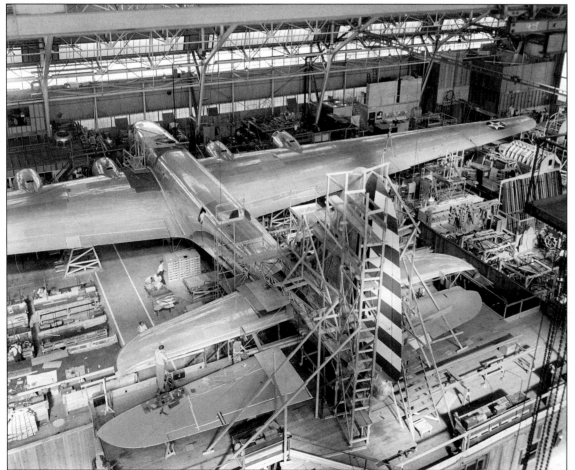

The massive Douglas XB-19 takes shape on the factory floor at Santa Monica. With a wingspan of 212 feet, it was the largest airplane yet built in the United States.

The Boeing XB-15, which came first, and the Douglas XB-19 were each the largest airplane yet to be built in the United States when they first rolled out—in 1937 and 1941, respectively. The XB-15 was 87 feet 7 inches long with a wingspan of 120 feet. It had a gross weight of 65,068 pounds and a range of 3,400 miles with 2,500 pounds of bombs. The XB-19 was 132 feet 3 inches long with a wingspan of 212 feet. It had a gross weight of 140,000 pounds and a range of 7,300 miles with 6,000 pounds of bombs.

The debuts of the XB-15 and XB-19 were long delayed. As they started to take shape in 1934 and 1935, both aviation technology and strategic doctrine were galloping at a much faster pace, and the big two were essentially becoming obsolete on the factory floors. As might have been expected, the big bombers met little enthusiasm in the War Department hierarchy. In October 1935, the Air Corps had requested funding for 11 XB-15s, but that number was cut to just the single prototype. In turn, Secretary

Initially ordered as the XBLR-2, the Douglas XB-19 did not make its first flight until June 27, 1941. It flew from the Douglas facility at Clover Field in Santa Monica to the Air Corps base at March Field in Riverside, California.

of War Harry Hines Woodring, who succeeded George Dern in 1936, had initially insisted that money to build the XB-15 program be deleted entirely and the funds reallocated for spare engines and parts for existing aircraft. Though the prototype was built, it was delayed for a year.

The once-secret XB-15 finally made a heavily publicized first flight on October 15, 1937. Complete with a kitchen and bathroom, it was so big that a person could enter the wing root and easily access the engines for inflight maintenance. In July 1939, the aircraft set world records for payload capacity, notably 71,167 pounds to 8,200 feet, and 4,409 pounds for 3,107 miles at 166 mph.

The vastly larger XB-19 made its first flight on June 27, 1941, after this debut was postponed several times by intermittent funding holdups. As with the XB-15, the program was limited to a single prototype, which was considered to be acquired mainly as a testbed to provide engineering data on very large airplanes.

Despite their size and promising performance, both aircraft had been overtaken by events and by other aircraft with more promising technology that were already flooding into the Air Corps pipeline. But thanks to the planning that went into them, especially by Boeing with the XB-15, the stage had been set for the Flying Fortress and aircraft like it.

Douglas crews polish the huge Douglas XB-19 on a hot summer day in 1941.

Chapter 2

BOEING OF SEATTLE

The story of the company that built the B-17 Flying Fortress is generally dated from July 4, 1914. It was on that day that a barnstormer named Terah Maroney was putting on a flying demonstration as part of the Independence Day festivities in Seattle, Washington. When he landed his Curtiss floatplane after an aerobatics display, Maroney offered to take passengers for a ride. A lumber company owner named William Edward Boeing came forward. A half hour later, the history of Seattle and of aviation had been changed.

Also taking a ride that day was Boeing's friend, George Conrad Westervelt, a naval officer and an engineer stationed at the US Navy shipyard in Bremerton, across Puget Sound from Seattle. Westervelt had studied aeronautics at the Massachusetts Institute of Technology (MIT), and the two men decided to build an airplane of their own. A single-engine, two-seat floatplane, it was built in the boathouse on Seattle's Lake Union where Boeing kept his yacht. Called the "B&W" after its builders and designated as Boeing Model 1, it made its first flight on June 15, 1916, with Bill Boeing himself at the controls. Westervelt was not there. He was on duty with the US Navy's Atlantic Fleet.

One month after the first flight, Boeing incorporated the Pacific Aero Products Company to build and market floatplanes. A year later, it became the Boeing Airplane Company. Through 1920, Boeing built more than 70 floatplanes and flying boats of a half dozen designs, including many for commercial customers and more than 50 examples of the popular Model C that were sold to the US Navy.

Boeing's first aircraft, the Boeing & Westervelt "B&W" aka Boeing Model 1, was handmade at Bill Boeing's boathouse on Lake Union in Seattle and made its first flight on June 15, 1916.

As his company expanded, Bill Boeing hired two recent graduates of the University of Washington engineering department: Clairmont "Claire" Egtvedt and Philip Gustav Johnson, who would be with the company for seven decades between them and who would lead the company after Bill Boeing departed in 1934. Both men would later be crucial players in the development of the B-17 Flying Fortress.

After World War I, Boeing built nearly 300 variations on the de Havilland DH-4 for the US Army. Through the 1920s and 1930s, Boeing's stock in trade became single-engine biplane fighters that the company designed and built for the US Army and the US Navy, especially the Army's P-12, of which over 350 were built through 1932, and the similar Navy F4B, of which nearly 200 were built through 1933.

Company executives assemble for a group photo on June 15, 1927. Seated (left to right) are Philip Gustav "Phil" Johnson and founder William Edward "Bill" Boeing. Johnson was president of the company twice, from 1926 to 1933 and 1939 to 1944. In the back row (left to right) are Clairmont L. "Claire" Egtvedt, Treasurer Edward "Eddie" Hubbard, W. G. Herron, and O. W. Tupper. Egtvedt served as president from 1933 to 1939 and 1944 to 1945. He also took over as chairman when Bill Boeing stepped down in 1934 and remained until 1966. Herron and Tupper were executives with Boeing Air Transport, the company's airline.

Boeing's first multi-engine bombers for the Air Corps came as part of the B-9 program (including YB-9, Y1B-9, and Y1B-9A), of which seven were built. They were twin-engine, open-cockpit monoplanes that were 52 feet long with wingspans just under 77 feet. First flown in 1931, they had a range of over 500 miles with a ton of bombs. However, in terms of performance, the B-9 was eclipsed by the twin-engine, enclosed-cockpit Martin B-10/B-12 series, of which the Air Corps bought more than 150.

Today known best for its commercial airliners, Boeing had been building planes that could carry one or two passengers almost from the beginning but truly entered the airliner field with the four-passenger Model 40 biplane series, which was first flown in 1925 as a two-passenger mail plane. In 1927, Bill Boeing went so far as to create a new airline, Boeing Air Transport (BAT), to fly airmail routes and passengers. In the first year, nearly 2,000 passengers would fly between San Francisco and Chicago aboard Model 40s. Boeing built more that 100 Model 40s and similar Model 95s, which were used by BAT as well as Western Air Express.

In 1928, Bill Boeing acquired Pacific Air Transport (PAT), which had a north-south route between Seattle and Los Angeles via San Francisco. In turn, Boeing Airplane & Transport Corporation (BATC) was created as a holding

Although Boeing is best known for larger, multi-engine aircraft, the company's biggest sellers in the early 1930s were single-engine fighters for the US Navy and Air Corps. This is a Boeing P-12E over Detroit.

company for BAT, PAT, and the Boeing Airplane Company. Also in 1928, Boeing unveiled the 12-passenger, trimotor Model 80 biplane. Said to be the first airliner to be staffed with flight attendants, it entered service with BATC.

The following year, BATC became the United Aircraft & Transport Corporation (UATC) and acquired several new subsidiaries, including aircraft engine maker Pratt & Whitney, Hamilton Standard Propeller Company, and the Chance Vought Corporation. In March 1930, UATC bought National Air Transport (NAT), an airline serving points from New York to Texas, whose route structure intersected BATC's at Chicago. Later in the year, UATC also acquired Varney Airlines, a major regional carrier in the West. In March 1931, United Air Lines was created as a management corporation to coordinate the operations of all of UATC's airline subsidiaries.

In February 1934, an airline industry corruption scandal resulted in President Franklin D. Roosevelt canceling all commercial airmail contracts. These were put out to bid again in June after four months of the airmail being flown by the Air Corps, but the Airmail Act of 1934 banned companies from owning both airlines and aircraft manufacturing companies. As a result, UATC was dissolved and United Air Lines and the Boeing Airplane Company were spun off in separate directions.

Boeing's first fully-enclosed airliner was the Model 80/80A series. Here is a Model 80A at Boeing Field in August 1929.

A disgusted William Edward Boeing left the business entirely, and Claire Egtvedt took the reins of the Boeing Airplane Company. Phil Johnson served for a time with United Air Lines before moving North to serve as vice president of operations for the newly-formed Trans-Canada Airlines.

Meanwhile, the company had been developing its Model 247, a new enclosed-cabin, twin-engine, monoplane airliner. As this writer wrote in his history of the Boeing Company, the 247 "made its first flight on February 8, 1933, marking the beginning of the era when air travel could truly compete with the Pullman passenger cars of the railroads for passenger comfort. In service, it became the first airliner to fly regularly scheduled transcontinental passenger service in less than 20 hours. A total of 60 aircraft were delivered to United Air Lines within a year, and an additional 15 were sold to other customers."

The next step in the Boeing airliner lineage was the 33-passenger, four-engine Model 307 Stratoliner. The first airliner to offer passengers a pressurized cabin, it could fly at 20,000 feet, well above most turbulent weather. By the time it made its first flight at the end of 1938, war clouds were gathering, and the airline industry was on the precipice of abrupt change.

Cited by myself in other works as probably the greatest of the Boeing prewar commercial aircraft was the Model 314 Clipper, an enormous, four-engine flying boat, of which a dozen were built for Pan American World Airways. Along with the Sikorsky S-42 and the Martin M-130, it was part of a triumvirate of great flying boats that Pan American used to pioneer its routes across the Atlantic and the Pacific during the late 1930s.

The driving force behind the Model 314 was Boeing aeronautical engineer Wellwood Beall, who played important roles in the development of the B-17 Flying Fortress, B-29 Superfortress, and the postwar B-52 Stratofortress. In 1936, with Beall basing his design on the Boeing experience with the ongoing XB-15 program, the company won a Pan Am contract for a new flying boat larger than the Martin and Sikorsky boats.

The first flight of a Model 314 came in June 1938, and the first Model 314, the *Yankee Clipper*, entered service with Pan American early in 1939. With a cruising speed of 183 mph, the Model 314 had a service ceiling of 13,400 feet and a range of 4,200 miles. It boasted plush seats in nine compartments on two decks for up to 74 passengers. For night flights, there were nearly 40 berths, depending on configuration. As I have noted, "the Boeing Clippers revolutionized air travel, and had it not been for World War II, they would have had a long and glorious career."

But World War II was indeed about to consume the world, and Boeing's role in the history of aviation was about to shift dramatically.

This 1941 billboard near Boeing Field clearly summarized the company's place in the world on the threshold of its greatness. From left to right, the airplanes depicted are the Model 314 Clipper, a truly intercontinental flying boat commercial airliner; the Model 307 Stratoliner, which was the first American airliner with a pressurized cabin; and the Model 299 Flying Fortress.

Chapter 3

ENTER THE BOEING MODEL 299

In the early summer of 1934, the US Army Air Corps issued Circular Proposal 35-26. It called for a design competition for a new multi-engined bomber to supersede its fleet of Martin B-10 twin-engine bombers that were only just beginning to enter service. While the Air Corps was generally pleased with the performance of the B-10, which exceeded that of previous twin-engine bombers, it was deemed important to start developing a successor because the process would be a long one.

The top speed of the new aircraft was to be between 200 and 250 mph at 10,000 feet, and the cruising speed was between 170 and 200 mph at that same altitude. These numbers were a modest improvement over the B-10, but improved endurance was the goal. The duration of flight was specified to be up to 10 hours with a range of 2,000 miles added in parentheses. This compared to 1,240 miles for the B-10. The service ceiling was specified at between 20,000 and 25,000 feet, which was about the same as the B-10.

This was, it will be recalled, the trough of the Great Depression, so there was a catch in the request for proposals. As Boeing's Donald Finlay wrote in 1951, in order to qualify, the bidder was required to submit "a complete and flyable airplane at his own expense."

Few manufacturers were ready to take such a gamble.

Glenn L. Martin, maker of the B-10 and the similar B-12, which were destined to be replaced by the new aircraft, naturally picked up the challenge and set to work developing their Model 146, which was developed from the B-10/B-12 types.

In Santa Monica, Donald Douglas was feeling optimistic. His DC-2 airliner had just gone into service with Transcontinental and Western Air (TWA) between Chicago and Newark, and it was already proving itself to be faster and more comfortable than the Boeing Model 247. Of course, as we know from hindsight, this was only a foretaste of the Douglas DC-3, first flown in 1935, which was to revolutionize global air travel.

Compared to Martin, the past bomber experience of Douglas Aircraft was limited to just eight B-7 bombers (variants of the O-35 observation plane) that were built around the time that Boeing produced seven B-9 aircraft. However, Don Douglas himself (working for Martin nearly two decades before) had designed Martin's first post–World War I bomber, the MB-1, which was the immediate predecessor of MB-2 that Billy Mitchell used over Chesapeake Bay in 1921.

When Douglas received the Air Corps Circular Proposal announcing the design competition for the new multi-engined bomber, he decided that he was halfway there. He had invested in developing a wing for the DC-2 that was up to date and certainly adequate for the task at hand. With this in mind, Douglas began work on a bomber fuselage that could

Clairmont L. "Claire" Egtvedt literally bet the company on the Flying Fortress. He was hired by Bill Boeing in 1917 straight out of the engineering program at the University of Washington. He took over as president in 1933, and in 1934, as the Model 299 was taking form on the drafting tables, he stepped into the chairmanship when Bill Boeing abruptly departed.

The first of its extraordinary lineage, the multi-engined Boeing Model 299 prototype was unofficially designated as XB-17, but it remained a company-owned aircraft.

For comparison: The twin-engine Douglas B-18 Bolo qualified as multi-engined and earned the bulk of the Air Corps orders—133 aircraft compared to just 13 Boeing Flying Fortresses.

be adapted to the DC-2 wing and began work on the Model DB-1 (Douglas Bomber, First).

As Circular Proposal 35-26 came across the transom in Seattle, the leadership role at Boeing was passing from founder Bill Boeing to young Clairmont Egtvedt, and the Boeing Airplane Company became an independent corporation called the Boeing Aircraft Company. The firm's experience with multi-engined bombers consisted entirely of just seven B-9 series aircraft, although on June 28, Boeing would receive a contract for design work and wind tunnel testing of its massive Model 294 (XBLR-1/XB-15), the Boeing entry in the Project A program.

While Martin, Douglas—and even the Air Corps specification writers themselves—took "multi-engine" as meaning "two" engines, Claire Egtvedt looked at the work then being done by Boeing on its four-engine Model 294 and the company's future plans for four-engine airliners and decided that "multi" could just as well mean "four." Four engines would give this aircraft greater range and payload capacity than two.

In their official US Air Force postwar study entitled *The Development of the Heavy Bomber*, Jean DuBuque and Robert Gleckner noted that "all but one manufacturer, perhaps in view of War Department economy policies, had assumed that only a highly superior twin-engine model of standard design was desired. Boeing engineers, however, noted the loophole allowed in the term "multi-engine" and launched as a private venture the pioneering development of a four-engine superbomber of radical design."

In fact, all of the aircraft developed under this program were "private ventures." The use of the term "loophole" by the Air Force is curiously ironic, as "multi" literally means any number more than one, and that prefix originated with the Air Corps.

According to Harold Mansfield, Boeing's public relations man at the time, Egtvedt traveled to Wright Field to discuss the number of engines face to face with Major Jan Howard, the engineering chief, to specifically ask him for confirmation. Apparently, Mansfield was present, as he recalled the conversation.

The laminated wooden wind tunnel model of the Boeing Model 299 as seen in October 1934.

"Would a four-engine plane qualify?" Egtvedt asked.

"The word is 'multi-engined,' isn't it?" Howard replied.

Boeing historian Peter Bowers wrote that preliminary work on this prospective multi-engined bomber began on June 18, 1934, and that construction started on August 16. The Boeing master list of model numbers shows that the program was officially designated as Model 299 on the latter date.

As Mansfield noted, the company was hanging by a thread financially that summer when Egtvedt had a conversation with William McPherson "Bill" Allen, the company lawyer and Boeing's postwar president.

"I don't want to jeopardize the future of this company," Egtvedt said. "You know what little we have left here. If we undertake this four-engine bomber, there'll be lots of unknowns. The design studies for the XB-15 make that clear enough."

"Do you think you can build a successful four-engine airplane in a year?" Allen asked.

"Yes. I know we can," Egtvedt said, looking out his window over the roof of the Boeing engineering building.

On September 30, the Board of Directors of the Boeing Airplane Company voted to spend $275,000 ($5.3 million today) for the design of the Model 299 and for the construction of a prototype aircraft that was to be delivered to the Army Air Corps Materiel Division (Materiel Command after 1942) at Wright Field in Ohio in August 1935 for flight testing. A further $150,000 was approved in December 1934 as the design process moved forward.

A maximum effort ensued in the engineering department with more than 100 hours spent testing models in the wind tunnel. The Model 299 was designed by a team of brilliant young engineers, notably Stanford-educated Edward Curtis Wells, who went to work for Boeing in 1931 and was only 24 when he became Boeing's project engineer for the Model 299 program three years later.

While incorporating the four engines of the Model 294, Wells and his team incorporated the clean lines and fully retractable landing gear of the new Model 247 airliner into the Model 299. Historian William Green later wrote that it was "as beautifully proportioned a military aircraft as had been conceived anywhere in the world at that time."

In *The Development of the Heavy Bomber*, DuBuque and Gleckner noted that "no bomber of such revolutionary structure had yet been produced in the United States. Numerous improvements in design were included which were more or less a composite of the best features of bombardment airplanes evolved since the MB-2 [of 1920]."

The handmade Model 299 prototype was rolled out on July 17, 1935, at Boeing's Plant 1, which was located at the 458-acre King County Airport (generally known as Boeing Field) on the south side of Seattle. The race to finish it had been such that day shifts and night shifts merged as everyone worked as long as they could to get the job done.

Delivered in natural metal with red and white Air Corps–style stripes painted on its tail, the company-financed and company-owned prototype was powered by four 9-cylinder Pratt & Whitney R-1690-E Hornet radial engines. It carried standard Air Corps insignia, but because it was still company-owned, it bore the civil experimental registration (X-13372) rather than a military tail number. Boeing would refer to the aircraft as the "XB-17" from the beginning, though the "B-17" designator was not yet officially assigned to the Model 299.

While the Model 299 had dorsal, ventral, and side blisters that could contain guns, the prototype was not armed. Nevertheless, the purpose of these was obvious. When a copy of the press photo of the rollout was handed to Richard Williams at the *Seattle Times*, for captioning, he wrote: "Declared to be the largest land plane ever built in America [the larger XB-15 was not yet completed], this 15-ton flying fortress, built by the Boeing Aircraft Co. under Army specifications, today was ready to test its wings."

For the rest of his life, Williams would be known as the man who coined the term "Flying Fortress," a label that was quickly and widely repeated throughout the national media and eventually became the aircraft's official name. Even Williams's 1989 obituary was dominated by this fact.

The Model 299 Flying Fortress took off on its nine-hour first flight at sunrise on July 28, a week and a half after the rollout, with Boeing chief test pilot Leslie R. "Les" Tower at the controls. Born in Polson, Montana, in 1903, he started at Boeing as a draftsman in 1925 and became a test pilot two years later. Thereafter, Tower had flown every aircraft Boeing had built.

Soon, when it was apparent that the first flight had been a success, all the Boeing executives gathered anxiously at Boeing Field breathed a collective sigh of relief. Harold Mansfield recalled that Boeing President Claire Egtvedt "shut his eyes and smiled" and that "[General Manager Robert] Minshall turned to Ed Wells, who had been promoted to project engineer [and said,] 'Nice work, Ed. Great work.'"

In the coming days, Les Tower flew out of Boeing Field on a series of flight tests over the Puget Sound area and then flew the XB-17 to Wright Field on August 20, averaging 252 mph over 2,100 miles.

At Wright Field, the Model 299 prototype proceeded to check the boxes of the Circular Proposal 35-26 requirements. It cruised at 200 mph at 10,000 feet and accelerated to 250 mph. It demonstrated a ceiling of 25,000 feet and an endurance of 10 hours. Major Oliver Echols, who had taken over from Major Howard as chief of engineering at Wright Field, seemed pleased.

Meanwhile, also arriving at Wright Field during August were the Douglas DB-1 and the Martin Model 146, each powered by a pair of R-1820 Cyclone 9-cylinder radial engines manufactured by Wright Aeronautical. As they too set out to prove themselves, the Martin aircraft fell short, but the Douglas bomber performed well.

By comparison, the Model 299 was 69 feet 9 inches long with a wingspan of 103 feet 9 inches; the DB-1 was 57 feet 3 inches long with a wingspan of 89 feet 7 inches; and the Model 146 was 52 feet long with a wingspan of 75 feet 1 inch. The respective gross weights were listed at 32,432 pounds, 20,159 pounds, and 16,000 pounds.

On October 30, 1935, the promising flight test program of the Model 299 ended in tragedy. That day at 9:10 a.m., the aircraft took off with Major Ployer "Pete" Hill in the pilot's seat and Lieutenant Donald Putt as copilot. Les Tower was aboard as an observer and so too were John Cutting and Mark Koogler, two civilian employees of the Materiel Division.

According to the subsequent Air Corps inquiry, the aircraft "immediately assumed an abnormally steep climbing attitude, continuing in this attitude until it stalled at approximately 300 feet altitude and then crashed, power on the airdrome, and immediately caught fire."

Edward Curtis Wells can be considered to be the father of the B-17 Flying Fortress. A Stanford University graduate, he joined the company in 1931 and was only 24 when he became project engineer for the Model 299 program in 1934. (Boeing Photo Courtesy of Mike Lombardi)

The rollout of the Model 299 was at Boeing Field on July 17, 1935. Later that day, across town at 1120 John St., Seattle Times caption writer Richard Williams was the first to call it a "Flying Fortress."

First on the scene were Lieutenant Robert Giovanelli and Lieutenant Leonard "Jake" Harman. They dragged Ployer and Tower out of the fire as the others scrambled out on their own. Caught in the flames from a fully fueled airplane, everyone was badly burned. Among the worst injured, Ployer died at the hospital, but Tower was expected to live. Claire Egtvedt, who was in Chicago, visiting United Air Lines on a sales trip, hurried the 250 miles to Wright Field.

The cause of the crash was quickly determined to have been that the rudder and elevator surface controls, which were typically locked when the

The complex frame for the nose and nose turret assembly of the Model 299, as seen in March 1935.

The completed and installed nose and nose turret assembly of the Model 299 around the time of the first flight in July 1935.

aircraft was stationary, had not been unlocked before the flight. Les Tower blamed himself, although it was not directly his fault, and Egtvedt told him so just before he died due to complications from his injuries.

The board of inquiry, convened by Brigadier General A. W. Robins, the commanding officer at Wright Field, determined that the crash was not due

The Model 299 in flight near Mount Rainier, the massive, 14,411-foot dormant volcano that is visible on a clear day from downtown Seattle.

to structural failure, malfunctioning of the flight controls or control surfaces, or failure of any of the four engines or propellers. The board also cleared the "structural or aerodynamic design of this airplane" and noted that the aircraft had exhibited no "undesirable or adverse flying or handling qualities."

Despite the crash, men throughout the ranks of the Army Air Corps—all the way up to Brigadier General Hap Arnold, the incoming assistant chief—were encouraged by what the Model 299 had accomplished in two months of tests, and they were pleased with the concept of a four-engine bomber.

According to a July 12, 1935, memo from the adjutant general to General Oscar Westover, the chief of the Army Air Corps, the airmen were so enthusiastic that they were now envisioning a new class of four-engine "heavy" bombers, of which the Flying Fortress would be but one, while all twin-engine bombers would be classified as "medium" bombers. Ultimately this did come to pass.

In the meantime, however, procurement decisions being made by the bean counters at the War Department relied on the comfort of the status quo rather than pushing the limits of the possible. The Douglas DB-1 had performed well, and when one compared price tags, there was no contest between it and the Model 299. In a lot of 25 aircraft, the unit cost of the DB-1 was $99,150, compared to $85,910 for the inferior Martin aircraft, while for the Boeing aircraft, the cost was $196,730, which was almost double that of the DB-1. In a lot of 220 aircraft, Douglas could bring the cost down to $58,500, while the unit price for the Boeing aircraft was $99,620.

In January 1936, the orders were placed. The War Department authorized the acquisition of 133 DB-1s under the B-18 (the prototype had been known unofficially as XB-18).

BOMB BAY, STA.5 FORWARD
MODEL 299
B213   7-26-35

A view inside the bomb bay of the Model 299, looking forward, in July 1935.

The Y1B-17 (Boeing Model 299B) is seen here in its original Air Corps livery. It made its first flight on December 2, 1936.

On October 30, 1935, the Model 299 prototype crashed at the Air Corps test center at Wright Field in Ohio. Someone had forgotten to unlock the rudder and elevator "gust lock" surface controls.

The flight deck of the XB-17 (Boeing Model 299) as photographed in July 1935. (Please refer to the control panel diagram in Appendix I.)

The flight deck of the Y1B-17 (Boeing Model 299B) as photographed in October 1938. (Please refer to the control panel diagram in Appendix I.)

The Air Corps, meanwhile, asked that 65 Flying Fortresses be purchased, a reduction in quantity from the 206 that had been requested in October 1935, along with the request for 11 XB-15s that had been cut to just 1. However, the War Department slashed that number of Flying Fortresses to just 13, with a 14th acquired as a structural test aircraft. Indeed, as late as June 1936, Brigadier General George Redfield Spaulding, assistant chief of staff of the US Army, had written in a memo that no tactical or strategic requirement existed for a service bomber with a 3,500-mile range.

Looking into the right wing toward the inboard engine nacelle firewall of a Y1B-17, October 1936.

Meanwhile, in a 1936 report issued by a board chaired by Major General William L. Bryden, an assistant chief of staff of the US Army, it was asserted that "the romantic appeal of aviation had induced a large section of the public and even a substantial element of the Air Corps to accept the conclusion that future wars would be decided by large independent fleets of super performing aircraft." The board implied that such a conclusion was, to borrow the colorful phrasing of Secretary of War George Henry Dern, the "fantasy of a dreamer."

Throughout 1936 and beyond, Air Corps Chief of Staff, Major General Oscar Westover, pushed continually for more money for long-range, four-engine bombers.

In the fall of 1936, Westover's deputy, Brigadier General Hap Arnold, lobbied for at least an additional 20 Flying Fortresses, citing the hardship that this placed on Boeing after all of the money that they had invested in the program. Addressing this issue, DuBuque and Gleckner noted that "in the case of unforeseen exigencies, such as reduction of appropriations and engineering and procurement problems, delays were understandable, but arbitrary changes without cogent reasons, when large private expenditures were at stake, would threaten the whole future of the aircraft industry."

For Boeing, the big immediate problem was that it had no place to build the Model 299s that the Air Corps had ordered nor the Model 307 and Model 314, which were large four-engine commercial transports that the company was planning. The first Model 299 had been handmade, but Boeing had outgrown its existing facilities and needed to find a place to build a large new factory, even if that meant abandoning Seattle.

As Boeing Historian Mike Lombardi recalled, "In an effort to keep Boeing in Seattle, a local truck farmer, Giuseppe Desinone, offered the company several acres of his land near Boeing Field for the price of $1."

On the strength of the Model 299 order and interest from Pan American Airways for its commercial airlines, Boeing undertook construction of the new facility, which came online in 1936 with 750,000 square feet of floor space across East Marginal Way South from Plant 1 and Boeing Field. Known as Plant 2, this factory complex would be expanded considerably over the ensuing years, growing to 1,776,000 square feet by the end of World War II.

Plant 2 actually consisted of several buildings. The giant, high-bay assembly building that is often referred to generally as "Plant 2," was officially designated as Building 2-40, while the building immediately behind it where fabrication work was done was designated as Building 2-41. Together, Buildings 2-40 and 2-41 were the centerpiece of the Plant 2 campus.

Boeing spent much of 1936 building up the tooling necessary for series production of the service test aircraft and hopefully for additional future production series orders. DuBuque and Gleckner note that there was now an extra emphasis on service test aircraft because of "numerous maintenance difficulties" that had been encountered with the Martin B-10/B-12 series that was "principally attributed to inadequate service test before accelerated production was begun."

The 14 preproduction Model 299s were purchased for $3,823,807.75 ($70 million today) under Contract W535 ac-8306, which was dated January 17, 1936. They were initially identified under the service test designation YB-17, but this changed to Y1B-17 on November 20, 1936, because they were being paid for with F-1 funding rather than regular fiscal year appropriations. This was a standard accounting procedure during the 1930s and is seen in many aircraft designations around this time. The letter "Y" with or without the number "1" identified the plane as a service test aircraft.

Internally, Boeing designated these aircraft as Model 299B.

While generally indistinguishable at first glance from the original Model 299, the Model 299B/Y1B-17 aircraft bore subtle differences, such as a single (rather than double) landing-gear strut and changes in the gun positions, in which guns were now actually installed. The number of crewmembers was also reduced from 8 to 6, although that number increased in later variants.

A big difference in the Model 299B/Y1B-17 was a change of powerplant. The Pratt & Whitney R-1690-E Hornet radial engines were exchanged for four GR-1820-39 Wright Cyclone 9-cylinder radials, delivering 930 hp. Variants of the Wright Cyclone were standard equipment on all future B-17 variants.

The first Model 299B/Y1B-17, and the first Flying Fortress officially acquired by the Air Corps, made its debut flight on December 2, 1936, wearing tail number 36-149. Several days later, after the brakes seized on landing and 36-149 nosed over, there were some angry words from Congress and nervous moments for Boeing and the Air Corps, but the aircraft was not badly damaged, and the incident was largely forgotten.

The remainder of the Y1B-17 aircraft were delivered by August 5, 1937. Some sources said that the second aircraft (36-150) was delivered in January, but Boeing historian Peter Bowers, who had access to Boeing records, put the date at March 1. At least this was the date that Major Barney Giles delivered the first Flying Fortress to the 2nd Bombardment Group at Langley Field in Virginia.

It was this group, commanded by Colonel Robert Olds, that would handle the service testing of these service test Flying Fortresses. Olds, along with Major General Frank Andrews, had been leading exponents of the acquisition of the Flying Fortress by tactical units. Twelve of the Y1B-17s gradually made their way to the 2nd during 1937.

The 13th Y1B-17 went to Wright Field for continued technical evaluation, along with the 14th airframe, which was ordered only for structural

tests and not meant to be flyable. As it turned out, the structural testing of the first-generation Flying Fortress happened, not by design, but by accident. One of the first dozen Y1B-17s (36-157) accidentally flew into severe turbulence, where it was badly wrenched and even tossed into an inverted position. When the pilot recovered and landed safely, it was evident by bends and popped rivets that the aircraft had been through a tempestuous mauling—and it had survived.

With the structural tests out of the way, the 14th Y1B-17 was made flyable and given tail number 37-269. It was known internally by Boeing as Model 299F and formally designated by the Air Corps as Y1B-17A on May 12, 1937.

This aircraft was powered by GR-1820-51 Wright Cyclones that were augmented by F-14 turbosuperchargers. The idea was to incorporate these on the subsequent B-17B variant, having used the Y1B-17A as a testbed.

Although invented by Alfred Büchi in Switzerland in 1915 and first used operationally a decade later, the turbosupercharger—known in the vernacular as a "turbo"—was refined and adapted for aircraft use by Dr. Sanford Moss of General Electric, who earned the 1940 Collier Trophy for this work. Working with Moss, engineers at the Air Corps engineering establishment at Wright Field developed superchargers for numerous aircraft during World War II, beginning with the Flying Fortress.

On May 12, 1938, three Y1B-17s based at Langley Field in Virginia successfully located the Italian liner Rex *when it was 680 miles at sea in the Atlantic, demonstrating the capability of the aircraft and of Air Corps navigators.*

Air Corps Y1B-17s of the 2nd Bomb Group over Lower Manhattan, New York City, in 1938.

As explained by Boeing public relations man Harold Mansfield, the turbosupercharger "was a turbine wheel with many little paddles like a steam or water-driven turbine, except that this one was to be turned by flaming exhaust gases. A supercharger was to be mounted on top of each engine nacelle, and the exhaust gas would be routed to take a torrid whirl through its blades, emerging on the surface of the nacelle before fanning away in the slipstream."

In his memoir, *Vision: A Saga of the Skies*, Mansfield explained that Ed Wells, the Model 299 lead engineer, who was to become Boeing's chief engineer for military programs, knew that "if they could get the B-17 up to high altitude with turbosuperchargers, it would be a tremendously effective airplane, much less vulnerable to attack."

The Y1B-17A made its first flight on April 29, 1938, but the turbosuperchargers proved problematic. Boeing initially installed the F-14 turbos on top of the engine, but as Mansfield recalled, this presented a serious stumbling block. He noted that Charlie Morris, who had been assigned to lead the supercharger installation told Ed Wells that "I'm worried about what these things are going to do to the airflow" if installed atop the engines.

However, as Mansfield explained, "They had already concluded this was the only place the turbos could go. The turbine wheels couldn't go on the bottoms of the nacelles because the landing gear retracted there, and besides, if there were ever a fuel leak, it would come right down into the turbo. The exhaust stacks were always put on top to avoid this danger."

To evaluate how much the turbosupercharger would disturb the airflow over the top of the wing, tufts of yarn were attached over the wing surface. Mansfield wrote that test pilot Lieutenant Colonel J. D. "Johnny" Corkille, the Materiel Command factory representative in Seattle, took off with the turbos disconnected. Meanwhile, Captain Clarence "Bill" Irvine from Wright Field was aboard to watch the yarn as the aircraft climbed to 10,000 feet. When the superchargers were engaged "there was a rumble throughout the ship and things began to shake. Irvine noticed the yarn tufts flapping idly over a 10-foot area behind each engine, not streaming with the wind as they should. Corkille turned the turbos off to reconnoiter."

"Watch the instruments," Corkille said as he again engaged the turbosuperchargers.

Alfred Palmer took this photo of a Y1B-17 in olive drab paint at Langley Field in 1942. It is equipped with a loop antenna, a characteristic of this variant. One of the Y1B-17s, originally a static test article, became the only B-17A. Note the Boeing B-18 and Douglas A-20 on the taxiway in the background. (Photo Courtesy Library of Congress)

One of the 13 Y1B-17 aircraft was painted in a distinctive but water-soluble temporary camouflage when it flew with the 20th Bomb Squadron during war games in 1938. (Photo Courtesy USAF)

As the instruments recorded a 25-percent increase in power, the air speed indicator dropped and the aircraft shook.

"Suddenly it grew violent, heaving and throwing them with a clapping of metal," Mansfield wrote. "Corkille snapped the turbos off a second time, drops of perspiration on his brow, and got the ship steadied. He looked around quickly. . . The disturbed airflow had whipped [the tail] mightily, but it was still intact. Corkille got back on the field as fast as he could."

"We'll not try that again," Corkille told Ed Wells. "Not me."

"We can't jeopardize our delivery schedule on the B-17B," Claire Egtvedt told Ed Wells. "If the turbo won't work, we'd better give it up."

"I think we can make it work," Irvine told the Boeing men.

"The contract allowed $75,000," Egtvedt said wearily. "We've already spent $100,000 on it. How much further can we go?"

Ed Wells pointed out that it had not yet been proven that the turbos could not be put on the bottom of the wing, and Oliver Echols promised to come up with some more money for wind tunnel tests.

The turbos were moved, the problems were ironed out, and they became standard equipment in future Flying Fortress variants.

As part of the service test program at the 2nd Bombardment Group, Colonel Olds sent his Flying Fortresses on several well-publicized demonstration flights during the first part of 1938. Olds himself set an east-to-west transcontinental speed record by flying from Langley to California in just under 13 hours, then turned around and flew back in less than 11.

When Roberto Ortiz was inaugurated as president of Argentina on February 20, 1938, the United States toasted him with a goodwill flight of a half dozen Langley Flying Fortresses in the midst of a 12,000-mile, mishap-free South American sojourn. Guiding this mission was the man whom Olds described to Colonel Ira Eaker as the "best damned navigator in the Army Air Corps." This man was Lieutenant Curtis LeMay, who as a general during World War II would do much with Flying Fortresses to realize the potential of strategic airpower.

On May 12, 1938, three Langley Flying Fortresses, again guided by LeMay, located the Italian ocean liner *Rex*, 680 miles off the Eastern Seaboard in the Atlantic Ocean. This demonstrated the accuracy of Air Corps navigation as well as the range and potential of the Flying Fortress, but it angered the US Navy. Thereafter, the Army's flyers were temporarily ordered not to fly farther offshore that 100 miles.

Through 1938 and into 1939, as the Flying Fortress fleet gradually completed its service test milestones—and flexed its versatility on long-range demonstration flights—the Y1B-17s were officially redesignated as B-17s, and the Y1B-17A became the only aircraft to be assigned the B-17A designation. However, by this time, an even larger batch of B-17B Flying Fortresses was taking shape on the factory floor at Plant 2 in Seattle.

The GR-1820-51 Wright Cyclone engines of the Y1B-17 were augmented by F-14 superchargers, first tested on the Y1B-17A.

A roster shot of the single Y1B-17A at Boeing Field on a rainy January day in 1939.

Demonstrating the operation of the M2 machine gun in the lower fuselage of the Y1B-17A.

The nose turret of the Y1B-17A when it was assigned to the 96th "Red Devils" Bomb Squadron of the 2nd Bomb Group at Langley Field circa March 1937.

Chapter 4

THE LIFE AND TIMES OF THE B-17B

The first true production series variant of the Flying Fortress was the aircraft that received the Air Corps designation B-17B. There is an old adage, erroneously described as an ancient Chinese curse, that declares, "May you live in interesting times." The B-17B certainly took shape in such times. Indeed, it was during these times that the world transitioned into World War II, and the US Army's official view of airpower transitioned from reluctant acceptance to amorous embrace.

As the design work for the B-17B was ongoing in 1936 and 1937, Boeing first designated it as Model 299E, identifying it as a sequential follow-on to the Model 299B that became the Y1B-17 and various intervening design studies that were designated but not produced. However, so many changes intervened that it was ultimately built as Model 299M.

The Model 299M/B-17B was similar at first glance to the Y1B-17A/B-17A aircraft, although there were numerous subtle differences. Its tail and flaps were larger, but the height of 15 feet and wingspan of 103 feet 9 inches remained the same as the B-17A. A redesigned nose section resulted in the overall length being reduced slightly from 68 feet 9 inches to 67 feet 11 inches.

The nose redesign involved installation of a 10-facet framed Plexiglas nose piece. This replaced a complex bomb-aiming window fixture in which the bombardier's section in the earlier variant was apart from a separate gun blister at the top of the nose. The multi-facet nose remained standard through the B-17E, after which it was replaced by the single-piece blown Plexiglas nose used in the

Test pilots compare notes by the tail of a B-17B at Boeing Field during the summer of 1939 as deliveries of the aircraft to the Air Corps were getting underway.

The first B-17B is seen here at Boeing Field on July 27, 1939, the day that deliveries officially began.

B-17F and B-17G. Such a nose had not been practical with 1930s technology.

Armament, as had been the case with the previous variants, consisted of five .30-caliber machine guns, one above, one below, one in the nose, and two in the waist.

Power for the B-17B was supplied by four Wright Aeronautical R-1820-51 Cyclone 9-cylinder radial engines rated at 1,000 hp with 1,200 hp for takeoff. These were augmented for high-altitude operations with B-3 turbosuperchargers. The same engine type had previously been retrofitted to the single Y1B-17A/B-17A aircraft.

At the time, the turbosupercharger was seen as the single most important new innovation to become standard in the B-17B. It was the feature that would allow the Flying Fortress to become what its advocates had long intended it to be. As Donald Finlay reflected, "The advent of the turbosupercharger brought about high-altitude bombing [capability], but this was not so much a change of [Air Corps strategic] philosophy as it was a realization of a previously desirable but unattainable characteristic."

The first order for the B-17B variant came with contract W535 ac-10155, awarded on August 17, 1937. It called for 10 aircraft to be delivered for a sum of $2,757,852.20 ($49 million today). Addendum CO.1, written the same day, added three more B-17Bs for $950,132.91. Addendum CO.2, issued on October 7, 1937, upped the order with an additional 13 B-17Bs for a contract price of $2,518,346.83.

Delayed for almost nine months because of budgetary issues and a continuing War Department bias against four-engine bombers, the final order for 13 B-17Bs, CO.5, was issued on June 30, 1938. With a price tag of $3,174,802.05, this deferred block of B-17Bs cost the government 20 percent more than the same number on the previous order and brought the total number of B-17B Flying Fortresses to 39.

While the Boeing Aircraft Company built all 39 B-17Bs with the consecutive company serial numbers 2004 through 2042, the Air Corps tail numbers were in nonconsecutive clusters, reflecting the sporadic nature of aircraft acquisition at the time. The first 13 were 38-211 through 38-223, and the second 13 were 38-258 through 38-270. However, the last group were scattered between two fiscal years as 38-583, 38-584, 38-610, and 39-1 through 39-10.

In the fall of 1938, as these purchase orders were being digested by Boeing in Seattle, momentous changes were taking place within the halls of power in Washington—and across the globe, where Europe was in crisis mode.

Adolf Hitler had begun flexing Germany's aggressive military might with a demand for the incorporation of the German-speaking Sudetenland, then part of Czechoslovakia, into the Third Reich. In an effort to stave off a war, the leaders of Britain and France met with Hitler in the infamous Munich Conference between September 17 and 23 and agreed to force Czechoslovakia to surrender the territory to Germany. British Prime Minister Neville Chamberlain spoke cheerfully of "peace for our time," but those who saw the agreement as a first step toward war were proven painfully correct a year later when World War II began.

When World War II broke out in Europe, President Franklin D. Roosevelt became an outspoken advocate of National Defense, and a large component of his advocacy was for increased numbers of military aircraft.

A B-17B taking off from Boeing Field, circa 1939.

The Munich Conference coincided with two important events in the evolution of American airpower. On September 29, 1938, Major General Hap Arnold suddenly became the Chief of the Army Air Corps after Major General Oscar Westover was killed in a plane crash on September 21. Less than three weeks later, on October 15, Brigadier General George Catlett Marshall became Deputy Chief of Staff of the US Army.

More amenable to airpower than almost anyone in the upper tier of the Army establishment, Marshall would come to wholeheartedly embrace the concept when he became chief of staff a year later on September 1, 1939. Close personal friends, Arnold and Marshall—both of them ultimately wearing five stars—would head their respective services through World War II.

Perhaps most important in the evolution of airpower doctrine within the American chain of command was the impact of Munich on the commander-in-chief, President Franklin D. Roosevelt.

On September 28, 1938, as the Munich summit was wrapping up, Roosevelt called a summit conference of his own at the White House. Secretary of the Navy Claude Swanson and Secretary of War Harry Hines Woodring were there, along with the Chief of Naval Operations, Admiral Harold Stark, and US Army Chief of Staff Major General Malin Craig. An old cavalry officer, Craig brought with him the opinion of airpower that still prevailed at the apogee of the US Army chain of command. Craig continued to firmly believe that the role of the US Army was to win wars on the ground and that the only possible role for airpower was to support this mission.

However, also present at the meeting were Craig's deputy and eventual successor, George Marshall, and Hap Arnold, who would formally assume command of the Air Corps on the day following the meeting.

"The heavy part played by [fear of] the Luftwaffe in the appeasement at Munich was not lost on the president," Arnold recalled of the meeting. "To the surprise, I think, of practically everyone in the room except Harry [Woodring] and myself, and to my own delight, the president came straight out for airpower. Airplanes—now—and lots of them! At that time, the War Department was handling the entire expansion for the ground and air forces, but FDR was not satisfied with their submitted report. A new regiment of field artillery, or new barracks at an Army post in Wyoming, or new machine tools in an ordnance arsenal, he said sharply, would not scare Hitler one blankety-blank-blank bit! What he wanted was airplanes! Airplanes were the war implements that would have an influence on Hitler's activities!"

Ironically, only three days later, France's President Daladier admitted to US Ambassador William Bullitt that "if France would have had 3,000 or 4,000 planes, there would have been no [capitulation to Hitler at] Munich."

After Munich, the president was not simply commander-in-chief but airpower-advocate-in-chief.

"Some of those present were obviously unprepared for the forceful way in which he had made up his mind," Arnold wrote in his memoir. "It was plainly a bolt from the blue, but the president, with equal plainness, made it clear that he had assembled this meeting to discuss aircraft production and airpower in general. He himself had some potent proposals which were obviously not made up on the spur of the moment."

In 1936, Congress had authorized 2,230 aircraft as a "minimum safe peacetime strength" for the Air Corps, although as of September 1938, the service had just 1,792. This was fewer than the number that had been authorized by the Air Corps Act of 1926!

"I left that meeting of the 28th of September 1938 with the feeling that the Air Corps had finally 'achieved its Magna Carta.'" Arnold said, summarizing his view of this turning point that came on the eve of his promotion. "It was the first time in history we had ever had a program—the first time we could shoot toward a definite goal of planes from the factories and men from the training fields. A battle was won in the White House that day which took its place with—or at least led to—the victories in combat later."

Though the president himself was using numbers in the low five figures, the practical implementation of the "Magna Carta" would travel a bumpy road. At a press conference on October 14, Roosevelt spoke in general terms about his desire to expand the Air Corps, mentioning 15,000 aircraft. Five days later, Arnold handed Woodring a detailed plan for a very modest—by Roosevelt's numbers—expansion to 6,360 aircraft by 1944. In retrospect, we know that this number was greatly overtaken by events, but in 1938, this was considered excessive in some quarters.

Nevertheless, with nearly a year left as chief of staff, Malin Craig vociferously resisted conversion. On October 24, 1938, he complained to Lewis Douglas, Director of the Bureau of the Budget, that the "defense of the country . . . rests with ground troops. What are we going to do with 15,000 airplanes?" Craig went on to tell Douglas that the money was better spent on weapons other than airplanes, which had a rapid rate of obsolescence.

However, Craig's platform was already crumbling. DuBuque and Gleckner recalled in *The Development of the Heavy Bomber*, that Marshall, as Craig's

A few years earlier, Boeing Chairman Clairmont L. "Claire" Egtvedt had literally bet the company on the Flying Fortress concept, but when the Roosevelt Administration started calling for increased numbers of aircraft, Egtvedt faced the problem of keeping up with the orders.

William McPherson "Bill" Allen was Boeing's corporate attorney and a close confidant of Claire Egtvedt during the Flying Fortress years. Between them, they hatched a solution to the production problem.

incoming deputy, "gave full support to General Arnold's vigorous effort to build up Army airpower with a strong force of heavy bombers. In November, he cited to Chief of Staff General Craig numerous reasons why it was essential to increase procurement of the new turbosupercharged B-17B. It could operate successfully in spite of partial engine failure; its long range permitted swift reinforcement of foreign garrisons; it could patrol wide sea areas and protect shipping; it possessed strong offensive power against enemy war vessels; and it could perform far greater counter air force operation than any existing twin-engine bomber."

In his November 29, 1938, memo to Craig, Marshall insisted that since the B-17 was considered "the outstanding heavy bomber of the world, it was essential, in order to meet the emergency procurement program established by the president for increased airpower, to purchase them in maximum quantities within the capabilities of existing aircraft facilities."

Craig was getting the message from both sides in the chain of command. President Franklin Roosevelt was among the first American civilian leaders to grasp the importance of airpower and the need to prepare for war while hoping for peace. Though the United States would remain neutral for three more years, it was time to start gearing up for what would later officially be called "National Defense."

The authorized strength of the US Army Air Corps of 2,230 aircraft seemed low to Roosevelt. In November 1938, as the Y1B-17A was nearing

Philip Gustav "Phil" Johnson was considered to be a mastermind of organizing mass production. He had been president of Boeing through 1933 but left the company. In 1939, Boeing needed him, so Claire Egtvedt and Bill Allen lured him back to the presidency.

flight test and the B-17B was on order, Roosevelt mentioned that perhaps that number ought to be raised to an astounding 20,000. By comparison, the German Luftwaffe was undergoing an extensive expansion and would take delivery of 8,295 aircraft in 1939 with more than 10,000 planned the following year.

On January 4, 1939, in a message to Congress, President Roosevelt insisted that "we have learned that survival cannot be guaranteed by arming after the attack begins—for there is new range and speed to offense."

It was widely rumored that the president would ask Congress for at least 10,000—half of his trial balloon figure—but in January 1939, he asked for merely 3,000, scarcely more that the current authorization. The politically skillful chief executive had gotten people used to a five-digit number, then he pleased fiscal conservatives with a small request.

Congress came on board incrementally. In their April 1939 Air Corps authorization, they appropriated $27 million (approximately $494 million in current valuation) immediately with $31 million for the coming fiscal year. An additional $89 million (1.3 billion today) was added in July.

Noting the quickening pace of warplane research and development among potential adversaries—especially in Germany—Roosevelt had observed in January that "information from other nations leads us to believe that there must be a complete revision of our estimates for aircraft . . . No responsible officers advocate building our air forces up to the total either of planes on hand or of productive capacity equal to the forces of certain other nations. We are thinking in the terms of necessary defenses, and the conclusion is inevitable that our existing forces are so utterly inadequate that they must be immediately strengthened."

The "information from other nations" to which Roosevelt alluded came from a 1938 Air Corps study that looked at "the development of foreign heavy bombers." According to DuBuque and Gleckner, these included the German Junkers Ju 89, first flown in 1938, and the Soviet Tupolev TB-6 (ANT-26), which had been around since 1928.

These were generally in the same size and weight class as the Flying Fortress. The former was a four-engine bomber, while the latter was powered by a dozen engines. They were perceived incorrectly as having superior speed and altitude performance, but the Ju 89 had set a world record by carrying a payload of 11,500 pounds to an altitude of 30,550 feet. There was no cause for concern, as neither entered production. The two Ju 89 prototypes were scrapped in 1939 or 1940, while only five TB-6s were built, and they were obsolete by 1938.

Though neither of these aircraft played a role in combat operations, the interest in them provides a look at the trajectory of Air Corps strategic thought as the Arnold era began in that service.

In the spring of 1939, as Congress was gradually increasing the Air Corps budget, the War Department was just as gradually increasing its own interest in airpower doctrine. On March 14, 1939, the War Plans Division was requested to prepare a comprehensive air force study, based on "accepted doctrines of aviation employment."

The conclusions reached by two specially appointed committees were to be analyzed and submitted in a final report to the Chief of Staff. It was the determination in these studies (issued in August 1939) that "(1) the initial air objectives of an enemy would be American air bases in Hawaii, Puerto Rico, Panama, and other exposed areas; (2) a well-led and determined air attack, once launched, could not be stopped by American defenses, although serious losses could possibly be inflicted upon the enemy; (3) it was the duty of the Air Corps to provide a powerful striking force and the necessary strategic bases; and (4) the land-based heavy bomber was declared superior for national security because of its flexibility of employment and strong offensive performance."

This memorandum, issued less than a month ahead of the opening salvoes of World War II, articulated the views that had been promoted by airpower advocates for two decades. The official attitude of the War Department rotated 180 degrees to an acceptance of the need for a coordinated effort to build up strength and expand industrial capacity.

In the meantime, the first of the 39 B-17Bs made its debut flight on June 27, 1939, at Boeing Field. The new Flying Fortress type was approved by the Air Corps and officially ordered into production. Deliveries started a month later on July 29, 1939, and concluded with the last delivery on March 30, 1940.

Just as September 1938 had marked witnessed turning points in the political evolution of American airpower, so too did September 1939. The first B-17Bs had just entered operations when September 1, 1939, marked the beginning of World War II, a most monumental milestone in

The right-hand-side gun blister on the B-17B, as seen from outside and inside in February 1940.

B-17Bs in production at Boeing's busy and crowded Plant 1. Note the Boeing Model 307 Stratoliner commercial airliners in the back-left corner.

A B-17B of the Air Corps 7th Bomb Group, based at Hamilton Field, California, in January 1941. (Photo Courtesy USAF)

world history. As Hitler's unstoppable blitzkrieg swept into Poland, Britain and France declared war. On September 8, President Roosevelt declared a state of National Emergency in the United States.

September 1 also saw the passing of the baton of US Army chief of staff from Craig to Marshall. This marked a major turning point in America's ability to meet the challenge of this greatest of mankind's armed conflicts.

Across the country, in Seattle, a turning point was reached at Boeing a week later on September 9, 1939.

Though the promise of significant Air Corps orders seemed to be on the horizon with Roosevelt's ambitious rearmament plans, the company was stretched thin by all of its own investment in technology for such projects as the Model 314 flying boat and the Model 307 airliner—with its pressurized cabin. The question at hand was whether the company could handle Flying Fortress production should orders begin to flow at a significant rate.

In August 1939, corporate attorney Bill Allen suggested to Claire Egtvedt that they try to lure former president Phil Johnson back into the company. Remembering the conversation, Harold Mansfield related that Allen told his boss, "The need now is production. That's Phil's long suit."

Mansfield noted that this proposal "rocked Egtvedt at first. But then, what Bill Allen was saying was true. Production was Phil's long suit. He had what the company needed now, maybe what the country needed. Egtvedt had to admit that his own heart had never quite left Engineering. If he were relieved of the management burden, he could better counsel the young engineers."

When Egtvedt contacted Johnson, he was reluctant to start something so daunting at a time when he was looking forward to retirement. However, when World War II began a few days later, Johnson agreed, and on September 9, he returned to Seattle as president of Boeing, and Egtvedt moved up to the chairman's role.

Before the month was over, the Air Corps had placed an order for 38 new Flying Fortresses under the designation B-17C.

Chapter 5

THE B-17C AND B-17D:
THE TRANSITIONAL VARIANTS

When World War II began on September 1, 1939, only half of the B-17Bs ordered back in 1937 and 1938 had rolled out the door at Boeing Field in Seattle. By the end of that month, though, Boeing had received its first order for the B-17C variant.

Air Corps Contract W535 ac-13257, issued on September 20, called for 38 B-17C Flying Fortresses for a total price of $8,102,892.20. Designated internally as Model 299H, these aircraft were assigned the consecutive serial numbers 2043 through 2080. In contrast with the B-17B program, where 39 aircraft were ordered in batches spread out over more than 10 months, all 38 B-17Cs in W535 ac-13257 were assigned consecutive Air Corps tail numbers. Reflecting the purchase being made with Fiscal Year 1940 funds, the tail numbers were 40-2042 through 40-2079.

Such an order was nice to have but not easy for Boeing to digest.

"We've got to get rid of the deficit, get some capital to work with," Phil Johnson told Bill Allen in a meeting reported upon by Harold Mansfield. Johnson asked Allen to start work on a plan to sell new stock, and in October 1939, Johnson and Allen travelled to Washington, DC, with two Seattle bankers to look into securing a loan from the Reconstruction Finance Corporation (RFC). Created in 1932, the RFC was established by Congress as an independent government agency whose original purpose was to facilitate economic activity by lending during the Great Depression. The RFC would make and collect loans, and buy and sell securities.

As Donald Finlay pointed out, with the B-17C contract, Boeing "began to suspect the nature of wartime production [tempos], when everything built is not only obsolete before it is finished, but the improvements have already been tried. The B-17C, then, represented a transition between the beginning B-17 and the end item."

Finlay added that "unnecessary soundproofing, carpeting, wiring conduits, and wiring shields were eliminated, aiding both production and field repair. Armor plate appeared."

The specified empty weight of the B-17C increased from 27,652 pounds in the B-17B to 29,021. Gross weight went from 37,997 to 47,242 pounds. The engines were now the R-1820-65 variant of the Wright Cyclone, which delivered 1,000 hp at 25,000 feet. The cruising speed was 250 mph with a top speed of 323 mph at 25,000 feet. The service ceiling was 37,000 feet, and it had a range of 2,400 miles with 2 tons of payload.

Edward Curtiss Wells, project engineer for the Model 299 Flying Fortress program, had seen great changes between 1935 and 1940, but no one could imagine what the next five years would bring to the program. (Boeing Photo, Courtesy of Mike Lombardi)

A B-17C (Boeing Model 299H) in flight over the Midwest in standard Air Corps livery and with the yellow Wright Field arrowhead on the aft fuselage. (Photo Courtesy USAF)

The protruding Plexiglas gun blisters on the sides of the earlier variants were superseded by flush (and therefore more aerodynamic) Plexiglas panels. The ventral gun blister below the fuselage aft of the wing that was part of earlier Flying Fortress variants was replaced by a tin bathtub fixture, which held a gun that could fire aft. It was roughly in the same place on the fuselage as the ventral ball turret of later, B-17E through B-17G, Flying Fortresses.

As with earlier Flying Fortresses, the B-17C was armed only with five hand-held .30-caliber machine guns not installed in turrets. In lieu of a nose turret, the B-17C nose position was innovatively equipped with six ball-and-socket mounts. As summarized in a Materiel Division internal memo of October 26, 1939, the gun could be moved around from place to place and used interchangeably with any of these mounts.

Gathering Urgency for the B-17C

Despite the newfound exigency brought on by the war, things moved slowly at Boeing Field, certainly more slowly than they would in the coming years. The last B-17B was delivered on March 30, 1940, and the first flight of the first B-17C was made on July 21. Thereafter the pace quickened. While it had taken nine months from first flight for Boeing to deliver 39 B-17Bs, it took only four months for 38 B-17Cs.

In the meantime, the Air Corps issued a second order for 42 additional B-17Cs. The addendum CO.2 to Contract W535 ac-13257 was written on April 17, 1940. The Boeing serial numbers would be 2087 through 2128, and the Air Corps tail numbers were 40-3059 through 40-3100.

As Finlay had observed, the momentum of technological progress meant that so many changes had been made in the overall design that the Air Corps would wind up redesignating these additional B-17Cs as B-17Ds.

Among other things, the fuel system was revised to reduce vulnerability, and the B-17D updates included the first production installations of self-sealing fuel tanks in Flying Fortresses. Cowling flaps were installed, but the B-17Ds were powered by the same R-1820-65 engine as the B-17C. The B-17D also carried a 10th crew member and had paired machine guns in its ventral "bathtub" turret.

According to Boeing Historian Peter Bowers, all of the B-17Cs and B-17Ds, like the previous Flying Fortress variants, were delivered in natural metal finish. However, as the world was now at war, the Air Corps decided to begin camouflaging its aircraft, and the B-17Cs and B-17Ds were all

B-17Cs take shape on a crowded factory floor in April 1940. Soon there would be a great plant expansion occurring at Boeing Field.

subsequently painted a dark olive green at Air Corps depots. Many subsequent Flying Fortress variants would be painted thusly at the factory.

The second order for B-17Cs that were delivered as B-17Ds came just eight days after the major German assault on Western Europe that began with the invasion of Denmark and Norway on April 9, 1940. The first flight of a B-17D came 10 months later on February 3, 1941. There were 48 B-17Ds built new and 18 B-17Cs converted.

After the invasion and occupation of Poland in September 1939, a feared attack to the West failed to materialize through the winter, but this changed on April 9. A month later, on May 10, Hitler's legions attacked into Belgium and the Netherlands. By May 28, those countries had surrendered, and German forces were pouring into France. By June 14, Germany seized control of Paris, having accomplished in five weeks what it had been unable to do in four years of protracted fighting in World War I. France finally surrendered on June 22.

A Suddenly Expanding Aircraft Industry

On May 16, 1940, two days after the Netherlands government fled in disarray ahead of Hitler's fast-moving blitzkrieg, President Roosevelt went before Congress to ask for more money for airplanes. Sixteen months earlier, he had floated a trial balloon of 10,000 aircraft but asked for 3,000. Now, the president took off the metaphorical gloves and proposed that Congress authorize funding for 50,000 airplanes!

For American planemakers, the worry of having enough work to fill their factories turned to a concern over whether those factories had enough floor space to handle the orders that began to flood in.

Three roster shots of the B-17C (Boeing Model 299H): front, side, and three-quarter view, taken on August 28, 1940. The first flight of the B-17C had occurred on July 21.

Nearly completed B-17Cs spill out of the factory onto the Boeing Field ramp for finishing touches.

With this in mind, Congress authorized the funding for industrial capacity beyond that which was necessary for the quantity of aircraft and other hardware that had thus far been authorized. This meant that the factories would be ready if and when the United States went to war. Among other measures, Congress passed H.R. 9822 on June 28, 1940, which was designed to expedite National Defense by streamlining "contracts for acquisition, etc. of naval vessels or aircraft."

The expansion of the aircraft industry that began in 1939 was part of a vast expansion of essential industries under the National Defense Program, which was managed by the National Defense Advisory Commission and the Office of Production Management (later the War Production Board). With this, the federal government found itself having to go into the business of building factories of all kinds. Roosevelt asked Secretary of the Treasury Henry Morgenthau to oversee much of this activity, while bringing in William S. Knudsen, the president of General Motors—the largest industrial company in the United States—to head the Office of Production Management with the rank of lieutenant general.

An Army Air Corps officer explains the new flush side windows, which replaced the protruding gun blisters of previous models, to a young woman out walking her dachshund.

On August 22, 1940, Congress chartered the Defense Plant Corporation (DPC), aka "Plancor," to facilitate the expansion of production capabilities for military equipment. The DPC would build and equip new facilities, as well as provide money to expand existing ones, through the Reconstruction Finance Corporation (RFC), which financed much of American industrial expansion during the war.

From 1940 through 1945, the DPC disbursed more than $9 billion for 2,300 projects in 46 states and overseas. The DPC added hundreds of thousands of square feet to existing aircraft factories, and financed the construction of many all-new, government-owned factories. Most of the latter were constructed away from potentially vulnerable coastlines. Among these were inland facilities for California planemakers, including factories

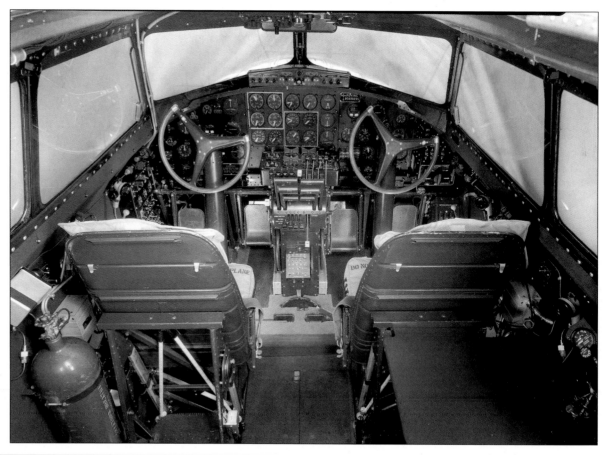

The flight deck of the B-17C, possibly that of the first B-17C, was photographed in August 1940, a month after this variant made its debut. (Please refer to the control panel diagram in Appendix I.)

for North American Aviation in Dallas and Kansas City, one for San Diego–based Consolidated Vultee in Fort Worth and the one near Chicago where Douglas Aircraft built C-54 transports that eventually evolved into today's O'Hare International Airport.

For Boeing, DPC funding permitted the company to build a new factory in Wichita, Kansas, adjacent to that of Boeing's Stearman Aircraft subsidiary. As discussed in greater detail in Chapter 6, Boeing entered into negotiations on this subject with the government in the spring of 1940 ahead of the formal creation of the DPC.

According to Boeing Historian Mike Lombardi, the only DPC contract at Plant 2 was Plancor 1577, which included a new office building on leased property across the street from the Boeing headquarters building as well as a parking lot and a bus terminal.

Funding for the expansion of the Plant 2 complex of buildings, formally designated as Project 3A, was authorized on October 18, 1940. Beginning at that time, Boeing was issued a series of Emergency Plant Facility (EPF) Project 3A contracts with the same W535 contract prefix as the orders for the Flying Fortress aircraft themselves. A series of further projects, numbered through Project 3A-11, followed through May 1945.

The flush side windows seen on these fuselage assemblies were an identifying characteristic of the B-17C and B-17D.

Exporting Heavy Bombers

In the August to October 1940 time period, as the DPC was ramping up to build factories and pay for projects such as the Plant 2 expansion, World War II continued to rage in Europe. Since June, Hitler now occupied and controlled all of continental Western Europe from the Arctic Ocean to the Pyrenees. With the fall of France, Britain stood alone to face the onslaught of Germany's might.

In August, the Luftwaffe began a brutal, unremitting bombing assault on Britain's ports, factories, and cities. The only thing that stood in the way of an easy victory was the courageous, but vastly outnumbered, pilots of the Royal Air Force. Despite the fact that the British had fewer than 1,000 fighters to face a Luftwaffe onslaught four times as large, the RAF was able to destroy 12 bombers for each one of their own losses. The Battle of Britain demonstrated the profound and significant role that would henceforth be played by airpower in modern warfare.

Against this backdrop, Britain's RAF, hungry for airplanes, became the second air force to operate the B-17C.

Though the process was complicated by restrictive American legislation, the acquisition of American warplanes by European air forces was not new. In the years leading up to World War II, German aircraft manufacturers had been going full bore to deliver fighters and bombers to the Luftwaffe while manufacturers in Britain and France, the two major countries opposing Germany, were racing to catch up.

The B-17C final assembly area at Boeing's Plant 2 in May 1941.

Looking across the Atlantic, they had established the New York–based Anglo-French Purchasing Board to acquire American aircraft for both the British Royal Air Force and the French Armée de l'Air. After the fall of France, this became the British Purchasing Commission.

Among other purchases, the British had come to Burbank, California, in 1938 to acquire Lockheed Hudson light bombers, and the French visited Santa Monica early in 1939 to buy the Douglas DB-7 attack bomber that was later in American service as the A-20. Ironically, a deal was cut for Boeing to build these Douglas airplanes for France under license.

Meanwhile, through the 1930s, Congress had passed a series of neutrality acts that greatly limited the sale of American arms to belligerents engaged in armed conflict. With the start of World War II and the declarations of war, sale of warplanes was greatly restricted. For example, shipping war materiel directly from US ports was prohibited, so crated airplanes were sent across the border to Canada, where they were picked up and taken to Europe. Roosevelt also adopted a "cash and carry" policy under which the British government paid for its goods from its gold reserves stored in the United States.

The B-17D variant, nearly identical to the B-17C, made its first flight on February 3, 1941. Subtle differences included engine cowling flaps, a tenth crewmember, and paired guns in the ventral turret.

The effort by President Roosevelt and Treasury Secretary Morgenthau (who favored arming countries opposing Hitler's Germany) to circumvent the neutrality laws eventually culminated in passage of the Lend-Lease Act on March 11, 1941. Technically, lend-lease involved the leasing of war machines, equipment, and other materiel to countries at war with Germany and its Axis partners, although very few of the leased items were ever returned. Under the program, $50 billion ($600 billion today) went to three dozen countries, with 62 percent going to the British Empire and 22 percent to the Soviet Union. The British entered into a repayment schedule with the Lend Lease obligation finally deemed repaid in 2006.

Of the 38 B-17Cs that had been ordered by the US Army Air Corps, 20 of them were diverted to the RAF, albeit with their having been assigned Air Corps serial numbers. In his memoir, Hap Arnold

In March 1941, the Air Corps began painting its B-17C and B-17D fleet in olive drab camouflage paint with a gray underside.

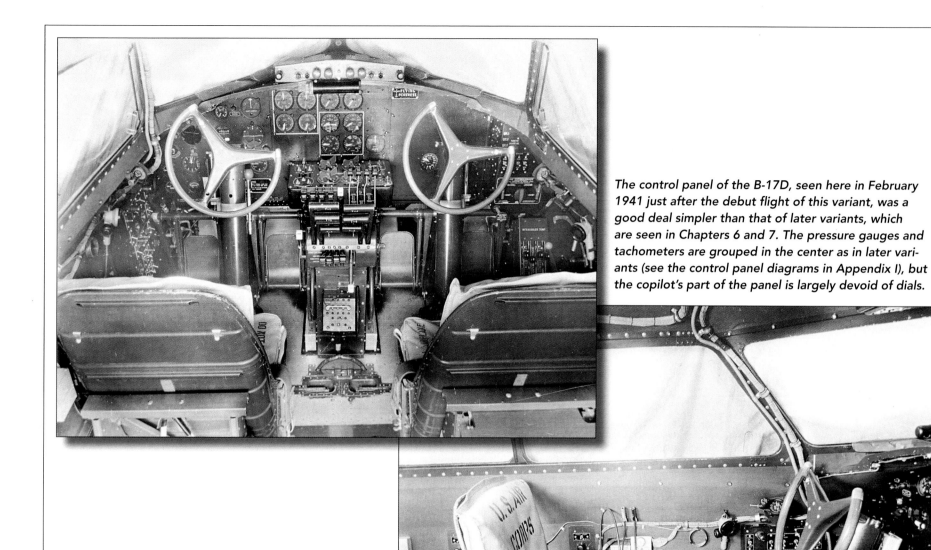

The control panel of the B-17D, seen here in February 1941 just after the debut flight of this variant, was a good deal simpler than that of later variants, which are seen in Chapters 6 and 7. The pressure gauges and tachometers are grouped in the center as in later variants (see the control panel diagrams in Appendix I), but the copilot's part of the panel is largely devoid of dials.

The basic layout of the side controls to the left of the pilot's position in the B-17D of February 1941 have a passing similarity to those seen in the control panel diagrams in Appendix I. The filter selector switch and interphone jackbox can be spotted, as can the cabin air-control lever just to the pilot's eft of the seat cushion.

reported that as early as August 26, 1940, the British had requested 68 B-17s and half of all of the Consolidated B-24 Liberator heavy bombers that were being produced.

A distinction between the foreign acquisition of the two types was that Consolidated sold Liberators directly, while Boeing undertook no direct foreign sales of the Flying Fortress. All of the Flying Fortresses that would be used by the RAF were acquired by the US Army Air Corps (and later the USAAF), then transferred to the British.

At the same time that Consolidated was producing the first B-24s for the Air Corps, it was also marketing an export version with the company's own "Liberator Bomber" designation, LB-30. In

A Boeing Model 299U in Royal Air Force markings runs up its engines at Boeing Field on January 28, 1941. This was one of 20 B-17Cs that were ordered by the USAAF but delivered to the RAF as the Fortress Mk. I.

On March 11, 1941, President Franklin D. Roosevelt signed the Act to Promote the Defense of the United States, better known as the Lend-Lease Act, which paved the way for the transfer of weapons to Allied countries—including B-17Cs to Great Britain. (Photo Courtesy Library of Congress)

April 1940, obviously not knowing that the disastrous German invasion was just a month away, the French Purchasing Commission placed an order for 168 "Mission Français" aircraft under the designation LB-30MF. None had been delivered when France was defeated, and the British took over the orders for about 135 of the aircraft, along with six YB-24s that became LB-30As, and they added some Liberators as LB-30B.

The first Flying Fortress reassigned to the RAF was the third B-17C off the assembly line, the one with the Boeing serial number 2044, which had Air Corps tail number 40-2043. The remainder were scattered throughout the production run with no more than three consecutive airplanes on the list. The final one was the last B-17C, with serial number 2080 and tail number 40-2079.

Although the RAF was not a direct Boeing customer, the aircraft were earmarked for export while on the assembly line, received their British insignia at Plant 2, and were designated by the company as Model 299U, distinguishing them from the B-17C, which was Model 299H.

These 20 aircraft received RAF serial numbers AN-518 through AN-537. Following the RAF practice of naming rather than numerically designating their aircraft, these were simply called "Fortress." In late 1942 and early 1943, when 19 B-17Fs were acquired by the RAF from USAAF stocks, these were designated as "Fortress Mk. II," so the B-17C equivalents then became "Fortress Mk. I." The RAF Fortresses first reached the United Kingdom in

May 1941 and entered combat two months later. During operations over occupied Europe, the RAF Bomber Command was disappointed with the performance of the aircraft, and by October 1941, most had been reassigned to the RAF Coastal Command for maritime patrol duty.

The lend-lease of aircraft, particularly heavy bombers, did not sit well with the Air Corps. Hap Arnold had been engaged in an ongoing feud with Henry Morgenthau ever since Roosevelt had put the Treasury Secretary in charge of production management.

"Does the Secretary of the Treasury run the Air Corps?" Arnold asked angrily before a Senate Military Committee meeting on January 24, 1939. "Does he give orders about Air Corps procurement?"

In his memoir, Arnold wrote that "it was the rosy dream of some Americans that we could save the world and ourselves by sending all our weapons abroad for other men to fight with."

Of course, this issue of foreign air forces poaching American aircraft that Arnold wanted was soon overtaken by events, as Congress was moving away from its accustomed sluggish reluctance to recognize the needs of Arnold's branch of the service.

Delivered to the RAF in August 1941, this Fortress Mk. I was originally the B-17C with tail number 40-2066. Having served in Egypt and India, it was returned to the USAAF in January 1942.

Chapter 6

THE B-17E BRINGS CHANGES IN PHILOSOPHY AND METHOD

Early in 1940, as Plant 2 was cutting metal on the B-17C orders, Ed Wells and his team were already a step ahead, inking the drafting vellum with a greatly updated design. The variant that Boeing designated as Model 299-O represented what Donald Finlay called "real change in appearance reflecting real change in design philosophy and method."

Visually, the 299-O, which the Air Corps would designate as B-17E, was dramatically distinguished from its predecessors by its tail. The big, rounded dorsal fin of the B-17E was nothing like those of the earlier Flying Fortresses, and it greatly increased the stability of the aircraft as a bombing platform. There was also now a gunner's position in the tail with a pair of .50-caliber tail guns.

Destined for its first flight on September 5, 1941, the B-17E had the same 103-foot, 9-inch wingspan as the preceding Flying Fortress variants, but it was larger on the other dimensions. At 73 feet 10 inches in length, it was 1 inch shy of being 6 feet longer. The new tail, at 19 feet 2 inches, lacked just 3 inches of being 4 feet taller.

The B-17E weighed 33,279 pounds empty (compared to 29,021 pounds for the B-17C), while it had a gross weight of 40,260 pounds (compared to 47,242 pounds for the B-17C). A maximum gross weight of 53,000 pounds was listed in the specs.

The Wright R-1820-65 Cyclone radial engine delivered 1,200 hp at takeoff and 1,000 hp at 25,000 feet. Specified performance was slightly inferior to that of the previous variant given that the B-17E

The first B-17E Flying Fortress (41-2393), seen here near Seattle, first flew on September 5, 1941, and was delivered to Wright Field on October 3.

weighed more and used the same engine type. The cruising speed was 210 mph, and the top speed was 317 mph at 25,000 feet. The service ceiling was 36,600 feet, and it had a range of 2,000 miles with 2 tons of payload.

Aircraft Turret Development Through 1941

As Donald Finlay later wrote, space considerations for future powered turrets were already being made as the earlier B-17C had been taking shape in 1939 and 1940.

However, the advent of powered turrets had not been as straightforward as it might seem in retrospect. Turret technology had progressed at a slow pace in the two decades since World War I. Perhaps the first aerial turrets had been circular plywood fixtures slotted to accommodate forked machine gun adapters that traveled on casters. Having been initially created in England for the Royal Naval Air Service by a warrant officer named Scharff, this contraption was called a "Scharff Ring" by the British, though the French called it a "tourelle." From that came the adoption of the term "turret" with its roots in an architectural term for a part of a fortress!

Soon, the wooden turrets gave way to machined metal rings as a support for the gun mounts. The challenges of a gunner in an open cockpit having to handle these in a slipstream led to the development of wind compensation mechanisms and eventually to thoughts of electrically powered turrets.

After the war ended in 1918, the rush to develop turret technology slowed to a snail's pace, especially in the United States. During the 1920s, powered turrets were deemphasized because they were considered by the Air Service Engineering Division to be cumbersome and overly complex, and they added excessive weight to aircraft. It was much easier to install fixed guns rather than flexible guns.

Captain Irving Holley, a historian with the Air Technical Service Command, writing in his 1947 study *Development of Aircraft Turrets in the AAF, 1917–1944*, noted that "flexible gunnery seemed to have become the Air Service's stepchild despite the lessons of World War I." He added that in the 1926 Aircraft Armament course at the Air Corps Engineering School at McCook Field, 27 hours were devoted to fixed gun installations and only 9 to all forms of flexible gunnery, machine guns, and gunsights.

He also cited a Langley Field memo from 1935 in which it was urged that guns smaller than .50 caliber should be adopted and that, rather than guns, "clouds, bad weather, and darkness should offer the greatest protection."

The .30-caliber machine gun was considered standard for bomber defensive armament because .50-caliber guns were seen as too heavy and awkward

The laminated wooden wind tunnel model of the B-17E, circa early 1941. This was the first variant with the completely redesigned vertical tail surfaces that would characterize all future Flying Fortresses.

This side view of the first-generation B-17E shows it with the remotely sighted lower turret that was installed in the first 112 B-17Es pending the delivery of the Sperry Ball Turrets. The tail turret, another B-17E innovation, was already installed.

for a gunner to handle and to fire with acceptable accuracy, especially in the slipstream. Holley added that "their bulk made internal structural interference an appreciably greater factor."

Meanwhile, experiments taking place at aircraft manufacturers such as Curtiss, Boeing, Douglas, and North American Aviation had confirmed that unpowered turrets required so much physical exertion to operate that accuracy and effectiveness would be compromised. These considerations would, of course, be eliminated if the guns were contained in powered turrets, although the latter were still considered unacceptably heavy.

While the US Army Air Corps considered flexible gunnery an experimental subject well into the 1930s, Holley cited memos from American military and naval attachés in Germany and Italy that told of much more advanced work being done. Meanwhile, companies such as Bofors in Sweden as well as Vickers, Bristol, and Armstrong-Whitworth in the United Kingdom were also making great strides in electrical and compressed-air turret drives.

It wasn't until April 1938 that Hap Arnold, now the deputy chief of staff of the Air Corps, commissioned a serious study of bomber defensive armament. He brought together representatives of the Air Corps, the Army Ordinance Department, and even the Navy, to look into the state of the art. Upon his becoming chief of the Air Corps five months later, Arnold fast-tracked flexible gunnery and turret development. He also tasked them with the studying and planning for the development of all the components of fire control systems from optics to gunsight computers.

The Air Corps Armament Laboratory at Wright Field took up the matter of turrets, initiating studies and mock-ups as well as negotiations with commercial sources. As Holley noted, by January 1940, they reported that experimental models of twin .50-caliber powered aircraft turrets would be available for testing "in the near future."

On the industry side, a great deal of studying had already taken place. The Sperry Corporation (Sperry Gyroscope Company, 1910 to 1933) was also moving toward development of aircraft gun turrets. Sperry was the apogee of high-tech for the era, being a world leader in analog computers, gyroscopic navigation, and naval fire control systems. As early as 1936, Sperry had proposed a turret and fire control system to the Air Corps Materiel Division. Though Air Corps funding was limited, Sperry had received a contract to design a turret for the Bell XFM-1 Airacuda bomber destroyer that

The powered top turret that was installed in B-17Es from the beginning marked a big change from the armament of early Flying Fortresses, and it became standard equipment in future Flying Fortresses.

Edward Curtiss Wells, the project engineer for the Flying Fortress program, studies the first installation of a Sperry Ball Turret in February 1941. (Boeing Photo Courtesy Mike Lombardi)

This interior view shows the Sperry Ball Turret as installed in February 1941. The first Flying Fortress to receive it was the 113th B-17E, tail number 41-2505, delivered in January 1942.

mounted 37-mm cannons in a manned nacelle on each wing. The Airacuda never reached production, but the project contributed to the aerial gunnery knowledge base. But there was still much to learn when it came to optics, analog computers, and ballistic trajectory calculations.

As so often is the case with evolving technology, it is the advent of a specific keystone device or mechanism that allows a technical breakthrough. In the case of American-powered aircraft turrets, this breakthrough device may well have been the Metadyne, which evolved into the Amplidyne.

Ernst Alexanderson and his team at General Electric had created these variable-speed electric drives for the US Navy for the purpose of facilitating the faster tracking of rotating systems (such as searchlights and naval gun turrets) where accurate, powered control was imperative. The idea was smooth movement with minimal or no lag between changes in the input and the position of the turret or other rotating system that needed to be on target at all times as they moved to track the target.

Invented by Alexanderson, the Amplidyne was essentially an electromechanical amplifier, consisting of an electric motor driving a DC generator in which the signal to be amplified is applied to the generator's field winding and its output voltage is an amplified copy of the field current. Amplidynes were eventually used in industrial applications involving high-power servo and control systems to amplify control signals for large electric motors.

An early installation of a Sperry Ball Turret in a B-17E, circa February 1942.

General Electric suggested these devices to the Materiel Division in July 1938 as a possible powerplant for a powered aircraft turret. Subsequent conversations ensued between Wright Field and General Electric with input from the Navy. Indeed, the Navy and Air Corps had formed a Joint Aircraft Committee (JAC) to coordinate their technical activities.

The Materiel Division was eager to take advantage of General Electric's expertise in addressing its fire control issues, but the company was heavily involved with Navy work.

As Irving Holley wrote, summarizing an October 17, 1939, Materiel Division memo, "However ready GE was to accept Air Corps projects, prior Navy obligations stood in the way. The [Materiel Division] Armament Laboratory was especially interested in securing details concerning the [General Electric] gyroscopically stabilized lead computer under contract at GE for the Navy, and the Chief of the Air Corps was called upon to obtain permission to do so officially."

General Electric did establish an aircraft fire control operation at its Schenectady, New York, plant, initially to develop turrets for the Douglas

The setup and test fixture for the Sperry Ball Turret in June 1942.

In this photograph of the Sperry Ball Turret assembly shop, probably taken in 1941 before America was in the war, there seems to be little urgency among the workers.

The Sperry Ball Turret is clearly visible in this color photograph of a B-17E on its March 3, 1942, delivery flight.

A-20 attack bomber. In 1940, the company entered into a collaboration with the Glenn L. Martin Company, which was developing turrets in-house for its B-26 Marauder medium bomber. These turrets utilized the General Electric Amplidyne system to provide speed control.

In the years before World War II, though, Air Corps funding, especially for cutting-edge technology, was greatly pinched. In 1939, the Materiel Division Armament Laboratory at Wright Field was staffed by three civilians and one uniformed officer. The budget for 1940 allocated $45,000 for fire control

A good close-up look at an early installation of the "Stinger," or "Steeplechase," tail turret in a B-17E, circa January 1941. It was first installed in the B-17E and remained standard equipment through that variant and the B-17F and into the first year of B-17G production. From June 1944, many B-17Gs were retrofitted with the Cheyenne tail turret.

A man kneeling in the tail gunner's position can barely be seen behind bulletproof glass in this straight-on view of the B-17E's Stinger Tail Turret.

and $25,000 for powered gun mounts.

Meanwhile, however, turret development in the United Kingdom (notably at Boulton-Paul and Frazer-Nash) had leaped ahead of that of the United States. The latter firm's turrets were coming off the assembly line at a rate of around 20 per day in May 1940. French industry (notably the Société Duplication de Machines Motrices) had also undertaken serious studies of powered turrets. If there was any good news on the world scene in this respect, it was that the Germans would continue to show little interest in powered aircraft turrets, despite their having control of French industry after mid-1940.

In the United States, meanwhile, there were American inventors outside the mainstream represented by General Electric who had ideas for turrets. One was Preston Tucker, an industrialist and race car developer based in Ypsilanti, Michigan. Though his ultimate impact both as an automaker and an armaments man was minimal in terms of volume and turnover, Tucker is worth a mention here because of his unique role in American industrial history. In the 1940s (like John DeLorean was in the 1970s or Elon Musk is in the 21st century), he created an iconic automobile that was the epitome of out-of-the-box thinking. In the late 1930s, though, he caught the attention of Hap Arnold with his ideas for a turret that Arnold described in a July 13, 1939 memo as "ingenious."

The Tucker turret featured a drive motor with glass-impregnated coils as a burnout deterrent, a communicator that did not arc under rapid reversals, and a lever-action, carbon-disc variable rheostat to control the field current for speed variations. At a Wright Field meeting, Tucker had tried to get a foot in the door by offering to build a power drive for an existing B-18 manual turret—for $10,000. The proposal was rejected because the B-18 was being sidelined by the B-17, but the Armament Branch did consider retrofitting Tucker's drive mechanism to B-17s.

Irving Holley noted that Tucker's participation in the Flying Fortress program was ultimately rejected because he did not have the resources to set up a production enterprise. As Holley said, "to perfect a turret and carry it successfully through the experimental stage to the threshold of production required either a government-financed experimental contract or a corporate organization of sufficient scale to absorb the unproductive immediate costs of the period of research and experimentation." His early interest notwithstanding, even Hap Arnold was unwilling to bet on Tucker.

Parenthetically, as Tucker's attempt to get into the turret business imploded, note that even corporations with very deep pockets did not always earn a seat at the Materiel Division table. A case in point was Westinghouse Electric, which was unable to prepare an acceptable response to an April 1940 Materiel Command request for powered turret proposals. On April 30, Captain P. E. Shanahan called it "very clumsy" and "unduly complicated."

Around the time that World War II began in September 1939, American industry was finally ready for a breakthrough. On its own initiative, Sperry was working on a comprehensive study of everything related to a comprehensive Central-Station Fire Control (CFC) system, in which multiple turrets could be controlled from a central location. It was an ambitious undertaking with an ambitious goal, but on June 23, the Air Corps finally authorized

A bombardier poses at his station above a shrouded Norden Bombsight in the nose of a B-17E. Forward-firing armament in this variant was limited, which would prove to be a critical weakness.

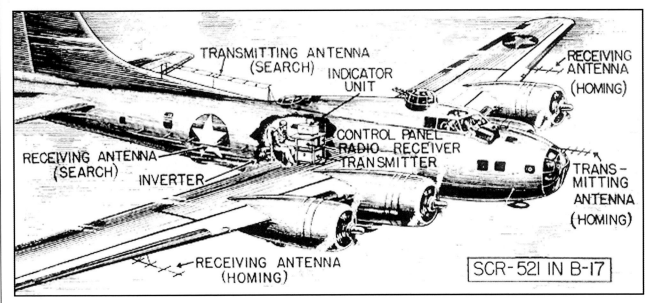

Labels on illustration: TRANSMITTING ANTENNA (SEARCH), INDICATOR UNIT, RECEIVING ANTENNA (HOMING), RECEIVING ANTENNA (SEARCH), CONTROL PANEL, RADIO RECEIVER TRANSMITTER, INVERTER, TRANS-MITTING ANTENNA (HOMING), RECEIVING ANTENNA (HOMING), SCR-521 IN B-17

The SCR-521 Radar installed in the B-17E was an airborne long-wave search system with a maximum range against surfaced submarines (broadside) of 6 miles. This data was summarized in the manual entitled FTP 217: US Radar: Operational Characteristics of Radar Classified by Tactical Application. *(Photo Courtesy Radar Research and Development Subcommittee, Joint Chiefs of Staff)*

these earlier variants had a 12-volt electrical system and the Sperry turrets were designed for a 24-volt system.

Initially, Boeing planned to build the turret dome, the gear trains, the ring gear mounts, and the gun mounts. Sperry would supply the computer, power units, controls, and gunsight. However, Boeing quickly decided that such a process of divided responsibility was too complicated and allowed Sperry to take it over and deliver completed turrets as Government Furnished Equipment (GFE), the term used for fully completed subassemblies that the government would buy under a separate contract and deliver ready to install.

On December 27, 1940, Sperry received Contract W535 ac-16235 for 540 "local" upper turrets for $7,185 each for a total of $3,879,900 (roughly $64,309,820 today). Also included was $1,274,075 for 113 lower turrets.

$8,000 of its own money for a .30-caliber flexible gunsight that the company had developed as part of its overall system.

By 1940, the state of the art had advanced to the point where turrets were being developed by multiple manufacturers, including major airframe builders, for a number of bomber aircraft. As Irving Holley noted, during the early months of 1940, the "handheld gunsight gave way to the turret system." In parallel with this new paradigm, expediency dictated that self-contained, "locally-controlled" turrets would take precedence over centrally-controlled turrets. According to memos dated on May 23 and June 17 of that year that were later obtained by Holley, Boeing had stated that it was unwilling to sacrifice its Flying Fortress delivery schedule for any "mythical anticipated development."

Holley pointed out that by May 1940, Boeing had come up with a turret plan that they expected to incorporate into the B-17C. The idea was for a locally controlled twin .50-caliber upper turret and a similar remotely controlled lower turret that used a Keuffel & Esser driftmaster non-compensating sight built into the turret itself. This plan was formally approved in July, but it was decided to skip the B-17C or B-17D and incorporate the turrets into the upcoming B-17E. One problem that needed to be addressed was that

So, few of the latter were ordered because the turrets being developed for the upper fuselage were less than ideal for the lower position. As Irving Holley pointed out, "No satisfactory solution had as yet been offered to overcome the difficulties of sighting below the fuselage level."

This sent Sperry's engineers scrambling back to their drawing boards and sent the Materiel Division to entertain lower turret proposals from the Bendix Aviation Corporation of South Bend, Indiana. Ultimately, the solution was found in Sperry's famous "ball turret," which is discussed in the following section. The adapted upper turrets were considered as an interim solution pending the arrival of the ball turrets, and 113 of these were ordered so as not to create a production bottleneck at the Boeing factory.

Bendix, meanwhile, would enter the Flying Fortress story a few years later as the creator of the famous "chin turret" that would define the profile of the B-17G.

With Boeing itself having declined to build the outer portions of the Sperry top turrets and their interim lower turret counterparts, Sperry the subcontractor was compelled to seek out a subcontractor of its own. Steel Products Engineering Company of Springfield, Ohio, was brought aboard, and the Briggs Manufacturing Company of Detroit took over heavy tooling and final assembly of the lower turrets. The Plexiglas was supplied by Rohm & Haas of Philadelphia. Ironically, Plexiglas had originated with the company's estranged German parent, Röhm & Haas AG.

As late as November 1940, anticipating potential delays, the Materiel Division was urging Sperry to engage Detroit automakers in the process, but Sperry resisted.

Despite the efforts made by ordering the interim turrets, the problem of turret acquisition caused delays in the whole Flying Fortress production program. Throughout 1941, the upper turrets were running two months behind B-17E production, while the lower turrets were four to five months behind schedule.

It should be pointed out that at the same time that the Materiel Division had picked Sperry as the purveyor of choice for Flying Fortress turrets, another company was emerging as a major player in the making of turrets. This was the Emerson Electric Manufacturing Company, a maker of compact electric motors based in St. Louis. Back in 1939, the manufacturing rights to some of the Tucker turret components were in turn acquired by Emerson, which also acquired turret manufacturing drawings from British manufacturers, such as Boulton-Paul.

Emerson went on to become a major supplier of other turrets, especially for the B-24 Liberator. In July 1941, Emerson would receive a Defense Plant Corporation contract that allowed for a massive expansion of its St. Louis factory. So large and capable was this new and modern facility that by 1942, the Materiel Division moved some of the production of Sperry's Flying Fortress turrets to St. Louis.

It was in the B-17E that all the work that had been ongoing with respect to gun turret development came to fruition. While the earlier Flying Fortress variants had carried fixed guns, the Model 299-O was specifically designed for the powered turrets top and bottom. The upper one was just aft and above the flight deck, and one was below the fuselage where the B-17C/B-17D had the "tin bathtub" gun position. It was remotely operated by the use of a periscope sight in a Plexiglas bubble a few feet behind the turret.

However, this turret was quickly superseded by Sperry's ball turret. Boeing historian Peter Bowers, citing aircraft serial numbers, listed 112 B-17Es that were equipped with the original turret and added that on the 113th airplane, the turret was changed. This agrees with the number mentioned in Contract W535 ac-16235.

The Sperry Ball Turret

This fixture was a locally controlled spherical installation roughly 3 feet in diameter into which the gunner inserted himself in a fetal position with his eyes roughly level with the pair of Browning .50-caliber machine guns. These extended through the entire turret and were located on either side of the

A view of the control panel on the flight deck of a B-17E as photographed in September 1941. (Please refer to the control panel diagram in Appendix I.)

gunner with the cocking handles operated through a system of cables and pulleys. A reflector gunsight was located between the gunner's feet. Because of the cramped interior, each ball turret gunner would be picked for his being the smallest man on his crew—and definitely someone not susceptible to claustrophobia!

Sperry outsourced production of the ball turret prototype to one of its subcontractors for other turret work—the Briggs Manufacturing Company of Detroit. Briggs was best known as the manufacturer of auto bodies for companies such as Ford and Chrysler. However, the Office of Production Management (OPM) had curtailed automobile production for the duration of the war. This left Briggs with plenty of production capability, although the company was quite displeased at losing lucrative contracts from major automakers.

Meanwhile, the Emerson Electric Manufacturing Company in St. Louis, which had been brought on board by the USAAF to produce the Sperry top turrets, was also in line to produce ball turrets when full-scale production got underway. However, coordination of the work became problematic, as Emerson was an Air Corps direct contractor rather than a Sperry subcontractor.

When the Sperry/Briggs prototype was delivered to Wright Field for testing in May 1941, one of the biggest concerns was whether a person could endure being cooped up in the thing for long periods of time. Although the determination was in the affirmative, Irving Holley noted in his *Development of Aircraft Turrets in the AAF, 1917–1944* that there remained concern for "the gunners' comfort."

Nevertheless, the Materiel Division gave a green light to Briggs for an initial order of 250 ball turrets in June, postponing full-scale production until the Production Engineering Section (PES) had conducted firing tests. Pending the completion of the tests and the production of production tooling, these 250 were handmade in Detroit at a cost of $20,300 each. The estimate for 2,050 production units was $14,099, including $3,700 for the gunsights.

A bottleneck in ball turret production was that only three machines in the United States (two at Ford and one at Chrysler) were large and sophisticated enough to cut the main ring gear for the ball turret. Likewise, there was a limited number of plants in the country that had the expertise to make other components for the ball turret. It was the tight timing imposed by the Air Corps that caused alarm at Sperry and Brigs. Holley noted that

This photograph of the left, or command pilot's, seat and the left-side instruments in a B-17E was taken in September 1941. (Please refer to the control panel diagrams in Appendix I.)

Here, we look right on the fight deck of a B-17E toward the copilot's seat and right-side instruments, circa September 1941. (Please refer to the control panel diagrams in Appendix I.)

"intrinsically, the ball did not represent an overwhelmingly difficult project, but a two-month deadline was hard to meet."

In September 1941, E. A. Burdy, head of PES, gave the project a "Number 1-AAA priority," having sent a memo to Lieutenant Colonel K. B. Wolfe at Wright Field on August 20 in which he said, "It's hot because we're short."

Even as the project finally got on track and the balls started rolling, other issues snarled it. Numerous modifications proved necessary in the early months. As late as November 1941, Sperry was still working on the computing gunsight. The list of complaints mounted. The sighting window became obscured by water and dirt on takeoff. The interphone and power switches did not work properly. The ammunition chutes jammed when the ammunition cans were half empty. While other issues were sorted out, the latter would take years of trying to fix.

Despite serious production delays in the early months, the ball turret became standard equipment for the B-17E, B-17F, and B-17G. Between them, Sperry, Briggs, Emerson, and a vast number of subcontractors would supply 12,485 Flying Fortresses with ball turrets over the next four years.

The Tail Turret

The B-17E would also be the first Flying Fortress variant with tail guns. Though it is perhaps hard to believe in retrospect, there had been an institutional skepticism of tail guns within the Air Corps Materiel Command. In his postwar book *Development of Aircraft Turrets in the AAF, 1917–1944*, Captain Irving Holley wrote that prior to 1940, "no extensive attempts had been made to place a gunner in the tail because of the weight and balance problems caused by such an installation, not to mention space limitations imposed by conventional designs."

In an October 1944 conversation, C. L. Anderson of the Aircraft Laboratory admitted to Holley that they had "assumed the impracticality of the tail gun [because] the pitch and yaw at the tail position would make sighting difficult if not impossible."

Meanwhile, W. G. McNeill of the Armaments Laboratory told Holley, also in October 1944, that it had been the belief that "tail gun positions would be impractical because of the high acceleration to which the gunner stationed there would be subjected."

Nevertheless, as much as this may have been the prevailing belief, it was not universally accepted. In a February 9, 1940, memo to Hap Arnold, Major R. C. Coupland had written that it had become necessary to redesign bombers to afford firepower from the rear that was "at least equal or better than can be brought to bear by the attacker in the rear cone of vulnerability."

This is a detailed view of the pilot's position in the B-17E, highlighting the control column installation as well as rudder and brake pedals.

For a definition of this "rear cone of vulnerability," look no further than a memo from February 19, just 10 days later, in which Captain P. E. Shanahan told Lieutenant Colonel Oliver Echols, then chief of engineering at Wright Field and later the chief of the Materiel Division, that it was "generally assumed that 80 percent of all attacks on bombardment airplanes would come within a 45-degree cone to the rear."

It is important to point out that the 1936 edition of the Materiel Command's own *Handbook of Instructions for Airplane Designers* had called for "specified fields of fire for bombardment aircraft covering the greatest possible portion of the forward hemisphere [and] complete protection of the upper rear quartersphere." The areas below and to the rear were not specifically addressed except to say that "intersecting fire from at least two guns should meet at 100 yards in every direction."

However, the 1937 revision of that book had been amended to read that protective gunfire was required for the "greatest possible portion of the entire sphere about the bombardment plane."

Looking forward through the B-17E radio operator's compartment, just aft of Bulkhead 5, in September 1941. The BC-348 radio receiver on the desk at the left remained standard equipment in this location through the B-17G.

Holley also reminded us that at this time, British manufacturers were designing heavy bombers with tail turrets. Indeed, the Avro Lancaster, Handley-Page Halifax, Short Stirling, and the Vickers Wellington would all operate with tail turrets containing four machine guns.

In the United States, manned tail turrets with paired Browning M2 .50-caliber machine guns became the norm for medium and heavy bombers, although the turrets themselves varied from aircraft to aircraft. While the Consolidated B-24 had a powered swivel turret built by the Emerson Electric Manufacturing Company of St. Louis, the Flying Fortress was equipped with the "Stinger" turret—also, but not often, called a "Steeplechase" turret. This was not so much a turret but a gunner's position built into the rear fuselage with the guns pointing aft.

In the defensive cone that the guns covered to the rear of the aircraft, they could be elevated 40 degrees from horizontal and depressed downward 15 degrees. They could be traversed 30 degrees to the left or to the right.

The gunner knelt, facing aft, forward of the twin M2 .50-caliber machine guns and behind the ammunition box. He was protected on the sides by armor plate and thick bulletproof glass in the windows.

The Stinger made its debut in October 1941 with the first B-17E and remained standard equipment through the end of World War II, although this turret was partially supplanted by the famous "Cheyenne" tail turret, which was introduced as an after-production modification in around 4,500 B-17Gs after May 1944 (see Chapter 8 under the heading "The Cheyenne Tail Turret").

B-17E Radar

The SCR-521 system used on the B-17E was an airborne long-wave search system for bombers that was used for locating and homing on ships or coastal targets as well as for navigation. It was based on the Air-to-Surface Vessel (ASV) radar developed and used by the Royal Air Force (RAF) to scan the surface of the ocean for both ships and surfaced submarines. ASV evolved from the testing air-to-air radar in 1937 and became operational in two stages in 1940 and 1941. The two ASV variants used by the USAAF were the SCR-521A (ASVC) 170-cm system and SCR-521B (ASE) VHF surface search system. (See the illustration on page 70.)

The pre-1944 "SCR-" prefix, often incorrectly interpreted as meaning "Signal Corps Radio," actually stands for "Set, Complete, Radio," as US Army Signal Corps radios and communications systems were thought of as "sets." A complete set was designated as "SC," while subcomponents had other designations such as "BC" for "Basic Component," etc.

As described by the Radar Research and Development Subcommittee of the US Joint Committee on New Weapons and Equipment in its 1943 FTP-217 Report, the SCR-521 radar had reliable maximum ranges for surfaced submarines (broadside) of 6 miles; for a 4,000 to 8,000-ton ship, 25 miles; and for a well-defined coastline, 60 miles. The minimum range was 350 yards. The sets covered 150 degrees forward when searching and 40 degrees when homing on a target. Range and left/right indication were provided on the radar scope. Identification Friend or Foe (IFF) identification signals were displayed directly on the scope.

In addition to B-17s, the SCR-521 was also used in the B-24, B-25, and B-34. It was noted in FTP-217 that the external antennas reduced an aircraft's top speed by about 5 to 7 knots, and the forward nose antenna interfered with the firing of the forward flexible guns.

Both SCR-521 variants were phased out of American production by the summer of 1943. (See Chapter 8.)

B-17E Production and Facilities

The Air Corps had been in discussion with Boeing about an initial order for 150 B-17Es even as President Roosevelt was unveiling his desire for 50,000 airplanes on May 16, 1940.

A month later, on June 14, Colonel Oliver Echols, assistant chief of the Air Corps Materiel Division at Wright Field, wrote to Phil Johnson to ask whether Boeing's existing facilities could handle the production work if the Air Corps was to increase the number of aircraft from 150 to 277.

In the reply to Wright Field on July 29, Boeing had said "no," this would be impossible without additional facilities. At the time, the company estimated that it would need approximately $6.3 million for 1,215,000 square feet of floor space and $2.7 million for tools, dies, jigs, fixtures, and machinery.

On August 7, after a meeting called by the National Defense Advisory Commission, Boeing presented the Air Corps with three options for B-17E

In this September 1941 photograph, we are looking forward from the tail area through the waist of a B-17E prior to installation of the waist guns at the two windows on the sides. On the floor just before Bulkhead 6 is the top of the Sperry Ball Turret.

In this January 1942 photograph looking forward from the tail area through the waist of a B-17E, the M2 waist guns have been installed, and a fender had been placed around the top of the ball turret in the background.

This B-17E, seen here on its February 26, 1942, delivery flight, survived the Battle of Midway in June 1942 but ditched in the Pacific in January 1943.

production. Plan A called for 1,250,000 new square feet in Seattle at a cost of $10 million. Plan B, which was seen as the least practical, would have added 800,000 square feet in Seattle and 1,555,000 square feet in Wichita. Plan C, the option preferred by the Air Corps, involved 800,000 square feet in Seattle and 350,000 square feet in Wichita—bringing Boeing's total square footage to 1.9 million square feet—at a total cost of $10.5 million.

The latter option was approved by General Bill Knudsen of the Office of Production Management on August 9, 1940, and forwarded to the War Department. According to an official postwar overview of the Plant 2 project, Assistant Secretary of War Robert Patterson "was rather reluctant to approve the Boeing-Seattle expansion, inasmuch as it was in a critical labor area and an unfavorable strategic location [i.e., it was not centrally located in the country, and being close to the coast, it was more potentially vulnerable to air attack.] However, he recognized that delay in production would result if a more acceptable site were insisted upon."

In turn, details of the plan were signed off by the Air Corps Materiel Division. Although the Materiel Division was headquartered in Washington, DC, the hands-on work was handled at the Air Corps engineering center at Wright Field in Ohio, where the man in charge of aircraft acquisition was Colonel Oliver Echols.

Looking very abstract in this September 1941 image is the underside of the pilot's cab assembly prior to installation. Note the circular cutout for the top turret.

As 1940 began, Major General George Brett was the chief of the Materiel Division, but during the year he was succeeded by Echols, who moved to Washington to assume command for the duration. Echols, who would be promoted to brigadier general in October 1940, and major general in February 1942, had been intimately involved in the Flying Fortress program since the beginning. He would go on to be the key man in USAAF aircraft acquisition during World War II. In March 1942, Echols' Materiel Division was upgraded in status and importance to become the Materiel Command.

In the meantime, as the government had gone into the business of building factories and facilities, the Materiel Division created its Industrial Planning Section, which was based at Wright Field and headed by Lieutenant Colonel (Colonel as of September 1941) Philip Schneeberger.

On August 30, 1940, through Echols, Boeing received the first order for the B-17E. W535 ac-15677 called for 277 aircraft at a cost of $70,449,955.20 ($135 million today) to be delivered before October 1, 1941. It was then augmented by a second B-17E order less than three weeks later on September 16. This one, W535 ac-15677 CO.1, called for an additional 235 aircraft to be delivered by April 1, 1942, for $56,917,000, bringing the total to 512.

The first batch of B-17Es carried Boeing serial numbers 2204 through 2480, and the second batch was numbered 2483 through 2717. The Air Corps tail numbers, reflecting acquisition with Fiscal Year 1941 funding, were 41-2393 through 41-2669 and 41-9011 through 41-9245, respectively. As discussed at length in Chapter 7, there were a number of B-17Es lend-leased to Britain as Fortress Mk. IIA in late 1942 and early 1943.

On October 18, 1940, with approvals from Echols, Brett, and Patterson in hand, Schneeberger's Industrial Planning Section formally authorized funding for the expansion of Plant 2, which was now officially designated as Project 3A. Boeing was issued Emergency Plant Facility (EPF) Contract W535 ac-16424.

Under the contract, Boeing received $7,368,849.13 ($134 million today) for construction of an assembly unit, primary shops, a warehouse building, hospital, office building, engineering space, storehouse for flammable materials, acetylene generator and gas storage building, and office building. Also included under EPF Contract W535 ac-16424 was the expansion of existing structures at or near Plant 2 that would be used for production, office space, and warehousing. Installation of tools and equipment as well as land improvements were also included.

Meanwhile, the sum appropriated had already been deemed insufficient, and a Project 3A-1 addendum added an additional $258,183 to the project on October 18, the same day as the contract.

Earlier in the year, the Air Corps had decided that its Flying Fortresses should be camouflaged to help prevent them from being targeted by air raids on airfields. They had done this work in-house with their small numbers of B-17Cs and B-17Ds, but with 512 B-17Es now in the pipeline, this promised to overwhelm Air Corps depot facilities. With this in mind, the service formally requested that Boeing paint the aircraft prior to delivery, and the formal request was made on October 23.

This October 1941 top view of the installed pilot's cab area of a nearly finished B-17E shows the flight deck and top turret.

This B-17E (41-2656), nicknamed "Chief Seattle from the Pacific Northwest," was financed by the people of the Puget Sound area who raised $280,535 in a war bond drive to pay for it. It was delivered in a March 5, 1942, ceremony at Boeing Field. "Chief Seattle" served with the 19th Bombardment Group in the Southwest Pacific and disappeared without a trace on an August 14, 1942, reconnaissance mission over Rabaul, New Britain, and the Solomon Sea.

On November 29, Boeing responded with a quote of $1,200 per airplane. The actual cost of applying the paint was $515.15, and the remaining balance was to be applied to the cost of building a new paint hangar at Boeing Field. The cost of the 40,000-square-foot hangar "suitably heated, ventilated, and equipped for spraying," was estimated at $169,800 to construct it and $350,000 to equip it, so it would seem that Boeing intended to amortize this activity over approximately 760 aircraft, more than the total B-17E orders then on the books.

As the schedule called for no B-17Es to be ready for paint until the fall of 1941 and because all parties had other fish to fry, approval for the paint hangar languished for half a year. By May 1941, the paint hangar had been rolled into a much larger program that was designated as Project 3A-2. This project was approved on May 21, although it was not signed off by Robert Patterson, now the "Under" Secretary of War, until June 28.

In the meantime, the Air Corps placed a third order for Model 299-O aircraft on June 2, 1941. This contract, W535 ac-20292, called for 300 aircraft to be designated as B-17E. However, with the progress of technology being what it was, these would be completed as the first batch of B-17Fs and are discussed as such in Chapter 7. In the context of the ongoing B-17E program, this order came at such a time as to underscore the urgency of the plant expansion requests.

In the meantime, big changes were afoot in Washington. On June 20, 1941, the US Army Air Corps and the tactical organization called General Headquarters Air Force, which answered directly to the Chief of Staff, were merged into a single entity to be called the US Army Air Forces (USAAF).

Reacting to the long-advocated creation of a "US Air Force" independent of the Army, US Army Chief of Staff General George Marshall had responded with a compromise that granted full autonomy to the USAAF within the US Army organization. Implicit in this action was an assumption that an independent "US Air Force" would be created when the war was over, which it was. It was reasoned that to do so in the midst of the war would not be expedient. Sorting out the unpredictable logistical complications of two parallel and competing bureaucratic infrastructures would create a needless distraction to fighting the war.

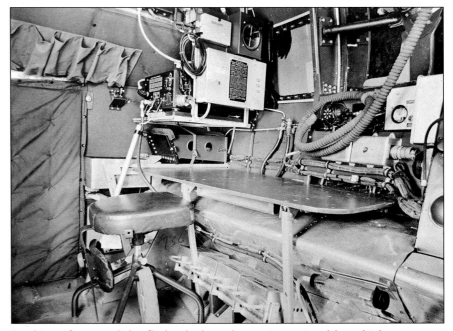

Looking aft toward the flight deck at the navigator's table, which was located on the left side of the nose behind the bombardier's station. This was a later-production B-17E (42-29467) photographed in December 1942.

As the first chief of the USAAF (Commanding General after March 1942), Marshall naturally picked Air Corps Chief Major General Hap Arnold. Promoted to lieutenant general in December 1941, he was given a seat on the Joint Chiefs of Staff (JCS) when that organization was formally created in early 1942.

Seattle Plant Expansion: 1941

The implementation of Project 3A-2 on June 28, 1941, was one of the first infrastructure actions taken under the new USAAF. On that day, Under Secretary of War Robert Patterson signed Emergency Plant Facility (EPF) Contract W535 ac-19670. Redesignated as Defense Aid Contract DA W535 ac-196 on July 8, this document described the scope of Project 3A-2.

A total of $15 million was appropriated for Project 3A-2, with $2.9 million to be spent on Plant 2 in Seattle, and the balance for plant expansion in Wichita. The Plant 2 work included the paint hangar as well as additions to other buildings, other tools, equipment and machinery, plus a boiler house. The total expansion would add 43,043 square feet of floor space.

During the summer, both Lieutenant Colonel Johnny Corkille and Lieutenant Colonel J. S. Griffith, the outgoing and incoming Materiel Division reps in Seattle, advised Hap Arnold's office in Washington of a pressing issue on the ground at Boeing Field. They reported that as production increased, serious congestion was likely to occur unless additional parking space for 15

to 20 completed aircraft was added near Plant 2 and that an effort should be made before the winter rainy season began.

Arnold replied in August that since King County owned the airport, improvements were their responsibility, adding the federal Civil Aeronautics Authority had already invested $274,470 in the airport. King County refused. The Board of County Commissioners told Boeing that it "did not have the power to transfer the land covered by these improvements to the [federal] government."

The Materiel Division blinked. On September 16, 1941, Colonel Philip Schneeberger's Industrial Planning Section recommended an appropriation of $50,000 for the project, although Boeing told General Oliver Echols that this money was "sufficient only to pave the parking area adjacent to the testing apron, and additional funds were requested." Schneeberger approved an additional $74,034 in November.

These conversations were overshadowed, however, by a major milestone in the evolution of the Flying Fortress: the debut of the B-17E.

The caption on this Signal Corps publicity photo of Boeing B-17Es under construction noted that it was "the first released wartime production photograph of Flying Fortress heavy bombers." It added that "Boeing exceeded its accelerated delivery schedules by 70 percent for the month of December 1942." (Photo Courtesy USAF)

USAAF Major General Oliver P. Echols was a production and management genius who oversaw the precision development and orderly acquisition of nearly 200,000 aircraft in the space of five years. He headed the Materiel Division until 1942, when it was upgraded to Materiel Command, whereupon he became its commanding general. (Photo Courtesy USAF)

The B-17E is Born into War

On September 5, 1941, the first of the new generation of tall-tailed B-17Es had taxied out onto Boeing Field to make its debut flight. This aircraft, tail number 41-2393, was delivered to Wright Field on October 3 and sent to Eglin Field in Florida a week later for armament evaluation.

The rate of production increased rapidly. New methods were already revolutionizing production. Boeing's Donald Finlay recalled that "the objection raised on the B-17B that production was slow because there was no room in the airplane to work was overcome by cutting the body and wings into sections so that many more workers could make installations simultaneously."

By December 6, 1941, the last day that the United States was not at war, Hap Arnold's USAAF possessed 145 Flying Fortresses of all types, a quarter of which were B-17Es that had been built, delivered, and accepted by the USAAF since October.

On December 7, 1941, the Japanese attack on Pearl Harbor in Hawaii brought the United States into World War II. The USAAF B-17s had their baptism by fire during the Pearl Harbor attack, as a half dozen Flying For-

Delivered in April 1942, this B-17E was painted in the high-visibility markings that had been common on prewar bombers but were phased out when the war began. This particular aircraft never went overseas. Instead, it was assigned to various locations in the States for test and training purposes.

This December 1942 photo was part of the same session that the Signal Corps referred to as "the first released wartime production photograph of Flying Fortress heavy bombers." (Photo Courtesy USAF)

tresses, four B-17Cs, and a pair of new B-17Es from the 38th Reconnaissance Squadron (inbound from Hamilton Field, California) arrived in the air space over Oahu as it swarmed with Japanese fighters. All of these aircraft were attacked but managed to land without crashing—although one set down on a golf course. Also, under attack by the Japanese was the USAAF's Hickam Field, which was immediately adjacent to the Pearl Harbor naval base. There were a dozen B-17Ds of the 5th Bombardment Group on the ground here, and eight were destroyed.

Across the International Dateline, where it was December 8, when the Pearl Harbor attack occurred, the Japanese conducted air attacks against the Philippines a few hours later, after word of Pearl Harbor had reached the Philippines and the USAAF Far East Air Force (FEAF). It was here that the Flying Fortresses would begin their first sustained combat operations. There were 35 B-17s in the Philippines, 16 of them at Del Monte Field on

the island of Mindanao, and 19 at Clark Field near Manila on the island of Luzon. The latter were ordered to get airborne to prevent being caught on the ground and to patrol the waters around Luzon. Unfortunately, many were back on the ground to refuel when the Japanese attacked, and most were destroyed.

Given the experience of the RAF with their Fortresses and the tactical failures that had befallen the USAAF in the Pacific, 1941 had not been an auspicious year for the combat credentials of the Flying Fortress, but the promising B-17E was finally rolling off the assembly line at Plant 2, the B-17F was just around the corner, and 1942 would be a very different year.

A moody nighttime view of a B-17E running up its engines on a foggy night at Boeing Field.

This B-17E carries the markings that had become standard for the Flying Fortress by March 1942: olive drab paint above with gray undersurfaces. Note that the red "meatball" at the center of the national insignia was deleted. This was to avoid confusion with the Japanese insignia in the heat of battle.

These B-17Es both rolled out in April 1942. The aircraft in the foreground is painted in a non-standard three-tone upper camouflage pattern. Although it wears British tail markings, it was never turned over to the Royal Air Force.

Chapter 7

THE B-17F AND SCALING UP FOR PRODUCTION

The story of the Flying Fortress variant that would wear the B-17F designation began three months before the first B-17E was delivered. Indeed, the F Model actually originated as the third order for the E Model.

As mentioned in Chapter 6, this third order for Model 299-O aircraft was issued on June 2, 1941. W535 ac-20292 (known as "Defense Aid" contract DA W535 ac-16 after July 1941) called for 300 aircraft at a cost of $89,851,680. The Air Materiel Command contract file indicates that a 6-percent fixed fee of $5,391,016.80 was added, which brought the total to $95,242,696.80.

These new aircraft, which were redesignated by Boeing as Model 299P before they entered production, were essentially identical in outward appearance to the Model 299-O/B-17E except for the single-piece blown Plexiglas nose. Aside from a flat Plexiglas bomb-aiming panel on the bottom of the nose, the framed "greenhouse" nose of previous variants was gone. This would be the principal feature distinguishing the B-17F from its predecessor.

Although the visible external differences between the B-17E and B-17F may have been negligible, inside the aircraft it was a different story. There were hundreds of changes between the variants, and these changes—some subtle and some more visible—would continue through a production run that lasted from June 1942 through October 1943 and delivered 3,405 aircraft. Internally, the last B-17F (June 1943) differed much more from the

Crowds gathered for the formal rollout of the first B-17F (42-5705) on May 4, 1942, at the Vega Aircraft factory in Burbank, California.

first B-17F (May 1942) than the latter differed from the final B-17E (June 1942).

Among the other less-visible features distinguishing the B-17F from the B-17E were an improved oxygen system, carburetor air-intake dust filters, a dual brake system, and revised engine cowlings that permitted propellers with wider blades to be feathered.

The B-17F was 74 feet 9 inches long, 11 inches longer than the B-17E (mainly because of the nose). Most sources give the B-17F variant a height of 19 feet 1 inch, although Peter Bowers lists it at 19 feet 2 inches, which is the same as the B-17E. The wingspan remained unchanged at 103 feet 9 inches with an area of 1,420 square feet. More-robust landing gear supported an empty weight increase from 33,279 to 34,000 pounds and a maximum gross weight increase from 53,000 to 55,000 pounds—although this data varies slightly by source and by subvariant.

The improved Wright R-1820-97 Cyclone air-cooled radial engines, initially pared with the A-11 turbosupercharger, provided 1,200 hp for takeoff and 1,000 hp at 25,000 feet with a war emergency power rating of 1,380 hp. The top speed was 299 mph at 25,000 feet with a top speed of 314 mph at its emergency rating. The service ceiling was 37,500 feet, and the B-17F had 1,300-mile range with 3 tons of bombs and a maximum range of 2,880 miles.

The June 1941 contract, W535 ac-20292 (aka Defense Aid contract DA W535 ac-16), for 300 B-17Es that were delivered as B-17Fs was followed by a few months by two supplemental orders. Contract DA W535 ac-16 Supplement 1, issued on September 6, 1941, put an additional 435 B-17Fs into the pipeline at a cost of $115,973,088 plus a 6-percent fixed fee of $6,958,385.28 for a total of $122,931,473.28.

After Pearl Harbor, all bets were off, and on January 14, 1942, the Air Materiel Command signed off on what was to be Boeing's largest order of any kind to date. Signed on January 30, Contract DA W535 ac-16 Supplement 2, called for 2,650 B-17Fs and spare parts for $683,709,672.50 plus a 5-percent fixed fee of $34,185,483.62. The total, $717,895,156.12, is equal to roughly $11 billion in today's valuation.

On September 6, 1942, a more modest DA W535 ac-16 Supplement 6 added an additional 350 B-17Fs. The estimated cost was $76,000,260, not including an additional 5-percent fixed fee of $3,800,013.

The BDV Committee

In May 1941, before W535 ac-20292 (DA W535 ac-16) was even issued, the USAAF had made the startling decision that the Flying Fortress program was so important that it was too big for Boeing!

The first B-17F-1-VE (42-5705) runs up its engines at the Burbank factory in May 1942.

The first B-17F-1-BO (41-24340) receives finishing touches on the ramp at Boeing Field in Seattle in June 1942.

26566 A.C.

Taken by Sergeant Stan Smith, this is probably the best inflight photo ever taken of a B-17F, and it has been called the best aerial combat photo of World War II. These B-17Fs are seen here during a mission with the 570th Bomb Squadron of the 390th Bomb Group to Emden in Germany on September 27, 1943. In the center is the aircraft named "Skippy" (42-3329), a B-17F-45-DL built by Douglas in Long Beach and delivered on May 14, 1943. In the background are the contrails of P-47 escort fighters. "Skippy" was lost in a crash over England on February 5, 1944, but the crew survived. (Photo Courtesy USAF)

Gladys Wright uses a power drill on the rear access door of a B-17F-5-VE at the Vega Aircraft plant in Burbank, California.

A powerful overhead crane deftly moved huge B-17F fuselage sections through Boeing's Plant 2 in Seattle.

An early Douglas B-17F, possibly the first B-17F-1-DL, is in the hanger at Long Beach in the summer of 1942. The absence of an astrodome on the top of the nose dates it as an early B-17F. The noses stacked in the foreground are not for Flying Fortresses but rather for A-20 Havoc or DB-7 Boston light bombers, which were also built by Douglas at Long Beach.

According to Irving Holley in his book *Buying Aircraft: Materiel Procurement for the Army Air Forces*, "A group of Douglas [Aircraft Company] engineers and production men were just leaving Washington after a conference when an air arm officer [unidentified, but presumably General Oliver Echols] suggested that it might be well if they returned to California by way of Seattle to discuss their common problems in person with the staff at Boeing."

From this evolved the revolutionary concept of a pool of three manufacturers to build the Flying Fortress. Douglas was first to join Boeing, followed by the Vega Aircraft Corporation, a subsidiary of the Lockheed Aircraft Company, at its new A-1 plant in Burbank, California. The new cooperative arrangement, known as the Boeing-Douglas-Vega (BDV) Committee, included representatives of each company and of the Materiel Command.

Although Douglas was based in Santa Monica, it would build its Flying Fortresses 22 air miles to the southeast at its plant in Long Beach. For the project, Douglas constructed its Building 12 and 13, totaling 1.4 million square feet of additional factory space.

Citing Mary L. McMurtrie in her 1946 *History of the Army Air Forces Materiel Command*, Major Michael Freeman wrote in his 2012 Air University study of Oliver Echols, that "as the production requirements continued to rise, it became apparent that multiple contractors would need to work together to meet the demands."

As McMurtrie explained, "The plane was Boeing's design, but because of the demands of the war, the company was willing to allow the other manufacturers to produce it."

Boeing provided all necessary drawings, patterns, and blueprints, and the three companies' committee coordinated production among themselves and all their subcontractors, having formulated a charter that authorized the committee to make all required decisions except for fiscal or contractual decisions. The executive committee was chaired by Major General Kenneth B. Wolfe, the chief of the Production Division of the Materiel Division (Materiel Command after April 1942) and composed of senior executives of the three companies who were empowered to make policy decisions.

Boeing Historian Mike Lombardi, writing in the August 2011 issue of *Boeing Frontiers* magazine, noted that the BDV Committee's members functioned "as if they belonged to one corporation. The committee took on many responsibilities, including coordination of tooling, coordination of design, and production changes, distribution of drawings,

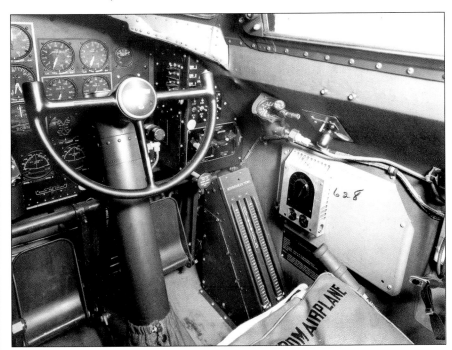

Two views of the right (copilot's) seat, control column, and auxiliary panel are shown in an early Block 1 Boeing B-17F in June 1942.

standardization of procedures, purchase of materials, and the management of subcontractors . . . In many instances, there were multiple subcontractors making similar parts that the committee had to ensure were 100-percent interchangeable."

The number of subcontractors was immense. Lombardi pointed out that "Boeing had 250 in 80 different cities and Douglas and Vega added another 350."

Coordinating the efforts of the members of the BDV Committee was a full-time job for many. Successfully herding the cats of the 600 or so subcontractors was a masterwork of organization.

Take for example a situation involving power inverters that arose in June 1943. As reported in the *Boeing Field Service News*, "inverters are now being supplied by Masters Electric Co. as well as Holtzer-Cabot. The products are essentially interchangeable except that the filter on those supplied by Masters Electric is slightly larger, causing an interference with the brace on the copilot's seat frame. To eliminate this interference and thus maintain interchangeability, the right-hand installation is moved 2 inches aft and raised by 1-inch mounting blocks."

The massive complexity of BDV Committee activities was to be dealt with calmly, simply, and without missing a beat in the tempo of production.

The "committee" approach to production was not unique to the Flying Fortress program. Freeman reported that "this model was so successful that it became a standard for joint aircraft production coordination. By the end of 1942, there were six of these committees operating."

The Consolidated B-24 Liberator heavy bomber was built by that company in San Diego but also by Consolidated at a new factory in Fort Worth, by Lockheed in Burbank, and by North American Aviation in Dallas—as well as by Douglas in Tulsa, Oklahoma, and by the Ford Motor Company in Willow Run, Michigan.

The Republic P-47 Thunderbolt fighter was built by Republic Aviation in Farmingdale, New York, but also by Curtiss-Wright in Buffalo. Boeing's great B-29 Superfortress was also produced in Atlanta by Bell Aircraft and in Omaha by the Glenn L. Martin Company.

After World War II, the US Air Force reused this template once. In the 1950s, the Boeing B-47 Stratojet medium bomber was also built by Douglas Aircraft in Tulsa, and by Lockheed in Marietta, Georgia.

The control panel and switch panel of a B-17F in September 1942 are shown prior to installation of the control columns and other components. (Please refer to the control panel diagram in Appendix I.)

The Block System

The subtle changes that distinguished the B-17F from the B-17E were only the tip of an iceberg. An avalanche of additional changes would soon wash over the B-17F and would continue throughout its production. The need to manage all these details through the manufacture of thousands of aircraft under frenetic wartime conditions was literally unprecedented.

The overhead instrument panel is shown in the top of a Boeing Block 1 B-17F flight deck, as seen in September 1942.

The basic dilemma, as explained by Boeing's Donald Finlay, was that "the multiplicity of installations dictated a certain sequence of operations. This sequence in turn established the points on the [assembly] line where operations were performed. Now, if it was desired to change, or add an installation, a motion study analysis had to be made and would often show that the change altered the sequence of some unrelated installations nearby, moving them and their parts somewhere else in the line, where room had to be made. Also, it altered the timing and the number of [workers], both of which had to be carefully worked out to keep the line moving in the space available. This was a tough situation at a time when the Air Force wanted airplanes in a hurry and also wanted to incorporate the lessons learned every day about component reliability, operational difficulties, tactical situations, enemy developments, and all the other things that change an airplane."

The situation with the Flying Fortress was just a microcosm of that which first began to confront the entire American aircraft industry in 1941. The scale of production and the problems inherent in administering it were staggering. The resolution of this predicament led to the production reorganization that was known as the "Block System."

Initiated by General Oliver Echols' Materiel Command as a concept in 1941 and shaped by the aircraft manufacturers over the ensuing years, the Block System made both high rates of production and rapid change possible. Airplanes of a single variant were now built in blocks of as few as a handful and as many as several hundred. The aircraft within the block were identical, but, as Finlay explained, "At the block change point, all accumulated changes were incorporated for the next block."

Finlay pointed out that the Block System accomplished three things: (1) it kept the line moving; (2) it allowed predictable time schedules of new or changed components; and (3) it gave each airplane a designation which could be traced through records to show what that particular airplane had in it.

The Block System necessitated the change of designation from B-17E to B-17F, as the former was already in process. Now, as it was being planned and organized, all of the production for the B-17F program could be subdivided into blocks.

The aircraft produced by each of the three companies of the BDV Committee were each given a designation with a two-suffix extension, identifying the manufacturer and the factory location.

The final suffix identified the manufacturing plant where they were made. Those built by Boeing in Seattle all had a "-BO" suffix, those built by Douglas at its Long Beach plant were designated with "-DL," and those produced by Vega in Burbank had a "-VE" at the end.

Between the variant designation (B-17F or B-17G) and the suffix, a block number was inserted into these designations.

For Boeing, the blocks ran from B-17-1-BO through B-17-130-BO. At Douglas, they ran from B-17F-1-DL through B-17F-85-DL, and at Vega they ran from B-17F-1-VE through B-17F-50-VE.

Normally, the blocks after "1" were numbered with numerals ending in "0" or "5," but there was a Block 27 among the Boeing B-17F aircraft and a Block 97 among Douglas B-17Gs.

All of the 300 B-17E aircraft of the June 2, 1941, order were completed as Boeing B-17F-BO and falling into blocks 1 through 27. They carried serial numbers 3025 through 3324 with tail numbers 41-24340 through 41-24639, being the only Fiscal Year 1941 B-17Fs.

The fact that the second B-17F order was issued to Boeing on September 6, 1941, one day after the debut of the first B-17E, shows how fast things were now moving. It called for 435 B-17Fs for a price of $115,973,088, with a 6-percent fixed fee of $6,958,385.28. This one and all subsequent orders were not new W535 orders but rather supplements to the ac-20292/DA-16 order of June 2.

The first Flying Fortress order issued to Douglas, meanwhile, was for 599 B-17Fs, which had serial numbers 3025 through 3324 and tail numbers 42-2964 through 3562. Two subsequent orders for just two and four aircraft brought the Douglas total of B-17Fs to 605. Vega, meanwhile received a single order for 500 B-17Fs. The orders other than the first one to Boeing were all based on Fiscal Year 1942 funding, so their USAAF serial numbers all had a "42-" prefix, or as written on the tails, a "2" prefix.

Individual changes were given numbered BDV identifiers, and these were promulgated simultaneously across the vastness of the program. They were not numerically consecutive nor were they supposed to be. In June 1943, for example, BDV 128 was issued simultaneously with BDV 664. In many cases, individual BDV-numbered changes went through a lot of changes within themselves, necessitating a single number becoming a series of numbers.

The left (pilot's) seat, control column, and auxiliary panel are shown in a Boeing B-17F in October 1942. Note the A-13 oxygen regulator on the bulkhead in the center. (Please refer to the control panel diagrams in Appendix I.)

In some cases, a single BDV number applied to numerous similar changes made over the space of several years. A good example is BDV 269A, which included numerous mandates with numerous suffixes for many separate metal shelving or flooring units to be converted from metal to plywood to conserve strategic materials.

Not counting all the suffixes, there were more than a thousand changes tracked by BDV numbers through the years. Smaller BDV numbers did predominate in the early years, though more than half of them had been assigned by the middle of 1943. Higher numbers came in 1944 and 1945. The exact number is elusive. In tracking available records, we find BDV 1097-1 and BDV 1114-2 being issued in July 1945 as Flying Fortress production came to an end.

Early Block B-17Fs

The first B-17F to take to the air was a Block 1 Vega-built B-17F-1-VE (42-5705) that flew out of Burbank on May 4, 1942. Boeing's first Block 1 B-17F-1-BO (41-24340) made its debut later in the month, on May 30, at Boeing Field. The first B-17F-1-DL was delivered to Wright Field on July 1. Before moving on to Block 5, Boeing built 50 Block 1 aircraft, but Douglas produced only 3, and Vega just 5.

Plant 2 hummed as Boeing moved quickly from Block 1 into Block 5 and Block 10, running parallel lines to deliver the first B-17F-5-BO on July 8 and the first B-17F-10-BO the next day. Vega started with its first B-17-5-VE on August 16, and Douglas followed on September 18. The Block 5 changes included armor around the circumference of the midsection of the aircraft to protect the waist gunners. Boeing and Vega added the SCR-269G Radio Compass at Block 5, but Douglas caught up to this change at Block 10.

The USAAF took delivery of Vega's first Block 10 B-17F on October 6, and Douglas followed on November 29. Among the Block 10 changes, Boeing modified the tail wheel structure, Vega introduced the SCR-535 radio, and Douglas added the waist armor and radio compass installed by the others in Block 5.

One change that was introduced in early block B-17Fs that was easy to see externally was the introduction of a circular Plexiglas astrodome in the center of the nose section above the navigator's station. This allowed the

Looking forward through the bombardier's station toward the Plexiglas nose of a B-17F in November 1942. Beneath this bombardier's seat is an early (and still classified) test installation of the Bendix Chin Turret that would become a standard feature of the B-17G half a year later. Note the absence of the Norden Bombsight.

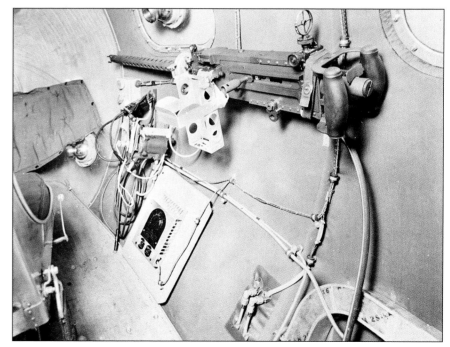

The flexible M2 gun installation in the right side of the B-17F bombardier's compartment in June 1942.

navigator to easily "shoot the stars" with his sextant to find his location at night. The astrodome appeared in Boeing Block 30 B-17Fs beginning in September 1942, and in Vega Block 15 aircraft, beginning in mid-November 1942. For DDD, the astrodomes were installed by Block 45 in April 1943 and probably before. Astrodomes would be standard equipment in B-17Gs from all three manufacturers. They were also retrofitted into some early RAF Fortress IIA aircraft, the B-17E equivalent.

As the astrodome example demonstrates, and as will be seen later as we discuss the unfolding story of block-by-block production, the same numbered block at each of the BDV Committee factories did not align chronologically with the blocks on the line at the others. In some cases, a given B-17F block might be on line in Seattle 2 to 6 months ahead of that same block number on a California assembly line. Thereafter, Boeing B-17F blocks lagged behind the others chronologically.

Completed aft fuselage sections for B-17F production are lined up and ready to install at Boeing's Plant 2 in Seattle. (Photo by Andreas Feininger, Library of Congress)

Introducing the Modification Center Concept

Another step in the massive production effort was the introduction of modification centers. Materiel Command chief Major General Oliver Echols had adopted the policy shortly after Pearl Harbor and issued a memo to that effect a month later on January 10, 1942. Echols formally presented the program to the War Production Board on February 10.

The concept is best summarized in the USAAF in-house manual, *The Official Guide to the Army Air Forces*:

"The tailoring job of the AAF fills the gap between the time we decide on an alteration of a plan and the time the factory can incorporate the change into production. To modification centers, operated by contract by commercial airline companies and manufacturers, go most of our airplanes before shipment overseas. Here they are modernized with the newest equipment available. Planes also are dressed up or stripped down according to the military requirements and weather conditions of the theater for which they are destined. Modification is continued on operational aircraft by service personnel in the theaters, where many modification ideas originate."

Some modification centers operated for a short time, while others remained in operation until mid-1945. Most of the centers were operated by aircraft manufacturers alongside their regular production operations, but others were run by commercial airlines that had operated repair and modification centers to serve their own fleets.

While numerous changes were incorporated into Flying Fortress production on the three assembly lines through the Block System, it was found that too many simultaneous changes created bottlenecks that slowed down the

Arlene Burton at work in the Vega Aircraft Company drafting room at Burbank in 1942.

Looking aft toward Bulkhead 6 at the M2 top gun and its flexible ammunition feed in July 1942.

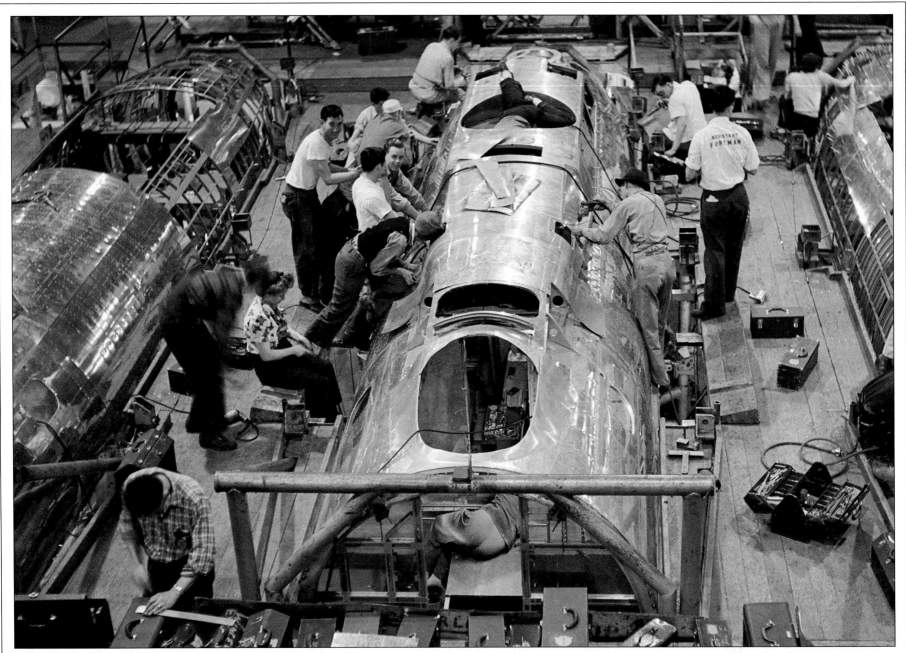

More than a dozen people lend a hand as a B-17F center fuselage comes together at Boeing's Plant 2. Two of the young men on the left are grinning at the Office of War Information (OWI) photographer taking this picture. The large oval opening in the foreground is the radio compartment hatch in which the M2 top gun would be installed beginning in early 1943. (Photo by Andreas Feininger, Library of Congress)

A Boeing Block 40 B-17F on its delivery flight on October 23, 1942. This aircraft later flew with the RAF as a Fortress Mk. II.

orderly flow of these lines. It was easier, therefore, to fly completed aircraft to other locations, where work could be concentrated on specific aftermarket revisions and additions. Meanwhile, the parts and subassemblies for these did not clog the logistical pipeline and warehouse inventories at the main factories. It was not unusual for aircraft to spend more days at a modification center than they had being manufactured at the original factory.

A Materiel Command directive of August 1, 1942, stipulated that "combat airplanes would be delivered from the factories in as nearly operational condition as practicable, but that modification centers would accomplish such changes demanded by the combat organizations as had not yet been introduced into the production lines."

Previously, a great deal of large- and small-scale modification work had been carried out at USAAF depots and subdepots, and it had been hard to coordinate. With massive numbers of aircraft starting to come through the system, the idea was now to funnel all non-factory work into the modification centers. Depots and subdepots were explicitly instructed not to make modifications without expressed direction from the Materiel Command, although compliance was difficult.

To each of the modification centers, as it did at the factories, the USAAF assigned a resident representative, who acted as a liaison between the center and the USAAF. Also assigned were a team of USAAF inspectors headed by an inspector-in-charge, who acted as an assistant to the resident representative.

The aircraft were parked briefly at or near the factories in a pre-modification pool until they could be turned over to the USAAF Ferrying Command and flown to the modification centers. After modification, they were again picked by ferry crews and now flown on to training or staging bases. More than half of these flights were flown by the women of the USAAF Women Airforce Service Pilots (WASP) organization.

It is important to point out that for more than two years, the USAAF checkout and formal acceptance of finished aircraft was at the factory. They each became government property prior to their going away to the modification centers. In June 1944, this would change for most modification centers—with the manufacturer then being responsible for each aircraft through its post-factory modification.

Virginia Toole, who wrote the official history of the program, entitled *The Modification of Army Aircraft in the United States* in 1947, detailed a list of 19 numbered modification centers, and three "temporary" centers. There were other smaller centers that were not on the numbered list.

Rows of Wright R-1820-97 Cyclone 9-cylinder radial engines await installation at Boeing Field in Seattle. (Photo by Andreas Feininger, Library of Congress)

The largest was the Lockheed Aircraft factory at Love Field in Dallas (Center No. 3), which was the first to begin operations in February 1942. This facility turned out 5,841 modified aircraft during the war, many of them Flying Fortresses.

A close second was that in Cheyenne, Wyoming (Center No. 10), which processed 5,733 aircraft, most of them Flying Fortresses. Owned by United Air Lines, the Cheyenne center was one of several that was run by airlines. There were also two operated in Atlanta by Delta Airlines and Eastern Airlines; one in Brownsville, Texas, managed by Pan American; the Denver operation of Continental Airlines; the center in Kansas City, Missouri, which was owned by Transcontinental and Western Airlines (TWA); and that of Mid-Continent Airlines in Minneapolis.

The Birmingham Modification Center (Center No. 14) in Alabama did not go online until March 1943, but it wound up as the third largest in terms of total output. Birmingham modified 5,506 aircraft during the war, although none were Flying Fortresses. Built and operated by the engineering and construction firm of Bechtel-McCone-Parsons, Birmingham was the largest USAAF aircraft modification center in terms of staffing with more than 4,400 employees at its peak in April 1944.

Although Cheyenne was the most important Flying Fortress modification center, other modification centers played a major role in the Flying Fortress program. In addition to Love Field (mentioned above), these were the Continental Airlines facility at Denver (Center No. 13), and Douglas Aircraft Company plant in Tulsa (Center No. 16).

The lines connecting the original factories with the modification centers crissed and crossed. While most Boeing Flying Fortresses went through Cheyenne and most Flying Fortresses originating with Douglas went to Continental Airlines in Denver, there were numerous exceptions.

The complex framework of the Flying Fortress is seen in this view of the waist section, looking aft, of a B-17F. The side windows where the waist guns will be installed are clearly visible. (Photo by Andreas Feininger, Library of Congress)

Early B-17F aircraft take shape at the Vega Aircraft factory in Burbank in the fall of 1942. Vega began adding a navigator's astrodome (absent here) on the top of the nose with its Block 15 B-17Fs in November 1942.

As Virginia Toole wrote, "The vast scope of wartime modification needs is indicated by the fact that during World War II, nearly 100 percent of the bombers and 50 percent of all other airplanes coming off the assembly line required some degree of modification before they could be declared fit to carry out their missions in competition with enemy aircraft."

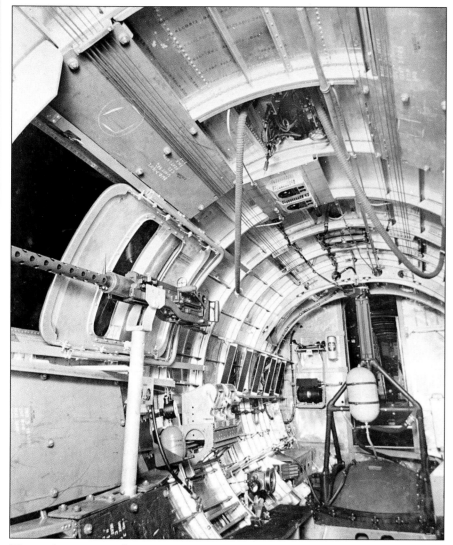

The waist section of a B-17F-40-BO is shown with the left-side M2 machine gun installed. Note the portable oxygen bottle on the bulkhead directly below the gun.

Meanwhile, the corresponding US Navy aircraft modification program was managed by the Bureau of Aeronautic (BuAer), the rough parallel of the USAAF Materiel Command. It operated the Naval Aircraft Factory (NAF) in Philadelphia and established the Naval Air Test Center at Patuxent River, Maryland, in 1942. In July 1943, BuAer created the Naval Air Materiel Center (NASC), which operated the Naval Aircraft Modification Unit (NAMU) at Naval Air Station Johnsville in Pennsylvania. NAMU became a key location tasked with preparing naval aircraft for overseas deployment and a parallel to the USAAF modification centers.

Seattle Plant Expansion, 1942

The mammoth volume represented by the orders placed under W535 ac-20292 would necessitate a massive expansion of the Plant 2 facilities at Boeing Field in Seattle. On January 14, 1942, according to the Air Materiel Command case history of Boeing's wartime production, the company sent a memo to Colonel Philip Schneeberger's Industrial Planning Section at

Sisters at work in the Vega Aircraft plant in Burbank, California, in 1942. Jean and Joan Wickmire rivet the aluminum skin of a B-17F from inside and out!

Wright Field in which it "indicated a willingness to increase its production from 75 to 165 [B-17] airplanes per month on condition that additional facilities would be provided for the increased production."

The Industrial Planning Section processed the request and passed it along to the War Department in Washington, where it was approved on January 27 as Project 3A-4, part of the Project 3A Emergency Plant Facility (EPF) program initiated in August 1940. The new program was divided into two segments (3A-4A and 3A-4B), which were authorized under EPF contracts W535 ac-26184 and W535 ac-26185, respectively.

The former, which included machinery and equipment, was written as a Special Facilities (SF) contract. The latter, which covered leasehold improvements and new buildings, was handled as a new EPF contract. These contracts were recommended for approval by Colonel A. E. Jones, chief of the Contract Section, at Wright Field on February 11 and approved by Major General Oliver Echols, Chief of the Materiel Division, on February 21.

In this view looking southeasterly toward the San Gabriel Mountains, a firefighting nozzle stands guard over this suburb that is not a suburb. Actually, it is a faux village that was part of the vast camouflage setup constructed on the tops of the factory buildings of the Lockheed and Vega plants in Burbank, California.

Under EPF Contract W535 ac-26185, Project 3A-4B would increase "productive floor space" at Boeing Field by 317,320 square feet to a total of 1,654,838 square feet, while "non-productive floor space" (offices and storage) would increase by 1,680 square feet to 359,105 square feet. The budget appropriated for this was $1,238,800. Meanwhile, the cost of Project 3A-4B machinery and equipment under SF Contract W535 ac-26184 was $2,180,391.04.

Project 3A-3, which came after the two sections of 3A-4, concerned improvements to Boeing Field, aka King County Airport, which were requested by Boeing on March 25, 1942. When the request was passed along to Materiel Division Headquarters in Washington by Industrial Planning Section on April 8, it totaled $268,000 and was itemized as $108,000 for an aircraft parking area, $90,000 for a concrete taxi strip, $35,000 for drainage, $11,000 for perimeter lighting, and $24,000 in a contingency fund.

Under Contract DA W535 ac-196, Project 3A-3 was approved on May 7 with an additional $2,680 for "interest" added to the budget and turned over to the Army Corps of Engineers who would manage the work. On July 25, the King County Board of Commissioners formally leased the west side of King County Airport, where these facilities would be located, to the US Government for 25 years.

On August 25, 1942, Boeing requested the first official change order to Project 3A-3. Approved three days later, Contract W535 ac-26185 called for the construction of a foundry building at "no extra cost." It would be paid for through cost reductions elsewhere in the Plant 2 expansion. Three days later, on August 28, Boeing submitted a request to add an Appendix A to Contract DA W535 ac-196 that would cover the construction of a new ground operations building and additions to the existing hospital at Boeing Field. This would be paid for by shifting funds already authorized.

In the meantime, on August 27, Boeing President Phil Johnson personally asked Colonel R. W. Propst, the assistant chief of the Industrial Planning Section at Wright Field to authorize the construction of a two-story building with 75,000 square feet of office space on the land that the federal government had leased from King County for Boeing plant expansion at Boeing Field. Perhaps Colonel Schneeberger, Propst's immediate superior, was on vacation.

As noted in Chapter 5, this building was part of the Defense Plant Corporation (DPC) contract Plancor 1577, which Boeing Historian Mike Lombardi pointed out as being the only DPC contract at Plant 2. He recalled that employees called this the "DPC Building."

The USAAF case study on Boeing's wartime plant expansion notes that "the expanded bomber program had overtaxed their available office facilities. In addition to the requirements of their own employees, additional space was required for personnel of the USAAF, representatives from other aircraft companies, and for the new administrative staff for training enlisted personnel under the training program of the Technical Training Command of the USAAF."

The "representatives from other aircraft companies" were, of course, employees of the other two members of the BDV Committee.

A detailed formal request sent to Wright Field on September 2, estimated the cost at $525,000. Having designated it as Project 3F, rather than another project under the 3A prefix, the Industrial Planning Section passed it along to Washington, DC, on November 21, recommending a cost reduction to $505,300, of which 62 percent would be construction cost, 36 percent for furniture and fixtures, and the balance for contingencies. Project 3F was finally approved on December 28, 1942.

The plant expansion was clearly justified. Boeing's Flying Fortress program had reached a milestone in October 1942, having increased from 240 per month, up from just 75 in January 1942.

Hidden in Plane Site

No discussion of wartime factories, and especially Boeing's Plant 2 complex, is complete without mention of the enormous efforts that were made early in World War II to hide them from the prying eyes of high-flying enemy bombardiers.

It was widely assumed on the West Coast during the early days after Pearl Harbor that the same Japanese war machine that had reached halfway across the Pacific to attack Hawaii could reach the rest of the way to attack America's Western states. Newsreel images of the London Blitz—less than a year and a half earlier—were still fresh in the minds of average people, and those in charge of public safety wanted to take no chances. Blackouts were ordered, and fearful eyes turned skyward, dreading the worst.

Amid this, there was a genuine fear that enemy bombs could soon be falling on Western factories, and there was an anxious desire to hide them. Within 48 hours of the attack on Pearl Harbor, Boeing President Phil Johnson put his men to work with buckets of black paint and by the end of the week, the company issued a press release tersely reporting that Plant 2 had been "entirely transformed from a daylight plant to a blackout plant, enabling all night operations during blackouts. This plant is believed to be one of the first, if not *the* first, major defense plant in the country to complete this transformation."

In the center of the picture is the neighborhood called "Wonderland" that was actually a hoax hamlet built to camouflage Boeing's Plant 2 in Seattle. The Duwamish River is in the foreground.

An item reported by the Boeing News Bureau a few weeks later added that "the suddenness of the Pearl Harbor attack and the urgency it created prevented wasting of any time in laying groundwork for the work of blacking out . . . painters, janitors, maintenance men—all available non-production workmen who had painting experience—were quickly rounded up and added to a crew furnished by Austin Construction Company."

The project had actually proven harder than the breezy release makes it seem. The crews had to experiment with five types of paint before they found a mixture that would stick to the windows. When they were done, the black windows created a reflection problem and had to be painted over with flat gray to match the rest of the building.

In Southern California, meanwhile, the problem of protecting aircraft factories was more acute. Companies such as Consolidated Vultee, Lockheed, Vega, Northrop, North American Aviation, and Douglas Aircraft—with locations from San Diego to Santa Monica—were all just a few minutes' flying time from the Pacific Ocean.

Here, the Army Corps of Engineers turned to a man uniquely qualified for the task at hand. Major John Francis Ohmer, Jr. was a World War I veteran who had recently assumed command of the 604th Engineer Battalion, transforming it into a camouflage unit. He was also an amateur magician and a photography hobbyist, who had had a serious interest in both the art and

This worker is leaning across the unskinned frame of a B-17F nose section. The circular frame for the Plexiglas astrodome is under her elbow. The astrodome installations at Boeing began with B-17F-30-BO aircraft. (Photo by Andreas Feininger, Library of Congress)

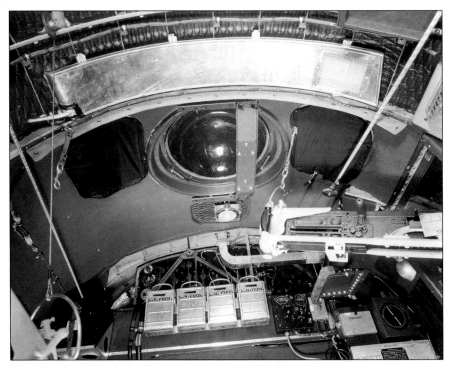

The view looking up and aft from the bombardier and navigator stations inside the nose of first B-17F-55-BO (42-29467) in December 1942. The astrodome is clearly visible at the top, and an M2 machine gun is in the foreground.

An installation crew inside the nose section of a B-17F attaches components just ahead of Bulkhead 2, which separated this area from the flight deck. (Photo by Andreas Feininger, Library of Congress)

the science of camouflage. Ironically, he had been sent to Hawaii earlier in 1941 to study defenses. He recommended an extensive plan to camouflage Wheeler Field on Oahu, about a dozen miles north of Pearl Harbor. The cost of the project was deemed "too excessive."

In December, with money no longer an object, the amateur magician was tasked with making California's aircraft industry disappear. His proximity to Hollywood gave Ohmer access to an incredible pool of talent in the form of the best set designers and large-scale scenic painters in the world. Ohmer and his team would eventually disguise nearly three dozen military air fields in Washington, Oregon, and California as well as Mills Field, the future San Francisco International Airport.

However, their most dramatic attention was reserved for the planemakers in the Los Angeles area, including Lockheed and Vega in Burbank. These facilities were made to appear like innocuous suburban neighborhoods to an observer flying at an altitude of 5,000 feet. Streets and greenery were painted on runways, and entire faux subdivisions were built on factory rooftops. Fake houses, as well as schools and public buildings, were made of canvas, and artificial shrubs and other ground details were created using burlap over chicken wire matrices. The overall terrain of the "landscape" was not flat. To compensate for the irregular height of various factory buildings, the subdivisions appeared at ground level to have been built on gently rolling hills.

The magician was, however, not the only practitioner of visual misinformation in town. Donald Douglas of the Douglas Aircraft Company decided not to wait for the Army Engineers, so he hired the legendary mid-century modern architect, H. Roy Kelley, to put fake ranch-style homes on his factory roofs.

For Boeing in Seattle, John Francis Ohmer dispatched John Stewart Detlie, an art director whom he had recruited off the Metro-Goldwyn-Mayer lot. Detlie's team created a large-scale, 26-acre neighborhood atop Plant 2 that came to be known locally as "Wonderland." The imaginary town had three major streets as well as alleys and driveways. The streets even had names and street signs. Though there was no way that a bomber pilot could read street signs from 10,000 feet, the people who built Wonderland had sense of humor and couldn't resist. Synthetic Street intersected Burlap Boulevard.

Wonderland had a total of more than four dozen homes, two dozen garages, three greenhouses, a small store, and even a gas station. All of them were built of wood and canvas like those that John Ohmer had designed in California. Many were only about 4 feet high at the eves, although some were taller, and there were even a few that represented two-story houses. Inside, most of the homes were furnished only with fire-protection sprinklers, although at least two were occupied—through 1943—by US Army personnel who manned antiaircraft guns. Fake streets and foliage detail were also painted across Boeing Field.

As had been the case in Southern California, some American pilots who had used the prewar Boeing Field were now so confused by the camouflage and the absence of familiar landmarks that when the field was covered by scattered clouds, it was very difficult to make it out from the air.

Enter the Superfortress

On September 21, 1942, as Flying Fortresses were lining the ramps and runways at Boeing Field, an entirely different airplane rolled across the tarmac, lined up on the runway, and unceremoniously took to the air on its first flight. It was 99 feet long and had a wingspan of 141 feet 3 inches, making it nearly half again larger than a Flying Fortress. It was the Superfortress. Known internally as Boeing's Model 345, it was designated as the B-29 by the USAAF.

It is mentioned because it was clearly an elephant in the room—or at Boeing Field—at the same time that the Flying Fortress program was unfolding there. Indeed, how can were speak of Boeing from 1942 to 1945 without a reference to the B-29?

Although it would not enter production for more than a year, the Superfortress was destined to be the ultimate manifestation of the strategic bomber

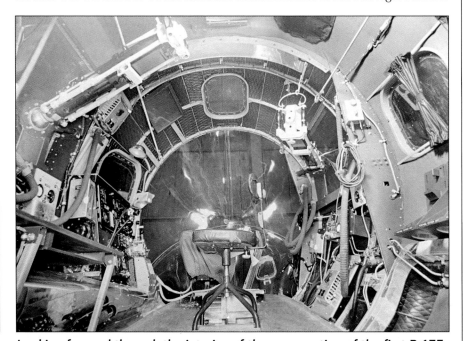

Looking aft through the interior of the nose section of the first B-17F-55-BO (42-29467) toward Bulkhead 2 in December 1942 after installation of all components, including the navigator's panel on the right and both M2 machine guns.

Looking forward through the interior of the nose section of the first B-17F-55-BO (42-29467) toward the nose in December 1942. The bombardier's station is in the center. Note the navigator's panel on the left and both M2 machine guns.

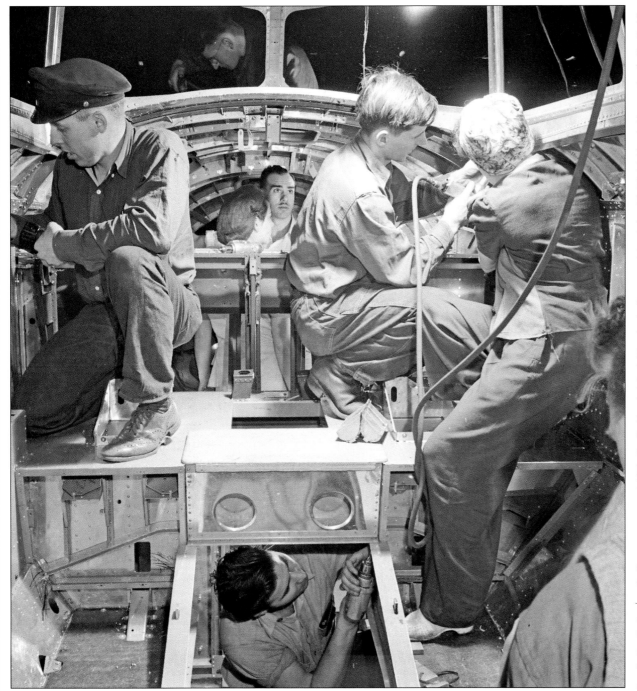

in World War II. With a pressurized cabin, it could be operated easily above 30,000 feet, and with a range of more than 5,000 miles, it was destined to be the weapon that crippled the Japanese war economy in 1944 and 1945.

In 1942 and 1943, however, it was a frightfully trouble-plagued program. Indeed, the second XB-29 prototype crashed with no survivors south of downtown Seattle in February 1943. It was forced into production before it was ready, and its difficulties drove both USAAF Commanding General Hap Arnold and Boeing President Phil Johnson to heart attacks. For Johnson, while on the production line in Wichita on September 14, 1944, it was a fatal heart attack. He was 49.

The B-29's problems, as much as they cast a shadow across Boeing, presented little impediment to the ongoing Flying Fortress program at Plant 2—indeed only the prototypes were built in Seattle. We mention it only because it cannot be ignored. Its shadow was never far away. The B-29 was the 300-pound gorilla in the Boeing board room and at USAAF headquarters throughout the war—first as a vexation of the highest order and finally as a triumphant weapon. It proved to be a worthy successor to the B-17 Flying Fortress.

The Modification Centers in 1942

Three modification centers began handling Flying Fortresses in March 1942. Both the Cheyenne and Denver Modification

Four people at work simultaneously on the flight deck of a B-17F, while others are visible on the other side of Bulkhead 2 and on the nose area. (Photo by Andreas Feininger, Library of Congress)

The completed instrument panel of the first B-17F-55-BO (42-29467) in December 1942. (Please refer to the control panel diagram in Appendix I.)

Centers, which would play a major role in the modification story, came online. As a footnote, the Mid-Continent Airlines facility in Minneapolis processed 18 Flying Fortresses between March and May 1942. A temporary plant, the Mid-Continent site operated only until May 1943, primarily to modify North American Aviation B-25s and P-51s.

In March 1942, Denver modified 16 B-17Es for the USAAF while Cheyenne turned out 7 for the Royal Air Force. Through the end of the year, Cheyenne modified 339 for the USAAF and 64 for the RAF and reached a peak of production with 84 aircraft in November. Denver modified 203 Flying Fortresses for the USAAF, reaching its peak of 38 in December.

The Douglas-operated Tulsa Modification Center joined the pool in August. There were 183 Flying Fortresses that passed through Tulsa in 1942, and a peak of 59 was reached in November.

Virginia Toole wrote in the official history, *The Modification of Army Aircraft in the United States*, that "the principal types of modifications assigned to the several modification centers during 1942 were (1) armament changes; (2) installation of radio, radar, and identification equipment; and (3) weatherization changes."

The latter two of these were given high priority because of the long-range delivery flights over the open oceans, especially the North Atlantic during the winter.

The implementation of the modification center process rode a learning curve that was not always smooth. The scale of the task and the bottlenecks that arose were frustrating.

A series of internal memos highlight several of the major issues that confronted the modification center program during 1942. Among those involved in these were Major General Oliver Echols, chief of the Materiel Command, and three officers reporting to him who were important to the program. These were Colonel Bryant Boatner, head of the Special Projects Section and soon to be head of the Modification Section; Major General Muir Fairchild, the Director of Military Requirements; and Brigadier General Bennett "Benny" Meyers, the commander of the Materiel Center at Wright Field.

From these, a picture emerges of four principal issues. First was the failure to deliver modified airplanes to operational units on time, and hence the bottlenecks. Second was "deficiencies in technical order compliances." Third was the reports of "apparent idleness or overemployment" at the

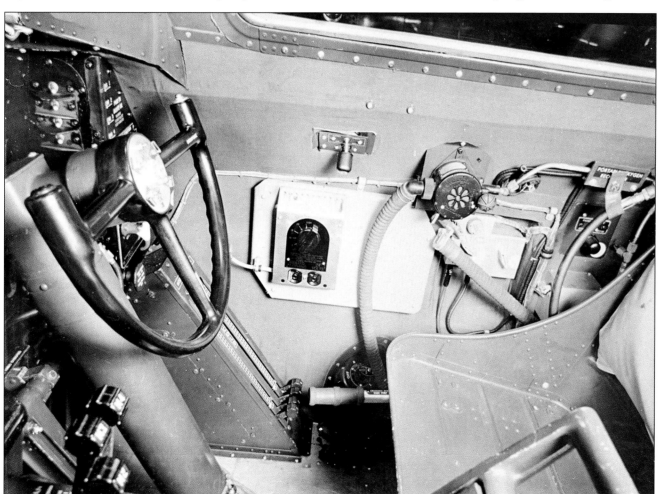
The right (copilot's) position and control column in the first B-17F-55-BO (42-29467) in December 1942.

modification centers. Finally, there was—as pointed out by Fairchild— "the fact that the same model of airplane sometimes received quite different modifications in different modification centers."

When Fairchild optimistically predicted to Echols on October 17, 1942, that "modification work would decrease shortly as modifications were introduced into the production lines," he was wrong. When 1942 ended, the modifications then being required for the B-17F were 30 percent more numerous than they had been when the centers had been inaugurated at the beginning of the year.

Boatner admitted to Echols on January 7, 1943, that the number of changes was growing despite "the fact that some of the changes had been incorporated at the factory assembly lines."

The frustration with the modification centers during their first year was perhaps most colorfully summarized in an August 28, 1942, memo that Mey-

ers wrote to USAAF Commanding General Hap Arnold. "It is a gigantic job to accomplish," he wrote. "We can't win this war with a pipeline bent square in the middle."

Royal Air Force Fortresses

Great Britain operated a modest number of Flying Fortresses, but it did not acquire them directly from Boeing or the other American manufacturers. As such, these are beyond the scope of this book. Nevertheless, RAF Fortresses are an important footnote to the development of the aircraft, so they are worth a mention.

As noted in Chapter 5, His Majesty's government, acquired 20 B-17Cs in 1941 before the United States entered the war. These were built under USAAF purchase orders and later transferred to the RAF under the name "Fortress" (later Fortress Mk. I). After an initial period of disappointment with the aircraft in the role of a long-range strategic bomber, the RAF assigned them to their Coastal Command, where they were used mainly as maritime patrol aircraft.

Two additional rounds of RAF transfers came in the winter of 1942–1943. First were 19 Boeing B-17Fs that were redesignated as Fortress Mk. IIs and given serial numbers FA-695 through FA-713. When a batch of 46 older B-17Es were transferred later, they were designated as Fortress Mk. IIAs. They were given RAF serial numbers FK 184 through FK 213, FG 449 through FG 460, and FG 462 through FG 464. In service, they were designated as Fortress GR.IIs and GR.IIAs when used by the Coastal Command, and Fortress B.IIs and B.IIAs when assigned to Bomber Command.

In 1944 and 1945, 98 Boeing and Vega B-17Gs that were acquired under USAAF purchase orders went to the RAF as Fortress Mk. IIIs. They were from throughout the production runs at Seattle and Burbank, with the earliest aircraft being B-17G-40-BO, serial number 42-97098, delivered to the RAF at Dorval, Quebec, on February 7, 1944. The highest number was 44-8970, a B-17G-90-VE that was turned

The left (pilot's) seat and control column in the first B-17F-55-BO (42-29467) in December 1942. Note the oxygen regulator on the bulkhead in the center.

The bombardier's station and the inside right of the nose section of the first B-17F-55-BO (42-29467) in December 1942.

This close-up shows the BC-348-H model radio receiver used in the B-17F manufactured by Belmont Radio Corporation of Chicago. It was a 28-volt DC low-frequency/medium-frequency/high-frequency set paired with the BC-375 transmitter and later redesignated as AN/ARR-11. (Photo by Bill Yenne)

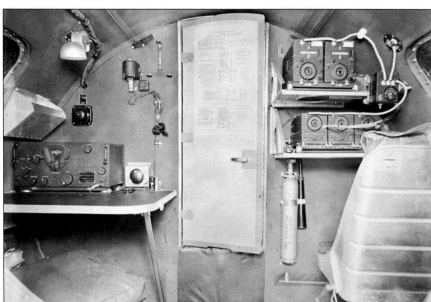

Inside the B-17F radio operator's station, just aft of Bulkhead 5. The Belmont BC-348-H radio receiver is on the radio operator's desk at left. On the high racks on the right are the SCR-274N two-way radios, of which at least two were typically installed.

The forward fuselage section ahead of Bulkhead 5 for a B-17F-55-BO is being hoisted from its cradle in rope slings for mating with inboard wing sections. Bulkhead 5, facing the camera, will form the front wall of the radio operator's station. (Photo by Andreas Feininger, Library of Congress)

B-17F fuselage sections on the floor at the Vega Aircraft plant in Burbank, California. The presence of a space for the astrodome dates these to late 1942 or early 1943.

B-17F inboard wing sections march toward completion at the Vega Aircraft factory in Burbank.

One step closer to rollout for these B-17Fs came as the inboard wing sections were mated with fuselage sections at the Vega Aircraft facility in Burbank.

B-17F fuselage sections at Boeing's Plant 2 in Seattle. In the background, wings and tails have been mated to the fuselage sections.

over to the Royal Canadian Air Force at Dorval on March 4, 1945. The former was one of 12 Fortress Mk. IIIs that were returned back to the USAAF at Eighth Air Force bases in England. The latter was among a small number that was received by the RCAF.

British serial numbers for Fortress Mk. IIIs included HB 761 through HB 820, KH 998 and KH 999, KJ 100 through KJ 127, and KL 830 through KL 837.

An additional 14 B-17Gs were given to the RAF near the end of the war as Fortress Mk. IIIAs and were assigned serial numbers SR 376 through SR 389.

With the exception of 64 B-17F/Fortress Mk. IIs that were modified at the Cheyenne Modification Center in March–July and October–December 1942, the modification of Fortress aircraft for the RAF took place after delivery in Canada or the United Kingdom. Modifications included radar countermeasures conversions that involved replacing the chin turret with a radome.

The Norden Bombsight

Of all the many components in that made up the B-17, there was no single piece of equipment that contributed more to its mystique in popular culture than the legendary Norden Bombsight. During World War II, the USAAF trained more than 45,000 bombardiers, and then entrusted them with a weapon that they were sworn to secrecy to protect with their lives.

Photographs of the Nordens were classified, and until late in the war, they were kept under armed guard when not in the aircraft.

Bombardiers had long faced the task of aiming ordnance from aircraft traveling several hundred miles per hour and often bouncing up and down and sideways at the same time. Surface gunnery delivers a projectile that has its own momentum, while aerial bombs are propelled at a much slower speed and pulled toward their targets only by gravity. Thus, bombs are much more susceptible to the whims of wind currents that often flow in opposite directions at different altitudes and change speed and direction invisibly.

Even today with the computing power of microelectronics, creating a calculating bombsight is a complex task, but in the years between the world wars, bombsight development was literally a hit-or-miss proposition.

The person who created what may well have been the most sophisticated aiming device in history not to use electronics was a Swiss-educated Dutch immigrant named Carl Lucas Norden. He joined the research and development staff at the Sperry Gyroscope Company in 1911, where he would be recognized as a pioneer in the field of gyroscopically stabilized naval gun platforms. He left Sperry in 1915 to strike out on his own, using his contacts within the US Navy Bureau of Ordnance to line up work. Because of his past performance on gyrostabilization, the Navy asked Norden to develop a bombsight for hitting maneuvering warships from the air.

Women are at work soldering, twisting, snipping, and securing at the wiring table inside the Vega Aircraft plant in Burbank.

In 1942, Virginia Harrigan and Gladys Wright were line inspectors in the electronics department at the Vega Aircraft plant in Burbank.

Norden began work in 1921 and delivered his Mk. III model two years later. Within a decade, Norden had worked his way up to the Mk. IV, a sophisticated gyro-optical device with a timing mechanism to tell the bombardier when to release the bombs. Provisions would be made to allow the bombardier to take lateral control of the aircraft from the pilot to line up the sight for the bomb run. Accuracy continued to improve, culminating with the Norden M-Series Bombsight delivered to the USAAF after 1943.

According to John Correll, writing in *Air Force Magazine* in 2008, postwar analysis showed that the Norden bombsight enabled the USAAF Eighth Air Force—the largest operator of Flying Fortresses—to put 31.8 percent of its ordnance within 1,000 feet of the intended targets from 21,000 feet. Such results were more disappointing than had been supposed during the war but certainly better than "hit or miss."

Being the most highly classified component in the Flying Fortress, the installation of the Norden Bombsight was the most sensitive step on any of the production lines. Numerous detail photographs were taken during manufacturing; many of them are reproduced here. However, when photographers came around, care was always taken to cover installed bombsights with a shroud.

Just as deployed Norden bombsights were removed from aircraft when not in use, Nordens were carefully guarded at the factories. Workers were

This template is being used to organize wire bundles into electrical subassemblies for a B-17F at Boeing's Plant 2. (Photo by Andreas Feininger, Library of Congress)

A Boeing worker installs electrical wiring behind the Plexiglas nose of this B-17F at Plant 2. The next step was installing the Norden bombsight.

Working toward the installation of this Wright R-1820-97 Cyclone 9-cylinder radial on the Burbank production line of Vega Aircraft.

Fine-tuning the attachment of the vertical stabilizer in the tail of this B-17F at Boeing Field in Seattle. Later factory photos of this sort did not have the tail numbers on the tails airbrushed out. This US Office of War Information photo, scheduled for release in early 1943, did not include any identifying serial numbers. (Photo by Andreas Feininger, Library of Congress)

Finishing touches are made to these Stinger-type B-17F tail turrets in preparation for the installation of the M2 machine gun pairs.

briefed not to discuss the Norden or even mention the name. It rarely appeared in any documentation, such as in BDV bulletins. Where it did, it was referred to as "the bombsight."

One of the few times that a reference to "the bombsight" appeared in the *Boeing Field Service News* during B-17 production was on December 18, 1944. A brief mention was made of the problem of vibration damage to the delicate instrument. To prevent this, BDV 1053 stipulated that the two adjusting plugs at the bottom plate were removed and reworked. The rubber pressure cushions were removed from the bottom plate recess holes and replaced with adjusting plug springs. The adjusting plugs were tightened

The Automatic Flight Control Equipment (AFCE) panel was located below the flight control pedestal and between the pilot and copilot seats on the flight deck. On the left is an AFCE panel from a B-17G-65-BO (42-29680) as seen in January 1943. On the right is a panel from a B-17G-120-BO (42-30735) in July 1943.

Not all wartime production photos carrying the caption "Rosie the Riveter" actually show riveting, but this employee of the Douglas Aircraft Company in Long Beach actually was a riveting machine operator. She is seen here joining sections of inboard wing assemblies. (Photo by Alfred Palmer, Library of Congress)

A Boeing Block 85 B-17F on its delivery flight in April 1943. The radio operator's compartment gun was stowed for this flight.

until "sufficient pressure is obtained to prevent play between the upper half of the mount and the base."

BDV 1053 had been implemented in Burbank with an early B-17G-70-VE (44-8512) delivered on October 3, 1944; in Long Beach with a late-production B-17G-65-DL (44-6701) on October 19; and at Plant 2 in Seattle in an early B-17G-105-BO (43-39083) on November 26.

Later in the war, the Norden was augmented by radar bombing systems for accurately dropping ordnance through cloud cover and overcast conditions. These systems included H2X (aka AN/APS-15), a derivative of the British airborne, ground-scanning H2S radar, which is discussed in Chapter 8 under the heading "H2X (AN/APS-15) Radar." The H2X made it possible for bombardiers to recognize ground features that were covered by clouds.

The Honeywell C-1 Autopilot

As with many aircraft in the USAAF arsenal during World War II, the Flying Fortresses were equipped with autopilots, electromechanical systems used to lessen pilot fatigue by automatically flying an airplane in straight and level flight.

For the Flying Fortress, the specific type was the Minneapolis Honeywell C-1. According to the official Air Force description, "When combined with the Norden bombsight, it created the stability necessary to bomb targets accurately from high altitude."

It consisted of two spinning gyroscopes located in cases attached to the airplane. One gyroscope, called the Flight Gyro, was located near the aircraft's center of gravity and detected changes in roll and pitch. The Directional Gyro, located in the bombsight stabilizer, detected changes in yaw. Using a series of electrical signals, the C-1 Autopilot controlled the aircraft with servos connected to the control surfaces. Either the pilot or the bombardier could take control of the aircraft.

Part of the C-1 system was the Formation Stick, a controller used to quickly maneuver the aircraft with minimum physical effort while the C-1 Autopilot was on and the aircraft was flying in formation with other Flying Fortresses as in a bombing mission.

The Formation Sticks were initially installed at the modification centers, but beginning in October 1944, provisions were made to the flight deck configuration under BDV 953 to pave the way for factory installation, a step first covered under BDV 953-1. This was a long process. For Vega, it started with Block 80 B-17Gs in November 1944, but it was January 1945 before the Formation Sticks were integrated into the B-17G assembly lines in Seattle and Long Beach.

The upper flexible gun mount, M2 machine gun, and ammunition feed in the hatch above the radio operator's compartment as seen in February 1943. This installation was mandated to begin within Block 85 in April, so this picture probably shows a developmental installation.

A Douglas B-17F over Southern California in early 1943. By the middle of the year, the "star in the circle" insignia had bars attached to either side.

The Formation Sticks were manufactured by Honeywell as well as by Jack & Heintz of Cleveland, Ohio.

B-17F Radio Installations

The radio receiver used in the B-17F, as well as into B-17G production, was the BC-348 (see page 110), which was a 28-volt DC variant of the BC-224, operating at 14 volts DC. These were designed as low-frequency/medium-frequency/high-frequency receivers for use in USAAF medium and heavy bombers as well as C-47 transports. In the beginning, they were paired with the BC-375 transmitter. Later in the war, when the BC-348 was redesignated as the AN/ARR-11, it was paired with the AN/ART-13A transmitter in the AN/ARC-8 system. The BC-224/BC-348 series included several variations during its long production history, which exceeded 100,000 units. The majority were manufactured by Belmont Radio of Chicago and Wells-Gardner of Milwaukee. A few were built under license by RCA and Stromberg-Carlson.

B-17F aircraft were equipped with SCR-274N AM radios with two-way continuous wave (CW), modulated continuous wave (MCW), and Morse code capability. As of mid-March 1943, two SCR-274N transmitters were installed. These were initially strapped to the floor but were soon moved to shelves, or racks, high on the wall of Bulkhead 5 on the right side of the radio operator's compartment opposite the radio operator's desk where the BC-348 radio receiver was located. Originally, the SCR-274N installation had been a modification center item, but it was initiated as a factory modification with B-17F-50-BO aircraft.

In the summer of 1942, the SCR-269G Radio Compass was an important and state-of-the-art system. By 1944, it had evolved into the similar but more advanced AN/ARN-7 Radio Compass. As the team led by Colonel Hobart Yeager of the Air Technical Service Command summarized in a system overview, the SCR-269G was a "radio receiver employing a superheterodyne circuit and certain additional essential circuits necessary for radio compass operation."

The SCR-269G "set" was a complete operable unit capable of providing the pilot with automatic bearing indication of the direction, relative to the line of flight, of the transmitter, thus creating the received signal. The set included

The Vega XB-38 Flying Fortress made its first flight on May 19, 1943. The aircraft was actually a Boeing-built B-17E (41-2401) in which Vega pulled out the four Wright R-1820 Cyclone radials and replaced them with Allison V-1710 V-type inline engines as were used in aircraft such as the Lockheed P-38 and North American P-51. After evaluating the reengineered aircraft for possible production, the USAAF canceled the project.

two remote controls and was manually tuned from either of two remote positions with the bands switched electrically from the position having control. It had a frequency range of 200 to 1750 kc, covered in three bands.

The Vega XB-38 Flying Fortress

It is important to point out that as early as March 1942, the USAAF was considering a parallel Flying Fortress variant with a powerplant other than the Wright R-1820-97 Cyclone air-cooled "radial" engine that was planned for the B-17F. On July 10, 1942, the Materiel Command officially issued a contract to Vega to experimentally adapt a B-17E to be powered by the Allison V-1710-89 V-12, water-cooled "inline" engines. These were the same engines being used to power the P-38 Lightning fighter that was built across the ramp in Burbank from where Vega would potentially build these new Flying Fortress aircraft that would be designated as B-38.

The first XB-38 Flying Fortress prototype (Vega Model V-134-1) was a converted Boeing B-17E (serial number 41-2401). As modified, it made its debut flight at Burbank on May 19, 1943. The Allison engine showed some improvement over the Wright radial, but a full comparison had not been completed when the sole XB-38 crashed on its ninth flight on June 16. The USAAF then decided not to proceed toward a B-38A, and conversion work on two additional XB-38s was terminated.

A worker with a power drill concentrates on a section of center fuselage for a B-17F at Boeing's Plant 2. (Photo by Andreas Feininger, Library of Congress)

Installation of a Plexiglas window in the nose section of a B-17F, which has been tilted up 90 degrees for easier access. (Photo by Andreas Feininger, Library of Congress)

Tokyo Tanks and the Spring 1943 B-17F Blocks

The first deliveries of Block 15 B-17Fs were on August 31, 1942, for Boeing; November 21 for Vega; and December 3 for Douglas. Changes were minimal in Seattle, but Burbank saw improved brakes and an alcohol-spray windshield deicer. In Long Beach, .50-caliber machine guns were installed that pointed out at a perpendicular angle from the sides of the nose. A-12 oxygen regulators were introduced by both Vega and Douglas.

In Block 20 B-17Fs, Boeing eliminated the ball-and-socket gun mounts in the Plexiglas nose, delivering the first B-17F-20-BO on August 30, 1942. Vega's first B-17F-20-VE arrived on New Year's Eve, and Douglas delivered its first Block 20 on January 2, 1943.

Boeing handed over its first Block 25 B-17F on August 2, 1942, ahead of its first Block 15 and Block 20 aircraft, but the second B-17F-25-BO came on September 14. Douglas's Block 25 B-17F deliveries began on January 7, 1943, and those of Vega on January 17. The changes at this block were minimal for Boeing and Vega, but Douglas now began to incorporate the famous Tokyo Tanks.

Tokyo Tanks were rubberized compound fuel cells that added 1,080 gallons of fuel to the 1,700 gallons carried in the six regular wing tanks, and the 820 gallons that could be carried in an optional auxiliary tank mounted in the bomb bay—for a combined total of 3,600 gallons.

The Tokyo Tanks were installed inside the wing structure, nine of them on each wing. Four were located in each inboard wing adjacent to the engines, and five were side by side in each outboard wing. Boeing began installing Tokyo Tanks in its Block 80 in March 1943, while Vega introduced them in its Block 30 the same month. Despite the auspicious nickname, the tanks did not give the Flying Fortress adequate range to reach Tokyo from any base in Allied hands.

An anomaly in the Block System came with Boeing's Block 27, which consisted of 55 B-17Fs delivered from September through December 1942. Changes included strengthening the landing gear drag strut and removing

Sharing a lighter moment deep inside the complex inner structure of a B-17F. (Photo by Andreas Feininger, Library of Congress)

The forward-firing M2 nose gun installation in a B-17F-85-BO in April 1943.

the .30-caliber machine gun from the nose. No other Flying Fortress manufacturer had a Block 27. These B-17F-27-BOs were also the last of the 300 Boeing aircraft that were part of the June 2, 1941, Fiscal Year 1941 order that had originally launched the B-17F program.

Boeing's first B-17F-30-BO was delivered on September 9, 1942, while that of Vega arrived on March 8, 1943, and Douglas's was a few days later on March 18.

In Block 35, Boeing eliminated armor in the tail gunner's position, Vega added gun ports in the nose, and Douglas incorporated improvements to the landing gear and braking system, increasing hydraulic capacity and added windshield wipers. The first B-17F-35-BO was delivered September 17, 1942, while Douglas delivered on March 15, 1943, and Vega on April 30.

The Block 40 changes were minimal, although Douglas used this point to eliminate the bomb bay fuel tank. Boeing began deliveries on October 4, 1942, while Douglas began on April 2, 1943, and Vega followed on May 30.

Douglas used the Block 45 changeover to introduce structural changes to the rudders while modifying and improving other tail surfaces. The noses of the B-17F-45-DLs also received reinforcement in the nose gun area and a new B-4 hydraulic pump. The other manufacturers made minor changes, including a B-5 drift meter at Boeing and the elimination of the D-16 fuel pump at Vega. Boeing began deliveries on October 26, 1942, with the B-17F-45-DL

coming on line on May 23, 1943, and the B-17F-45-VE on June 28, 1943.

In Block 50, Vega introduced some of the tail surface modifications that Douglas had done in its Block 45, while smaller Douglas innovations included a change of landing gear motor. Boeing added heavy-duty braking and a flexible trace feed for the waist guns, delivering its first B-17F-50-BO on November 18, 1942. Initial deliveries for Douglas and Vega were on May 20 and July 28, 1943, respectively.

External Bomb Racks

In early 1943, it was perceived that the addition of external bomb racks could increase the "hitting power" of Flying Fortresses, and a good deal of complicated engineering went into the project. Specifically, provisions were made for mounting a 1,000-, 1,600-, 2,000-, or 4,000-pound bomb under each wing.

The *Boeing Field Service News* reported that Technical Order 01-20EF-19, dated January 20, 1943, described the retrofit work necessary for installing the racks and the electrical release mechanism. However, work had already begun. The *Boeing Field Service News* of April 26, 1943, noted that Boeing B-17Fs with USAAF serials 42-5050 through 42-5484 and 42-29467 through 42-29831 "left the factory without external bomb racks, but wing fittings and

The view from the inside: the side-firing M2 nose gun installation in a B-17F-85-BO in April 1943.

The view from the outside: the right-side M2 nose gun installation in a B-17F-85-BO in April 1943.

Looking up and rearward into the top turret in a B-17F-85-BO in April 1943. The pair of M2 machine guns are pointed aft. Note the gunner's oxygen supply hose.

Tail assemblies for B-17-30-VE await installation at the Vega Aircraft factory in April 1943. At this time, the aircraft were still getting their olive drab warpaint at the factories, a practice that was phased out later in the year. The tail numbers had not been censored in this photo.

A view from above of the forward section of a B-17F at Boeing's Plant 2 shows the top turret rotated forward to a 1 o'clock position.

Completed inner wing sections for B-17F aircraft on the floor at the Vega Aircraft factory in Burbank in 1943.

Attaching a right outer wing section of a B-17F-35-VE at the Vega Aircraft factory in Burbank in May 1943.

As their fellow workers look on from inside the flight deck of this B-17F, these two men at Boeing's Plant 2 are installing the right inboard Wright R-1820-97 Cyclone 9-cylinder radial engine in the aircraft. (Photo by Andreas Feininger, Library of Congress)

The M2 machine guns in the top turret of this B-17-85-BO are pointed aft for its April 6, 1943, delivery flight. The nose gun was not part of its final delivery package, but cheek guns had been installed.

controls were installed so that the bomb racks might be added at a later date."

These deliveries included Boeing's Blocks 30 though 55 and were delivered between September 9, 1942, and January 3, 1943. Vega began delivery of aircraft fitted with these controls on December 31, 1942, with its Block 20 B-17Fs, and Douglas followed two days later with its own first Block 20 B-17F. Beginning on February 24, 1943, with Boeing's first Block 75 B-17F (42-29832), the external bomb racks were installed at the factory.

Meanwhile in February 1943, as summarized in Boeing Service Bulletin D-4105-22, kits containing 250 sets of complete bomb-rack assemblies and installation parts were furnished to the USAAF for field installation in B-17Fs where attachment provisions had been installed without the racks. These kits contained complete installation instructions in blueprint form.

As described in the technical bulletins, the external bomb rack beam was "an aluminum alloy extruded channel with attachments for the bomb

At work on the covering of a deicer boot between the two engines on the right wing of a B-17F at Boeing's Plant 2 in Seattle.

Installing the left inboard Wright R-1820-97 Cyclone in a B-17F-505-BO. (Photo by Andreas Feininger, Library of Congress)

hoists, shackles, A-2 release units, and for the sway braces." Also included were fittings provided to fasten the beam to semipermanent brackets.

The external racks were mechanically controlled by a bomb-release lever or by emergency-release handles through the same linkage as controls the internal racks. Electrical connections were provided on each rack for two positions of an A-2 release unit and for a type A-1 bomb-arming control used with nose-fused bombs. Arming control was by a toggle switch on the bombardier's panel that operated the arming units on both racks simultaneously.

Loading the bombs required removal of the racks, which were then reinstalled with the rack and bomb hoisted as a unit. The bomb to be loaded was placed under the airplane wing immediately below the position it will take when hoisted. Sway braces were adjusted to the diameter of the bomb, and the shackle was attached to the bomb lugs. The same bomb-hoist drums used for internal bombs (and which were furnished with the airplanes) were

Workers at Boeing's Plant 2 bend and cut structural components that will become the skeleton of a B-17F. (Photo by Andreas Feininger, Library of Congress)

A crew at work on the inner structure of a B-17F wing section at Boeing Field in Seattle. (Photo by Andreas Feininger, Library of Congress)

attached to the beam by means of support assemblies, one hoist being used at each end of the beam.

The release procedure for the external racks was similar to that for the bomb bay, except that external bombs could be dropped electrically while the bomb doors were closed as long as the bombardier's control handle was in the "selective" position and the proper rack selector switch was closed. The external racks incorporated a bomb-arming control for use with all nose-fused bombs.

The Achilles heel of the external bomb racks was their effects on performance because of increased aerodynamic drag, and range was decreased because of higher fuel consumption. A 4,000-pound bomb that was carried externally reduced the aircraft's true airspeed by about 25 mph at 10,000 feet

and about 30 mph at 30,000 feet. The external racks installed without bombs reduced the speed about 8 mph at 10,000 feet and about 10 mph at 30,000 feet.

Effective at the time of Boeing's Block 95 B-17F, which came in May 1943, the external bomb racks would no longer be installed.

A crew attaching the sheet metal skin to the wings of a B-17F wing section at Boeing Field in Seattle. (Photo by Andreas Feininger, Library of Congress)

Sharon Arnott, a punch-press operator, is at work on a wing rib for a B-17F at Boeing's Plant 2. (Photo by Andreas Feininger, Library of Congress)

Seattle Plant Expansion: Early 1943

On January 9, 1943, Major J. H. Williams of Materiel Command Headquarters in Washington, DC, wrapped up a visit to Boeing in Seattle with a memo that read in part, "Growth has been rapid during the past two years, but a balance has been maintained by careful planning. The result is an expanded organization of balanced strength."

Such statements are often followed by a "but," and the Williams memo was no different. He went on to say that Boeing's Plants 1 and 2 were "approaching maximum efficient production . . . unless additional floor space could be made available."

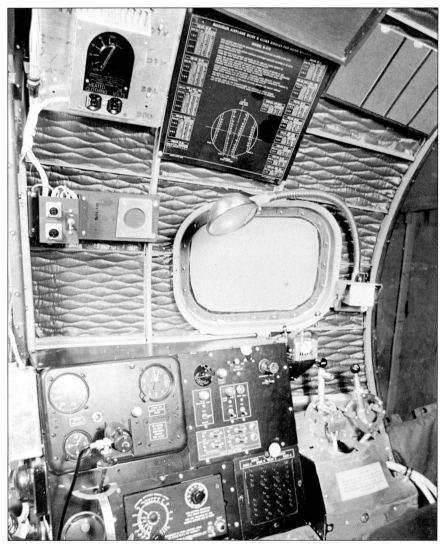

Aft lower fuselage sections for B-17Fs are ready for installation at Boeing's Plant 2 in Seattle. (Photo by Andreas Feininger, Library of Congress)

The left side of the bombardier's compartment just to the left of the nose in a B-17F-95-BO (42-30323) in May 1943. Note the bombardier's panel.

The left side of the B-17F bombardier's compartment just to the left of the nose in June 1943. Note the bombardier's panel and release stand, lower center. Just behind it on the right is the shrouded Norden Bombsight, and above that is the handlebar controller of an experimentally installed chin turret.

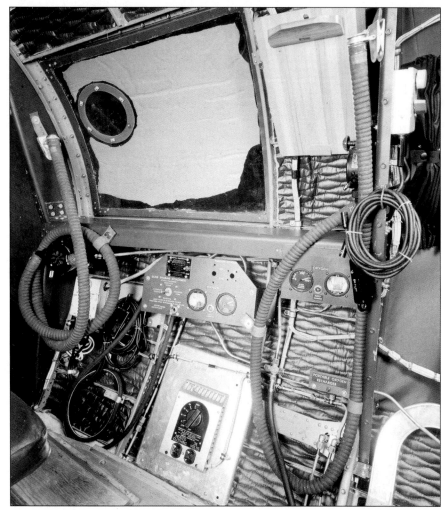

The right front of the bombardier's compartment just to the right of the nose in a B-17F-95-BO (42-30323) in May 1943.

A USAAF bombardier is seated in the right front of the B-17F bombardier's compartment with the nose visible on the left. Note the M2 machine gun in the top foreground.

The left front of the bombardier's compartment just to the left of the nose in another B-17F-120-BO (42-30734) in July 1943. Note the bombardier's panel. No chin turret controller is seen here.

The navigator's station on the left side of the nose section, just aft of Bulkhead 2 in the first B-17F-105-BO (42-30432) in May 1943.

Blackout curtains are in place in the right rear of the bombardier's compartment just forward of Bulkhead 2 in the nose in a B-17F-120-BO (42-30734) in July 1943.

The navigator's table on the left side of the nose section, just aft of Bulkhead 2 in a B-17F-110-BO in June 1943.

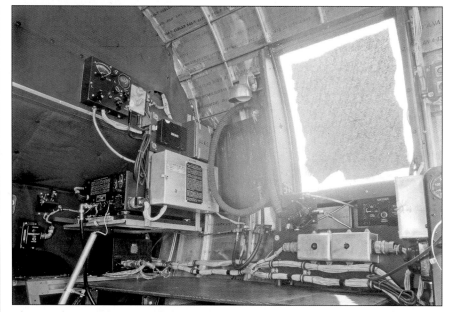

This is a low-angle view of the navigator's station on the left side of the nose section just aft of Bulkhead 2 in the third B-17F-120-BO (42-30734) in July 1943.

Change orders Number 3 and Number 4 of Contract DA W535 ac-196 were forthcoming on January 11. They specified a reallocation of the existing budget rather than calling for additional funding. However, on January 28, 1943, Boeing applied for funding for additional facilities in the amount of $2,290,522, suggesting that this might be approved as an appendix to a contract from a year earlier—this being Contract W535 ac-26184 of January 27, 1942. This, Boeing contended, would allow for monthly production of 270 Flying Fortresses.

On March 15, 1943, Robert Patterson, the Under Secretary of War for Air, personally approved Boeing's request without a reduction in estimated cost.

The complex framework of the Flying Fortress is seen in this view of the nose section, looking aft, of a B-17F. The openings for the astrodome and the window above the navigator's station are clearly visible. (Andreas Feininger, Library of Congress)

Designated as Project 3A-5, it included $1,404,181 for machinery and equipment, $289,379 for furniture and fixtures, $198,004 for mechanical building installations, $195,976 for laboratory and testing equipment, $125,322 for portable tools, and $77,660 for automotive equipment. Wright Field's Production Resources Section had found the costs "reasonable, adequate, and necessary."

The Boeing payroll topped 30,000 in early 1943, which was up from just 5,000 in the summer of 1941. This mushrooming number of personnel came with requirements of its own. Project 3A-6, which evolved at the same time as Project 3A-5, was not directly related to Flying Fortress production but directly to Boeing workers. It concerned the expansion of the two Boeing Field employee parking lots, and the desired construction of bus-stop shelters and a bus terminal before the winter's rainy season.

Boeing had started out with a request to the King County Transportation Commission, but the county responded that it "could not legally provide any funds" for such a project. Meanwhile, Charles Wartelle, the Seattle City Engineer, was unable to obtain the required signatures of adjacent homeowners that were needed before the city could finance the project.

Having hit bureaucratic roadblocks at the local level in Washington state, Boeing turned to Washington, DC, specifically to the Resources Division of the Materiel Command, headed by Brigadier General Frederick M.

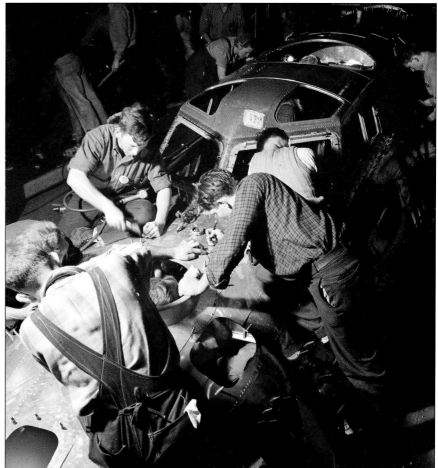

Crowded, but with carefully choreographed activity, work proceeds on the top of a B-17F forward fuselage section, each person concentrating on a specific task or component installation. (Photo by Andreas Feininger, Library of Congress)

The pilot's control column and sidewall panels prior to installation of the pilot's seat in the first B-17F-105-BO (42-30432) in May 1943.

Looking up into the flight deck area of the third B-17G-120-BO (42-30734) in July 1943. The pilot's seat is on the left, the copilot is on the right, and the control panel is visible in between. In the lower center between the seats is the Automatic Flight Control Equipment (AFCE) panel. The gunners access to the top turret, as well as his oxygen line, are visible at the top of the photo.

The right side of the copilot's instrument panel in the first B-17F-95-BO (42-30232) in May 1943. (Please refer to the control panel diagrams in Appendix I.)

Hopkins. He processed the request, the cost of which Boeing had estimated at $655,000 under the Project 3A-6 designation on August 19, and passed it up the chain of command. On September 13, Under Secretary Patterson signed off on the project, albeit with the budget reduced to $649,000.

The cost of the parking lots and the bus terminal was ultimately covered as part of Plancor 1577, the Defense Plant Corporation (DPC) contract that also financed the DPC Building, which was the office building across the street from Boeing Headquarters.

Middle Block B-17Fs

The final Vega Block 50 delivery, that of aircraft 42-6204 on August 21, 1943, marked the end of the 500 B-17Fs produced by Vega, which then slid seamlessly into B-17G production. Boeing and Douglas continued through Block 130 and Block 85, respectively.

Boeing began its Block 55 with a new batch of five-digit tail numbers with the delivery of B-17F-55-BO number 42-29467 on December 20, 1942.

A B-17F-105-BO is on the ramp at Boeing Field in June 1943.

A B-17F-115-BO on the ramp at Boeing Field in July 1943. This aircraft reached the 385th Bomb Group in England in August 1943 and was lost on a mission to Rostok during the Eighth Air Force Big Week campaign in February 1944.

A B-17F-120-BO on the ramp at Boeing Field in July 1943. The new insignia with sidebars was introduced around this time. For a short time, it was outlined in red, as can be deduced here, but this was soon changed to an outline in the same shade of blue as the circular background of the star.

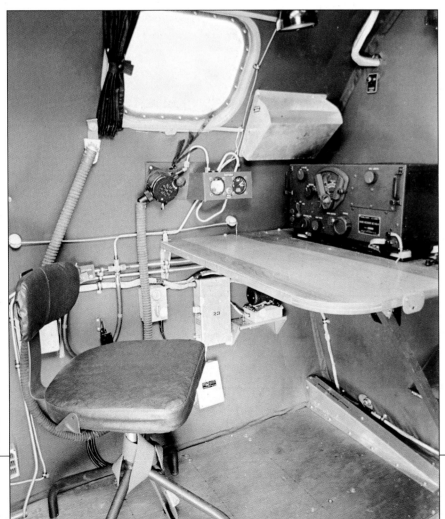

With this, Boeing introduced the alcohol-spray windshield deicer that Douglas had incorporated into its Block 15, the first of which (42-3004) had been turned over to the USAAF less than three weeks earlier on December 3. In its own Block 55, which was first delivered with aircraft 42-3394 on June 2, 1943, Douglas added provisions for an auxiliary powerplant for the electrical system, a B-3 bomb release control, and an AN-5790 thermometer.

Block 60, which began for Boeing with the delivery of 42-29532 on New Year's Eve in 1942 and for Douglas with 42-3420 on June 16, 1943, saw minimal changes coming through Seattle, but from Burbank, bombardiers got a windshield wiper and SCR-287 radio equipment.

In Block 65, Boeing reinforced the outer wing panels and added P-1 generators with a first delivery on March 14, 1943. Douglas updated the A-12 oxygen system and controls for external bomb racks that had first been incorporated in its Block 15 and Block 30, respectively. The first B-17F-65-DL was delivered on June 18, 1943.

Beginning around March 15, 1943, early in Boeing's Block 65, semitempered glass was introduced into windshields in an effort to eliminate cracks that were "believed to have been caused by gunblast." The new windshield had the same overall thickness as the previous type and was interchangeable with it. However, as noted in the *Boeing Field Service News*, "The thickness of each of

The radio operator's station in the mid-fuselage of a B-17F-115-BO (42-30621) in June 1943. Note the Belmont BC-348-H radio receiver on the desk. The chair was now a movable desk chair rather than a fixed seat as in previous variants. The fixed seat returned in the B-17G in 1944, but chairs were to be found once more in 1945 B-17Gs.

The upper gun mount with M2 machine gun is shown in firing position with its flexible ammunition feed. It is seen here in the hatch above the radio operator's compartment in a B-17F-110-BO (42-30542) in June 1943.

The center fuselage of a B-17F, the section between Bulkheads 5 and 6 containing the radio operator's compartment, is seen here tipped upright for access. (Photo by Andreas Feininger, Library of Congress)

The right-hand M2 waist gun installation with ammunition feed and plywood ammunition box is seen looking aft toward the tail in the third B-17F-120-BO (42-30734) in July 1943. Note the portable oxygen bottle on the bulkhead, lower left.

the two plies of glass which form the inner pane of the double-pane window is increased from 0.078 to 0.109. The two plies of the outer pane remain at their original thickness value of 0.109. All plies are semitempered glass."

Boeing's first Block 70 B-17F was delivered on February 11, 1943, with changes including the installation of the D-16 emergency fuel transfer pump. The 9-volt D-16 was two pounds lighter than the previous D-15. Meanwhile, the auxiliary powerplant was fitted for operation in the stowed position by providing an exhaust line through the skin that is reinforced with a stainless steel patch.

Changes previously accomplished at modification centers or as a modification item at the factory continued to be moved back to become regular production-line items at the factories. For example, according to the *Boeing Field Service News* of March 1, 1943, effective with the first Boeing Block 70 B-17F (42-29732) stowage for a spare antenna was routinely provided on the inside of the right waist gunner's ammunition box. The reel was bolted to the lower portion.

Another former modification-center job brought onto the assembly line at the time of Boeing's Block 70 was the installation of curtains that could be

Finishing touches are applied with the aid of a light in the dark recesses just aft of Bulkhead 5 in the area that would soon be fitted out as the radio operator's compartment in the B-17F center fuselage. (Photo by Andreas Feininger, Library of Congress)

A well-lit view of work being done in the area aft of Bulkhead 5 in a B-17F center fuselage. The door leads into the bomb bay. Bulkhead 5 was distinguishable from Bulkhead 6 in that the doorway did not reach all the way to the floor. (Photo by Andreas Feininger, Library of Congress)

snapped into position during combat "to protect the lower turret from spent cartridges and other debris."

Meanwhile, deliveries of Boeing Block 75 B-17Fs began on February 24, 1943, with minor reinforcements in the nose section, a radio-compartment upper gun hatch. There were also the provisions for an auxiliary powerplant for the electrical system that were similar to what Douglas did with its Block 55 B-17Fs after June 1943.

As summarized in the *Boeing Field Service News* of March 29, 1943, design changes incorporated with the first Boeing Block 80 B-17F included BDV 432, new brackets to accommodate larger landing-gear motors; and BDV 540, tail-gear limit switches changed to an "instantaneous" action type. BDV 648 "completely eliminated the carbon dioxide engine fire extinguisher system [which saved] about 78 pounds, simplifies manufacturing, and does not greatly affect safety." Nevertheless, this change would be reversed under BDV 648.1 eleven months later.

Boeing began installing Tokyo Tanks in its Block 80 B-17Fs, which were first delivered on March 13, 1943. Douglas had begun incorporating Tokyo Tanks in its Block 25 B-17Fs two months earlier in January 1943, but Vega started installing them at about the same time as Boeing. According to the *Boeing Field Service News*, this "outboard wing tank installation" was done under the change order identified as BDV 358.

For Boeing, the first delivery of Block 85 B-17Fs on April 2, 1943, saw improvements to the main landing gear and braking system as well as provisions for a remote-reading compass.

Block 85 also saw the augmentation of the existing glycol heating system for the crew areas of the aircraft through the addition of an auxiliary heating system. As described in the *Boeing Field Service News* of April 12, eight radiator fan assemblies connected by glycol tubing with the No. 3 engine nacelle system were installed in the astrodome, the navigator's compartment, the top turret, the cockpit, the radio compartment, the ball turret, and the tail turret."

Recirculating radiators, consisting of a radiator core and an electric fan assembly, were arranged to draw air from inside the airplane. Non-recirculating heaters had a radiator-fan assembly as well as an air scoop to provide a continuous flow during flight. Dampers were provided to permit discharge of any desired proportion of the heated air inboard of the recirculating radiators.

The right-hand M2 staggered waist gun installation with ammunition feed is shown looking aft toward the tail in a B-17F-115-BO (42-30631) in August 1943. This was a developmental placement, as staggered waist guns did not become standard until early 1944 during the B-17G production run. Here, the barrel extends through an opening in a Plexiglas panel, another feature due to become standard in the B-17G.

The left-hand M2 waist gun installation with ammunition feed and plywood ammunition box is shown looking forward in a B-17F-125-BO (42-30880) in August 1943.

Douglas Aircraft Company employees work in Long Beach on the center fuselage of a B-17F. In this view, we are looking aft toward the tail, with open-ings for the waist guns prominent on either side. (Photo by Alfred Palmer, Library of Congress)

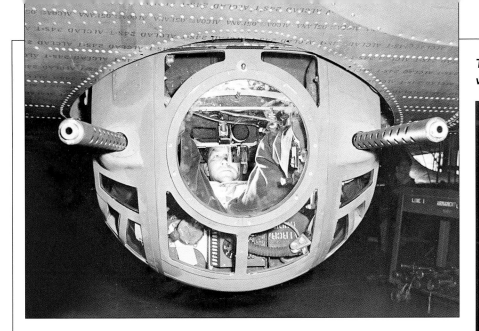

This view of a B-17F ball turret is a good illustration of how the gunner would position himself within its catastrophic confines.

The Stinger Tail Turret assembly for a B-17F, minus the pair of M2 machine guns. In this view we are looking aft. The gunner knelt here with his head in the cupola at the top. The guns protruded from the opening in the back.

Sally Wadsworth works on wiring connections beneath the tail of a B-17F-40-VE at the Vega Aircraft plant at Burbank in June 1943. Into the space where she sits will slide the Stinger Tail Turret assembly.

Later Block B-17Fs

Automatic Flight Control Equipment (AFCE) had been installed in Boeing B-17Fs as early as Block 65 aircraft at the beginning of 1943, but BDV 685 mandated an improved version that began appearing in April 1943 with Boeing Block 90 aircraft. These improvements were first incorporated into Douglas B-17F-40-DL number 42-3250 and Vega B-17F-30-VE number 42-5879 on April 8 and April 14, 1943, respectively.

At this point, BDV 685 also mandated that two resistor units be added into the AFCE junction box to develop finer control in the aileron and rudder circuits. These latter changes also reached Douglas and Vega during that same week in mid-April. For the former, it was with aircraft 42-3250 in the middle of its Block 40, and for Vega, it came on 42-5879, which was a B-17F-30-VE.

In its Block 90, Boeing also initiated BDV 492-1, the removal of seats in the radio compartment "in order to facilitate installation of a fatigue bench at the AAF modification center . . . Stowage space will probably be provided beneath the seat. To accommodate this change, the interphone jackbox has been moved slightly forward and the heated-suit rheostat and portable oxygen bottles moved."

The single-piece Plexiglas nose is installed into a B-17F at Boeing's Plant 2. This fixture was one of the most visually prominent features of the B-17F, which differed from earlier variants that had faceted Plexiglas noses.

A Vega employee prepares one of the B-17F's 56-inch tires for instillation onto the main gear strut. The gear and tires retracted into the inboard engine nacelles on each wing.

Vega's Betty McDonald performs wiring work inside the nose of a B-17F on the ramp at Burbank in the warm California sunshine. Because of the warmer climate, much final assembly work in Southern California could be done outdoors.

A nearly completed B-17F is about to be rolled out the factory door with dozens more soon to follow. (Photo by Andreas Feininger, Library of Congress)

Other changes that began with aircraft number 42-30132, the first B-17F-90-BO, included such minutia as BDV 269A-47, the elimination of flexible conduit in the junction boxes on top of the propeller feathering motors. This relatively modest change is a nice illustration of the complexity of managing parallel changes across the breadth of the BDV Committee factories.

The California planemakers began incorporating BDV 269A-47 three months later. Vega did so with aircraft B-17F-45-VE number 42-6089, which was delivered on July 17, 1943, in the middle of its Block 45. BDV 269A-47 was to have appeared in what was ordered as Douglas Block 75 B-17Fs (starting with aircraft 42-3504), but that group was redesignated as Block 5 of the subsequent B-17G variant—first delivered on July 16, 1943.

Boeing's Block 95, which followed on May 3, saw several important changes to the Boeing B-17F, including tail stabilizer modifications to improve their interchangeability, reinforcement in the mid-fuselage near the radio room because of accidental machine gun discharge, and the introduction of the JH-3R starter. It was from this stage of production that external bomb racks were no longer installed.

The Boeing Block 100 B-17Fs, which began to appear on May 15 with aircraft 42-30332, had small electrical system changes and one physical change, designated as BVD 269A-52, that was illustrative of the mood of the times with regard to conservation of materials vital to the war effort.

"As a means of further conserving strategic materiel," reads the internal description of BVD 269A-52, "the tail gunner's ammunition stowage box has been redesigned and will hereafter be made of wood. The new box is

This photo of a fire drill at Boeing's Plant 2 complex on August 14, 1943, provides a good view of the lay of the land. On the left, across East Marginal Way South, is Boeing Field with completed B-17Fs ready for their delivery flights. On the right is Building 2-40, the big high-bay assembly building that was the centerpiece and dominant fixture at the Boeing Plant 2 complex. On its roof, one can see the artificial trees that were part of "Wonderland," the phony subdivision created to fool enemy bombardiers looking for Plant 2. In the center is a line of recently completed B-17Fs awaiting their trip to the paint hangar. Aircraft in the foreground is a B-17F-115-BO about to depart for Ladd Field in Alaska for cold-weather testing.

Final engine checks are carried out for the R-1820 Wright Cyclones installed in these B-17Fs. (Photo by Andreas Feininger, Library of Congress)

interchangeable with the old. It is also directly adaptable to the use of the flexible feed track, which is to be incorporated on Boeing 42-30532 [Boeing's Block 110 B-17F]."

For Boeing, Block 100 of the B-17F saw a significant change to rudder balance control. This came under BDV 128, an unusually low-number designation for the middle of 1943. This indicated that it had probably been in the works for some time. For Douglas, it appeared with B-17F 42-3268 in Block 40, and Vega's Block 35 B-17F numbered 42-5949. The aircraft were delivered on April 18 and May 28, 1943, respectively.

BDV 128 was undertaken because "in order to reduce the control force necessary to operate the rudder, the rudder trim tab operating mechanism has been revised to provide a servo action. Thus, when the rudder is swung in one direction, a linkage moves the tab in the opposite direction. The tab projected into the airstream in this manner produces a resultant force which aids the pilot in overcoming the air forces on the rudder. This opposite motion is accomplished by mounting the forward end of the tab operating shaft and the operating drum in a fixed position on the underside of the lower rudder-hinge bracket rather than on the front face of the rudder spar as heretofore. In this manner, the forward end of the shaft remains fixed with respect to the airplane instead of moving with the rudder as it formerly did. The drum centerline is also shifted 1.06 [inches] to the right of the rudder centerline."

Boeing's Block 105, first delivered on May 30, had small changes to the remote-reading compass and fuel valves as well as the removal of the landing-gear warning horn. Changes were also minimal when Boeing's Block 110 appeared on June 18 with a changed thermometer system and installation of flexible ammunition boxes.

On duty. A guard watches over completed B-17Fs after the manufacturer had officially turned them over to the government. His armband reads "MP," but his helmet suggests that he might be a member of the State Guards organization, which was supplied with surplus equipment dating to 1918. They were deployed as a substitute for National Guard units that had been federalized and deployed overseas with the US Army. (Photo by Andreas Feininger, Library of Congress)

Ready to go. A lineup of completed B-17Fs is on the Boeing Field ramp across East Marginal Way South from the Plant 2. (Photo by Andreas Feininger, Library of Congress)

By the summer of 1943, the tens of thousands of different kinds of parts flowing into three factories presented a logistical challenge, rivaling even that of the armed forces with their operations across a half dozen continents. It was logistics on a scale that no one could have envisioned even 18 months earlier.

Examples mentioned in the June 7, 1943, issue of the *Boeing Field Service News* include such esoteric components as Type B-2 landing light relays and Type AN5735 directional gyro indicators. Existing B-2 relays had proven "unsatisfactory in service due to their low current rating." It was reported that "the products of four manufacturers, which are similar to the Type B-2 relay, have been investigated and found satisfactory by reason of higher performance ratings."

In naming these items, we get an idea of the scope of the subcomponents that the BDV Committee had to track—without modern computers—on an immense scale, and a partial roster of electrical subcontractors. The products that were ordered to "hereafter be used exclusively in place of Type B-2 relays," were the Guardian Electric 34420, the Cutler-Hammer 6041-HS7, the General Electric CR-791-A1O1A3, and the Struthers-Dunn 62HXX1OO.

A larger electronic component, but one still small enough to fit in the palm of your hand, was the AN5735 Directional Gyro. It was being supplied by two companies, the Ternstedt Manufacturing Division of General Motors and the Sperry Gyroscope Company. They were each satisfactory, but they were not entirely compatible with one another in the control panels of the aircraft.

"The indicators are identical in operation, but the housings differ in that the vacuum ports are not located in the same relative position," read a description. "The Ternstedt instrument has the port at the lower part of the case instead of in the center as in the Sperry instrument . . . Since there is no distinction in part numbers, it is very probable that a Ternstedt instrument, having the vacuum port in the lower portion of the case, may be supplied as a replacement. . . In that event, the existing metal tube connection to the manifold will not fit. It should, therefore, be replaced by a length of BAC884-6-84 hose or its equivalent, AN884-6-84. The 811FT-6D fitting at the manifold and 811CT45-6D fitting at the indicator are also to be replaced by an AN840-6 nipple and BAC535-12 hose clamp at each point." Whew.

Such were the complexities that were met and overcome every day—if not every hour.

Starting on June 29, 1943 with Boeing's Block 115 aircraft, extra SCR-287 radios were no longer installed, and beginning on July 21, Block 120 included a number of further changes. These included those to the life raft hatch door, the bombsight mount, and the A-3 oxygen flow indicator. The D-16 emergency fuel transfer pump, which had been part of Boeing's B-17F package since February, was now deleted. Vega had made a point of also removing it from its Block 45 B-17Fs around the same time.

Also in the Boeing Block 115 aircraft, the M2 .50-caliber "cheek" guns were installed in small enclosures on the sides of the nose, which protruded slightly to provide better forward visibility for the gunner. They first appeared in the B-17F-115-BO (42-30631) on July 31, 1943. Guns had been previously installed pointing straight out of the sides of the nose or in the Plexiglas nose or windows. These had appeared in various configurations on variants going

Crews fuel a B-17F in preparation for its delivery flight to a modification center, a USAAF training field, or another facility. (Photo by Andreas Feininger, Library of Congress)

Ready to go to war, but most likely on its way to an interim stop at a modification center in preparation for its combat career, a completed B-17F takes off from Seattle's Boeing Field. (Photo by Andreas Feininger, Library of Congress)

back to the B-17D and B-17E, but the side-mounted, forward-firing nature of the cheek guns was a substantially more complex engineering project.

Credit for designing the metal enclosure for the cheek gun is credited to W. W. Erickson of United Air Lines, who was at the Cheyenne Modification Center where many Flying Fortresses were going for modification.

Beginning in June 1943 with USAAF tail number 42-3483, Douglas Block 70 B-17F aircraft were rolled out with chin turrets and were promptly redesignated as B-17G-1-DLs. The Block 75 Douglas aircraft, which began to be delivered in July, were redesignated as B-17G-5-DLs. (These variants, and those originally ordered from Douglas as Block 80 and 85 B-17Fs, are dis-cussed in Chapter 8.)

Boeing's B-17F Block 125 changes, first delivered on August 5, 1943, were again minimal, but those of Block 130 from August 23, included the rein-forcement of the nose that would be necessary as Boeing began the transi-tion to the B-17G variant with its Bendix chin turret. Boeing's final Block 130 B-17F, which carried the company serial number 6145 and the USAAF tail number 42-31031, was the final B-17F. It was hand delivered to the USAAF on September 4, 1943.

Boeing had now produced 2,300 B-17Fs, while Douglas built 605, and Vega rolled out exactly 500.

Chapter 8

THE B-17G: THE ULTIMATE FLYING FORTRESS

Although the B-17G was the climactic and definitive Flying Fortress variant, its transition from the B-17F was so seamless it was hardly noticeable—aside from the addition of the Bendix Chin Turret described below. The first Block 1 B-17Gs from each of the three factories of the BDV Committee members bore a company serial number and a USAAF tail number just one digit advanced from those of the final B-17Fs.

The Douglas B-17G-1-DL was the first, having been ordered and carried on the books as a B-17F-70-DL. It was delivered on June 20, 1943, complete with its chin turret. It bore company serial number 8419 and USAAF tail number 42-3483. Vega's B-17G-1-VE was next on August 24 with company serial 6501 and tail number 42-39758. Boeing's debut B-17G aircraft, bearing company serial number 6146 and the USAAF number 42-31032, was delivered to the USAAF on September 4, 1943, the same day as its final B-17F. Like the B-17F, the Boeing B-17G carried the Model 299P designator.

The specifications were largely unchanged from the B-17F. As with the B-17E and B-17F, the wingspan was 103 feet 9 inches, with an area of 1,420 square feet. Most sources give both the B-17F and B-17G a height of 19 feet 1 inch.

The B-17G was 74 feet 9 inches long—the same as the B-17F. The eventual adoption of the Cheyenne Tail Turret, with is discussed in detail later in this chapter, reduced the length of effected B-17Gs by about 5 inches. Sources that give the length of the B-17G as 74 feet 4 inches without mentioning the Cheyenne Tail Turret are being misleading. Sources that give the length of the B-17F as 74 feet 4 inches are incorrect.

General Henry Harley "Hap" Arnold, the Commanding General of the USAAF (left), with General George Marshall, Chief of Staff of the US Amy. The two men at the top of the chain of command were most responsible for the might of American airpower in World War II. Both achieved five-star rank in December 1944. Arnold was both a visionary and a brilliant executor, while Marshall recognized this and gave the USAAF what it needed to excel.

Excellent side views of B-17Gs, circa 1944, prominently show their defining chin turrets and cheek guns. Seen flying a mission against the Third Reich, these are from the 532nd Bomb Squadron of the Eighth Air Force 381st Bomb Group based at Ridgewell. The aircraft in the center closest to the camera is the second B-17G-70-BO, delivered on May 19, 1944. It flew more than 55 missions and returned home in May 1945. It is the only aircraft in this photo with a Cheyenne Tail Turret. The aircraft in the lead as seen here is a B-17G-35-DL that was delivered on February 24, 1944. A P-51B Mustang "Little Friend" is seen top right.

A weight comparison between the B-17F and B-17G shows an increase in empty weight from 34,000 pounds to 36,135 pounds, and an increase in maximum weight from 55,000 pounds to 65,500 pounds, although this data varies by source and by subvariant, as it does with data on all Flying Fortress variants.

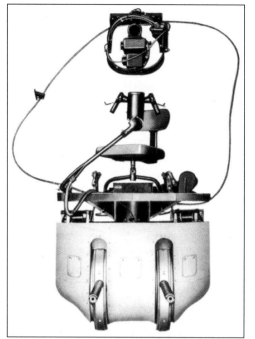

This drawing illustrates the operational Bendix Chin Turret. The actual turret is at the bottom, and the gunsight is at the top. In the center is the bombardier's chair and the handlebar controls, which could be tilted to the bombardier's right when he needed to concentrate on his bombsight. (Photo Courtesy USAF)

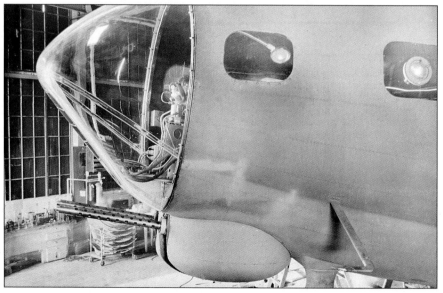

These two photos show an early experimental installation of a prototype chin turret in a B-17F in November 1942. It is much flatter and shallower than the operational chin turrets that were ultimately made standard equipment in the B-17G. Note the handlebars of the gun control. (Boeing Photos Courtesy of Mike Lombardi)

The Wright R-1820-97 Cyclone 9-cylinder, air-cooled radial engines that had been used for the B-17F continued into B-17G production. Developed by Wright Aeronautical, the Cyclones were manufactured by Wright in Patterson, New Jersey, as well as by licensees, notably Studebaker. According to USAAF records cited by Irving Brinton Holley in *Buying Aircraft*, his postwar study of wartime procurement, Studebaker produced 63,789 Cyclones in South Bend, Indiana.

The Cyclones were initially equipped with the General Electric B-2 turbosupercharger, but during 1944, these were gradually upgraded to the B-22 type. The manual lists the B-2 with a governed speed of 23,400 rpm and the B-22 with a governed speed of 26,400 rpm. Although there were multiple subcontractors making the B-22, those used in Flying Fortress production were sourced mainly from General Electric as part WW8456556.

Edward Curtis Wells contemplates a B-17 chin turret. Wells had been the lead engineer on the Flying Fortress program since its inception in 1934, and by the time the B-17G arrived on the scene in 1943, he was Boeing's chief engineer for military programs. (Boeing Photo Courtesy of Mike Lombardi)

The turbosupercharged engines delivered 1,200 hp for takeoff, 1,000 hp at 25,000 feet, and a war emergency power rating of 1,380 hp. Although data varies by source and subvariant, the cruising speed was between 160 mph and 182 mph. The top speed was rated at 300 mph at 30,000 feet, and the war emergency rating was 302 mph. The service ceiling was between 35,000 and 37,600 feet (depending on the source). The B-17G had a 2,000-mile range with 6,000 pounds of bombs, and it had a maximum ferry range of 3,400 miles.

The Bendix Chin Turret

The defining feature of the definitive Flying Fortress variant was the Bendix Chin Turret. The idea of a chin turret emerged as one of the solutions to the serious problem of defending bombers against frontal attack by enemy interceptors. Most bombers, including the earlier variant Flying Fortresses, were defended by fixed nose guns. A notable exception was the Consolidated B-24 Liberator, which came to be defended by the A-15 nose turret. Developed by the Emerson Electric Manufacturing Company in St. Louis, this was a variation on the tail turret that Emerson was then producing for the B-24. First tested on some B-24Ds, the nose turret became standard equipment with the B-24H variant in 1943 and was also installed in the later B-24J.

For the Flying Fortress, the front-firing guns would be in a chin turret produced by the Bendix Aviation Corporation of South Bend, Indiana. Bendix had been a participant in earlier powered turret programs, but its performance had not been stellar. Had it not been for wartime urgency, the company never would have received a chance at the chin turret. Materiel Command historian Irving Holley wrote that "Bendix turrets were far from being ideal," and he described an earlier Bendix lower turret as "a collection of malfunctions."

Citing a transcript of a July 22, 1941, phone call between Major S. R. Brenthall, the Materiel Division rep at Bendix and Colonel K. B. Wolfe at Wright Field, Holley observed that "Bendix deliveries were so much in default that the Materiel Division contemplated throwing half the Bendix contract to Emerson."

On October 10, 1941, a memo from Brigadier General Ralph Royce, the American air attaché in London to the Office of Production Management paraphrased a British turret expert named Speckley, who called the Bendix turret "completely hopeless due to improper control and poor design in general."

Had it not been for wartime exigency, Bendix would probably have been banished entirely by the Materiel Division, but production capacity was in urgent demand. Bendix had a lot to prove.

Bendix had been working on the chin turret concept since July 1942, when it hand-built two examples as proposals for possible use in the B-17 and the B-24. The one designed for the B-17, which used indirect sighting (with a gunsight on an arm located away from the guns) was deemed to be the best choice. It was considered for both aircraft, but when a full rotating turret was picked for the B-24, the chin turret was earmarked for the Flying Fortress alone.

Given Bendix's spotty production record and the reputation of its products as "a collection of malfunctions," the development of the chin turret was anything but straightforward.

Delays dragged on, memos to and from Major General Oliver Echols, the head of the Materiel Command, indicate a great deal of skepticism about the ability of Bendix to meet the demands of mass production. In a January 27,

A detailed view is shown of some of the armament in the YB-40 aircraft. This armament also included the Bendix Chin Turret. The YB-40 was developed in parallel with the evaluation of the Bendix Chin Turret in B-17F aircraft. The YB-40 designation went to a group of service test aircraft that might have led a series of heavily armed Flying Fortresses that would escort B-17 bombers. A dozen of them flew missions with the 92nd Bomb Group in May–July 1943. The defensive fire concept worked, but the weight of the armament dangerously slowed the YB-40.

1943, Echols complained that "the history of the Bendix Company in turret production does not bear out any optimistic assumption as to their capacity to better the delivery schedule."

By June 1943, Bendix was able to produce 150 chin turrets monthly, but they proved impractical, and it was back to the drawing board. Chin turrets with indirect sighting were experimentally installed in some B-17Fs as well as in the XB-40/YB-40 aircraft, which are discussed later in this chapter and were modified and heavily armed B-17Fs.

A redesigned direct sighting system, which had fortunately been in the works since earlier in the year, was incorporated into the Bendix Model D Chin Turret and ready for installation in time for the first completed B-17G to roll out in Long Beach on August 6, 1943.

According to Boeing Historian Mike Lombardi, credit for the chin turret as it went into production goes to Boeing's own B-17 Armament Group and to Keith McDaniel, who was a member of that organization. In a conversation with Lombardi many years ago, among the stories McDaniel related was that the Plexiglas nose used in the B-17F series tended to shatter when the guns were fired at full elevation, leading to the development of a flatter nosepiece in the B-17G.

Technically speaking, the Bendix Chin Turret Model D was an electrically driven power turret working off the B-17G's 24-volt DC system with the peak starting current for the motor amplidynes being at 1,280 amps and the maximum current draw running at full load being 92 amps. The turret mounted two .50-caliber Browning M2 machine guns that were equipped with a recoil-absorbing mechanism, firing solenoids, and manual gun chargers.

The Bendix Model D weighed 438 pounds without the guns or ammunition. The two M2 Browning machine guns weighed 65 pounds each, and the 900 rounds of .50-caliber ammunition added 297 pounds, bringing the total weight of the fully armed turret to 865 pounds. The external turret assembly (with the exception of the gun barrels that protruded through canvas-covered, zippered slots) was enclosed in a movable aluminum housing to minimize wind resistance. Plexiglas windshields sealed the space at the floor of the aircraft around the turret.

The guns rotated 172 degrees in azimuth (86 degrees to the left and to the right of forward), and they swung from 26 degrees above horizontal to 46 degrees below. In the event of electrical power failure, the turret could be rotated in azimuth and the guns swung in elevation by use of a hand crank.

The turret was mounted at floor level in the bombardier's compartment and manned by the bombardier. The turret was operated by lifting a latch and swinging the turret controller column from its stowed position against the right side of the fuselage to the combat position, which was in front of the gunner. The sight was suspended at eye level from the top of the fuselage above the operator's position. The main power switch was on the front of the controller column.

The ammunition containers were attached to the movable housing and equipped with guide chutes that allowed the .50-caliber rounds to flow into the guns while they were rotating in elevation and/or in azimuth. Empty shell casings and belt links were ejected through the bottom of the housing.

The gunner could follow a target freely, firing as required without the guns striking the fuselage or firing into any part of the aircraft. The limits of the gun movements in azimuth and elevation were automatically controlled by switches. Turret motion was stopped by releasing the control handle safety switches on the side of the control handles.

The direction and speed of the guns were controlled by handlebars. Each handle contained a safety brake switch for stopping the turret should the gunner relax his grip, spring trigger switches for firing the guns, and a high-speed switch for fast tracking speeds.

In turn, the movements of the control handles in azimuth and in eleva-

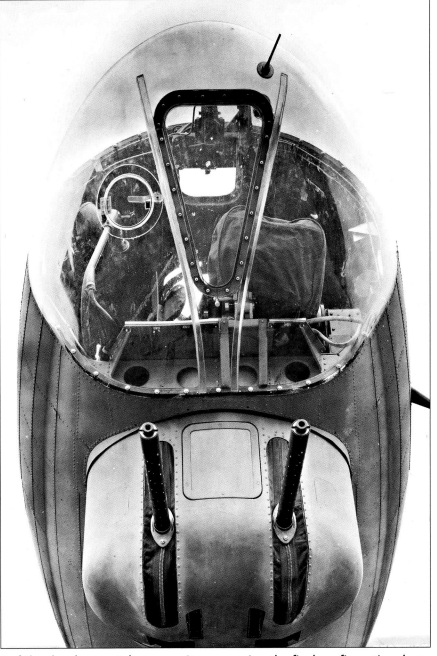

This prototype Bendix Chin Turret was installed in a B-17F in April 1943 as part of the developmental process. It was nearing the final configuration, but changes were still to come, including a reduction in size of the panel between the guns. Note the shroud covering the Norden Bombsight in the nose.

tion moved potentiometers that varied the control fields of the azimuth and elevation Amplidyne generators.

The variable output of the Amplidyne generators controlled the direction and speed of the azimuth and elevation turret drive motors. The Amplidyne system of control automatically furnished a constant speed for any setting of the control handles regardless of the change of torque.

The open gunsight was synchronized with the movements of the gun in azimuth and elevation, and it was driven by tachometer shafts from the azimuth and elevation gear trains. Thus, the gunner's field of view moved with the guns and always included the direction in which the guns were pointed.

The center of the field of view was marked by a center dot that indicated the point upon which the guns were trained. The dot and circle were used in the same manner as a ring sight and bead in a flexible machine gun installation. The sight was equipped with a rheostat to control the intensity of the light of the circle, which was projected on the sight glass. The intensity of the light could be varied according to operating conditions—from bright sunlight or night flying.

Bendix went on to be vindicated. The company whose turrets were once characterized as "completely hopeless" redeemed itself with 8,680 chin tur-

rets installed in B-17G aircraft. As these aircraft armed with those turrets became the backbone of the strategic air campaign against the Third Reich, countless Luftwaffe interceptors fell to the streams of .50-caliber lead from the chins of those thousands of bombers.

The XB-40/YB-40 Flying Fortress

The Bendix Chin Turret evolved in parallel with the perceived need for an escort aircraft that was even more heavily armed than the aircraft already known as the Flying Fortress. The B-40 project dated back to November 1942, a time when Luftwaffe interceptor opposition to Eighth Air Force B-17 missions over Europe was so severe that the USAAF was grasping outside the box for a solution. (See photo on page 152.)

The B-40 was conceived as an ultimate manifestation of the Flying Fortress idea. As it had evolved, the B-17F was armed with 11 .50-caliber machine guns: two each in the nose, tail, waist, dorsal turret, and ventral ball turret, and one in the radio room. The B-40 would have an additional dorsal turret, plus twin gun mounts on either side of the waist, plus the chin turret. The ammunition load would increase from 11,000 to 17,000 rounds.

 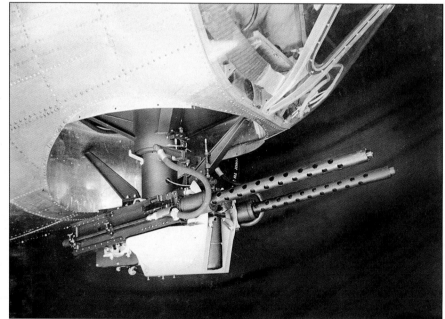

These two photos illustrate an operational production-series Bendix Chin Turret installed in a B-17G-10-BO (42-31285) in October 1943. One image shows the turret with the housing removed to reveal the M2 machine guns and the internal mechanism.

The XB-40 testbed was converted from the second Boeing Block 1 B-17F (41-24341) and made its first flight on November 10, 1942. An additional 20 service test YB-40s and four TB-40 trainers were converted from B-17Fs built by Vega in Burbank. They were fitted with their armament by Douglas at its Tulsa Modification Center. It was here that things got creative. Some YB-40s received quad tail guns, and some had 40-mm cannons installed. At least one had 30 guns.

A dozen YB-40s flew nine operational missions between May 29 and July 4, 1943, with the 327th Bomb Squadron of the Eighth Air Force's 92nd Bomb Group based at Alconbury in the United Kingdom. While they could defend themselves well, the weight of their armor and armament made it hard for them to keep up with the conventional Flying Fortresses that they were supposed to protect.

Irving Holley noted that on a July 1943 mission, one YB-40 gunner reported that he was unable to track more than one target with an early-generation chin turret "because of the difficulty of picking up targets attacking in rapid succession."

As the aircraft proved to be ineffective in many ways in defending the other aircraft around them, the YB-40 program was canceled and filed away.

A technician adjusts the remote control line on a B-17G Bendix Chin Turret. In the center is the combination case and clip cartridge ejection chute.

This test and evaluation rig for the Bendix Chin Turret was used in the development process for designing subsystems.

The lasting legacy of the YB-40 is, of course, the first, albeit ineffective, combat tests of the chin turret that defined the B-17G.

Beginning B-17G Blocks

With the exception of the Bendix Chin Turret, the first B-17Gs from each member of the Boeing-Douglas-Vega Committee were nearly identical to the last Boeing B-17Fs from each company. Indeed, in the transitions, the first B-17Gs bore serial numbers only one digit higher than the respective final B-17Fs.

Douglas and Vega both delivered ahead of Boeing, the originator of the Flying Fortress lineage. In fact, Douglas delivered all of its Block 1 and Block 5 B-17Gs before Boeing started delivering its first Block 1 B-17Gs. This was in part because they had been ordered under the B-17F (Douglas Blocks 70 and 75) designation and were already in the pipeline in the summer of 1943.

The aircraft that were intended to be delivered as the final four Douglas B-17F production blocks (70, 75, 80, and 85) were redesignated before they were built, and they became the first four of the Douglas B-17G blocks. The first Douglas B-17G-1-DL, which had existed on paper as the B-17F-70-DL, was delivered on June 20, 1943. Its USAAF tail number was 42-3483, just one digit higher than that of the last Douglas B-17F-65-DL. Likewise, its Douglas serial number (8419) was one digit beyond the last Douglas Block 65 B-17F.

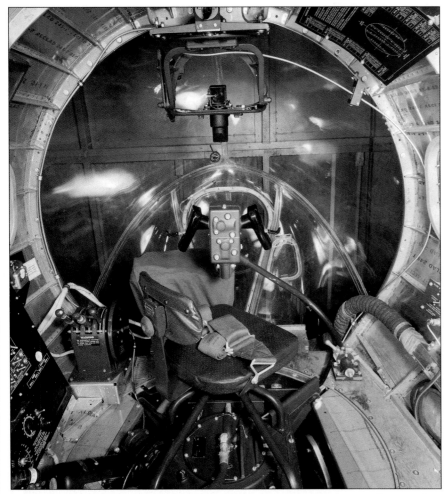

Looking forward through the bombardier's station in the nose of a B-17G-10-BO. Note that the handlebar controller for the Bendix Chin Turret (looking a bit like a video game controller from far in the future) is in the operating position.

Patricia Rogers works inside the nose of a B-17G at the Vega Aircraft plant in Burbank in late 1944.

The fuselage section for a Vega Aircraft Block 5 B-17G glides effortlessly through the air across the Burbank factory on a massive, heavy-duty crane. When completed, this particular aircraft was delivered on September 25, 1943.

Vega delivered its first B-17G-1-VE on August 24, 1943, nearly two weeks ahead of Boeing's first Block 1 B-17G. It incorporated the same mid-fuselage reinforcing around the radio room, which Boeing had introduced in its Block 95 B-17Fs in May 1943, and the remote-reading compass that Boeing had been incorporating since its Block 85 B-17Fs in April.

It was hand delivered on September 4, 1943, which was the same day as the last Boeing B-17F. That company's first Block 1 B-17G carried Boeing serial number 6146 and the USAAF tail number 42-31032, which was only one digit removed from those of the last B-17F. The block changes incorporated into the B-17G-1-BO were minor electrical modifications and the A-1 bomb control system. Changes to the B-17G-1-BO codified under BDV 803 and BDV 806 also called for the elimination of some bulkhead armor and certain bomb hoist cables and pulleys.

The Douglas B-17G-5-DL (formerly B-17F-75-DL) was first delivered on July 17, 1943, incorporating the A-3 oxygen flow meter that Boeing started putting into its Block 120 B-17Fs that same month. Vega's first Block 5 B-17G was delivered on September 23 with minimal electronic upgrades and the emergency hydraulic brake system no longer part of the package. Boeing handed off its own first Block 5 B-17G one day after Vega. It incorporated a supplementary oxygen feed for the ball turret gunner and some fuel valve alterations.

Douglas Block 10 B-17Gs, first delivered on August 6, 1943, incorporated the same mid-fuselage reinforcement that Boeing had added on Block 95 B-17Fs in May and which Vega was doing on its Block 1 B-17Gs in August. Vega and Boeing Block 10 B-17Gs were first delivered three days apart on October 19 and 22, 1943. Boeing's came with wiring changes and breech heaters for the upper turret (BDV 781-1), while Vega's aircraft carried modified A-2A ball turrets. The latter were adopted by Boeing for its Block 15 B-17Gs.

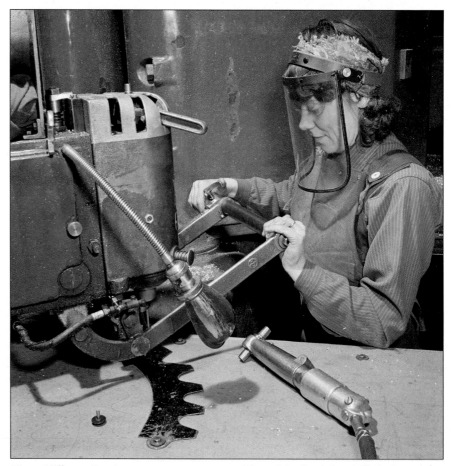

Checking and balancing the rudder on a B-17G at the Vega Aircraft factory in Burbank, circa September 1943.

Mary Miller, a Boeing router operator at Plant 2 in Seattle, drills holes in a part for a Flying Fortress. (Photo by Andreas Feininger, Library of Congress)

For its B-17G-10-BO, Boeing also added a .032-gauge "J"-shaped guard to the emergency bomb release pulley bracket above the forward entrance door. The purpose of the guard was said to be "to avoid possible fouling when cable is rewound after an emergency release." Curiously, the paperwork for the change, designated as BDV 459-2, emphatically stated that Douglas and Vega "will not incorporate" this component.

The first Boeing B-17G-15-BO was delivered on October 19, with the first B-17G-15-VE coming on November 15. Douglas had made its first Block 15 delivery on September 6.

Noticeable changes that took place in Flying Fortress deliveries over the summer of 1943 were in their appearance. There was the introduction of the new national insignia with the white sidebars added to either side of the star in a circular blue field.

Meanwhile, the USAAF was also in the process of phasing out the requirement that its aircraft be painted in olive drab camouflage. The Air Materiel Command first considered this change as early as November 1942 because it could reduce weight and aerodynamic drag, thereby increasing speed. By 1943, the threat of attack on the ground by enemy bombers was nonexistent or greatly diminished in many theaters, although paint was still seen as a protective barrier to corrosion under humid conditions.

In June 1943, USAAF aircraft that were not deployed overseas, such as trainers, were officially exempted from camouflage paint. In October 1943, service bulletins carried the notice that Flying Fortresses could officially be delivered in natural metal finish, and the change was mandated by BDV

These photographs show the complex task of constructing electrical and electronic wiring assemblies for Flying Fortresses at Boeing's Plant 2 in Seattle. Not visible here is the comple spectrum of color-coded wires. (Photo by Andreas Feininger, Library of Congress)

889. This change was not implemented overnight. Some combat aircraft were delivered without camouflage paint early in 1943, but others were still being painted as late as January 1944. In general, the final phaseout of factory-camouflaged B-17Gs came during the deliveries of Boeing and Douglas Block 35 aircraft and Vega's Block 20.

The *Boeing Field Service News* noted on January 31, 1944, that this change "effects a weight saving of approximately 98 pounds, but performance is not appreciably changed. Olive drab anti-glare panels are painted forward of the cockpit on the top inboard quarter of the nacelle surfaces and on the top portion of the tail gun enclosure to eliminate sun glare."

An important innovation introduced by the BDV Committee members in late 1943 was the improved Emerson A-2A variant of the ball turret with its oxygen swivel gland designed to ensure a flow of oxygen to the gunner regardless of how much swiveling he did in his spherical "cage." The A-2A reached Vega B-17Gs at Block 10 in October, Boeing at Block 20 in November, and Douglas with Block 30 in early December.

September 29, 1943, marked the first Douglas Block 20 B-17G delivery. Those of Boeing and Vega followed on November 11 and December 5,

Workers at the Cheyenne Modification Center rivet a panel just aft of the big 25-inch LP-21-A Radio Antenna Loop used on B-17Gs for radio and navigation.

A line inspector checks things over inside the nose section of a B-17G at the Vega Aircraft plant in Burbank.

respectively. Changes were minimal, although Vega did add ammunition storage for the tail guns, and Boeing incorporated the A-2A ball turret.

Plywood in Flight

In the fall of 1943, an interesting trend emerged amid the piles of BDV-designated change orders that were drifting into the inboxes at Burbank, Long Beach, and Seattle. The BDV prefix was "269A" and the operative word was "plywood."

It will be recalled that in May 1943, with the beginning of Boeing's Block 100 B-17Fs, BVD 269A-52 stipulated that the tail gunner's ammunition stowage box would now be made of wood in an effort to "conserve strategic materiel." Indeed, the ammunition boxes for both waist guns were also now being made of plywood, although the ammunition boxes for the ball turrets were still made of sheet metal.

The fall of 1943 brought more such BDV 269A mandates. BDV 269A-55 specified that "the wing break junction box shield, located on the compression strut just aft of Bulkhead 4 in the bomb bay, is changed to wood to conserve strategic materials." Meanwhile, BDV 269A-57 stipulated that the command radio transmitter support should be "redesigned to further conserve materials and is now fabricated of plywood."

These changes both applied to the Boeing Block 10 B-17Gs, first delivered on October 22, 1943. BDV 269A-57 reached Vega with Block 5 B-17Gs, first delivered on September 23. BDV 269A-55 was implemented by Vega with Block 20 from December 5. Both changes affected Douglas Block 35 B-17Gs during January 1944.

On the heels of these wood conversions came BDV 269A-56, which called for the flooring in the aft section of B-17G aircraft to be changed to plywood. The order took effect with Douglas Block 10 B-17Gs from August 6, 1943, in Vega Block 15 B-17Gs from November 15, and in Boeing Block 25 B-17Gs after December 14, 1943.

It is fascinating to reflect upon the fact that the making of one of the most sophisticated weapons in the American arsenal, circa late 1943, was affected by the pervasive pressure throughout the country to conserve metal for the war effort.

Also worth mentioning is the ready availability of wood products, especially in the Pacific Northwest. Aside from the extensive aircraft, ship, and railcar manufacturing in the Seattle area, the timber industry was probably

Looking forward from the waist of the fourth B-17G-20-BO (42-31435) in October 1943. In the center foreground is the rounded top of the Sperry Ball Turret, which was standard equipment since the early B-17E.

Looking forward from the waist of a restored B-17G-85-DL (44-83575) that was delivered in April 1945. In the center foreground is the rounded top and gunner access door of the Sperry Ball Turret. Note that the position of the yellow oxygen bottle had changed since paired bottles were being installed 18 months earlier. Also note that the ammunition boxes were metal for the ball turret but plywood for the waist guns. (Photo by Bill Yenne)

The right-side M2 .50-caliber waist gun aboard the first B-17G-15-BO (42-31332) in October 1943. The big 600-round ammunition boxes for the waist guns were made of plywood.

the leading economic powerhouse across the entire region.

Of course, it is part of the story to remind ourselves that Bill Boeing himself had achieved success as a lumberman before he saw his first airplane.

The Modification Centers in 1943

In her history of the modification program entitled *The Modification of Army Aircraft in the United States*, Virginia Toole spoke of the "steady upward trend" of the USAAF modification work as 1943 began. In October 1942, Major General Muir Fairchild, the Director of Military Requirements, had predicted to Major General Oliver Echols, chief of the Materiel Command, that "modification work would decrease shortly as modifications were introduced into the production lines." However, by January 1943, the number of changes in the Flying Fortress program increased by 30 percent since early 1942.

Nevertheless, there were those at the Materiel Command who still

The right-side M2 .50-caliber waist gun aboard a B-17G-80-BO in December 1943. Over the course of the preceding two months, changes in the B-17G production line had seen the plywood ammunition boxers move from floor to wall mounts. Note the one-piece fixed Plexiglas window that was introduced at the same time as the idea of staggering the waist gun placement.

Looking forward toward the flight deck through the bomb bay of a B-17G-85-DL (44-83575) that was delivered in April 1945. (Photo by Bill Yenne)

wanted to modify the modification system itself. On February 26, 1943, Colonel Bryant Boatner, head of the Modification Section, proposed that the modification centers run by the airlines be phased out in favor of giving the manufacturers primary responsibility.

However, as Virginia Toole observed, "The slowness with which modifications were taken up by the factories as well as the press of work rendered the release of the airline facilities impossible, despite General Boatner's determination to make all modifications the direct responsibility of the prime contractors in their own centers."

Instead, Echols advocated an expansion of the facilities at the modification centers. His team proposed such changes as streamlining the bureaucracy and doubling of the 4 million square feet available for modification at the existing centers. By July 1943, all 19 of the numbered centers—including 6 that were run by airlines—were in full operation.

The Cheyenne Modification Center in Wyoming that was operated by United Air Lines (Center No. 10) continued to be the principal Flying Fortress facility. Indeed, while some centers handled a variety of aircraft types,

Cheyenne processed almost nothing but Flying Fortresses. During 1943, Cheyenne handled 2,372 Flying Fortresses, which was up from just 403 in 1942. Cheyenne set a monthly average of just over 200 aircraft monthly in 1943 and reached a peak of 243 in December.

The Denver Modification Center managed by Continental Airlines (Center No. 13) modified 1,431 Flying Fortresses in 1943, which was up from 203 in 1942. As in Cheyenne, it reached its peak in December, as 202 aircraft passed through.

Workers assemble CD346 oxygen regulators at the Cheyenne Modification Center for installation in various crew positions throughout the B-17G.

Looking forward toward the flight deck through the bomb bay of a B-17G-10-BO (42-31264) in October 1943.

The Tulsa Modification Center operated by Douglas Aircraft (Center No. 16), which had modified 183 Flying Fortresses in 1942, handled just 51 in 1943, and 31 of these were in January with the rest coming in September and October. The Lockheed Aircraft Company's Dallas Modification Center at Love Field (Center No. 3) processed 218 Flying Fortresses between May and October; 66 of those came in September.

Through 1943, individual records show that the first hop made by Flying Fortresses built by Vega in Burbank was not to a modification center but a flight of just 29 air miles south to the Douglas Aircraft plant in Long Beach, where they resided in a "premodification pool" for several days before moving on to Cheyenne, Denver, or Tulsa.

Overall, the archipelago of USAAF modification centers processed 22,007 aircraft of all types during 1943 (compared with 4,038 in 1942).

Late 1943 B-17G Electronics Systems

Most Allied aircraft were equipped with Identification Friend or Foe (IFF) systems by which Allied radar operators could identify friendly aircraft and confirm that they were not hostile. The British had been working on such

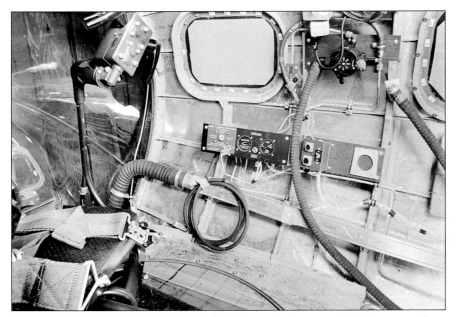

The right side of the crowded bombardier's compartment in the nose of a B-17G-5-BO (42-31150) prior to its being retrofitted for a first-generation cheek gun. Note the handlebar controller for the Bendix Chin Turret.

systems since 1940 (Mark I and Mark II) and developed the Mark III, which remained operational even after the war.

The summer and fall of 1943 marked the operational deployment of the Mark III IFF aboard Flying Fortresses. The British Mark III system was designated as ARI-5025, while the US Army Signal Corps Mark III IFF system was designated as SCR-595 or SCR-695. B-17G Flying Fortresses were built with provisions for these systems beginning with the Boeing Block 10 aircraft and the Block 15 from Douglas and Vega.

Other Flying Fortress electronics upgrades in mid-to-late 1943 included the adoption of the SCR-522 very high frequency (VHF) four-channel command radio system, the British Standard Beam Approach (SBA) blind landing radio navigation system, and the RC-103 Airborne Localizer Receiver.

Introduced in various Flying Fortress production blocks in 1944, the RC-103 aided instrument approaches. It was based on the German "Lorenz beam" Landfunkfeuer (LFF) ultra-short-wave landing radio beacon. The RC-103 was also installed during the war in B-24s, C-47s, and other aircraft. The RC-103 evolved into the AN/ARN-5, and in various forms it continued to be used for many years after the war.

In addition to the SCR-522 VHF radio, the B-17G aircraft were also equipped with the SCR-274N AM radios that had been installed in B-17Fs for more than a year. Whereas a B-17F of early 1943 had two transmitter units and a receiver, two to four SCR-274N transmitters and three receivers were installed side by side on shelves or racks high on the wall of Bulkhead 5 on the right side of the radio operator's compartment.

H2X (AN/APS-15) Radar

Known operationally during the war as H2X, the AN/APS-15 system was introduced into the Flying Fortress electronics package in mid-1943 and first used operationally over Europe in late September of that year. It was an early form of ground-scanning radar that was to be widely used in both B-17s and B-24s. H2X was an American adaptation of the British H2S radar and a precursor to the postwar higher-resolution AN/APQ-7 Eagle and AN/APQ-14 radar systems.

H2S had been the first operational airborne, ground-scanning radar system, having evolved from airborne-intercept radar when it was discovered in 1941 that different ground objects have different radar signatures. When scanning the ground, the magnetron in the radar showed that bodies of water looked different from open land, which in turn looked different from urbanized terrain.

The H2S developed for the Royal Air Force Bomber Command was first used operationally in January 1943 with radar-equipped Pathfinder aircraft leading the bomber formations. Bomber Command flew its missions at night to reduce the threat of German interceptors or antiaircraft fire, so targets were hard to see visually, but neither darkness nor cloud cover deterred the H2S.

The H2S concept was seen as a possible solution to the single most limiting factor in USAAF daylight bombardment operations: the weather. When a target was obscured by clouds, which seemed to be the case more often than not, over occupied Europe, precision bombing using the Norden Bombsight was impossible, so bombers had to forego an attack on the primary target to search for targets of opportunity.

Although the RAF was acquiring H2S equipment as fast as it could be manufactured, the Eighth Air Force managed to get its hands on a small number of sets and began installing them in its bombers. Flying Fortresses thus equipped formed the nucleus of the 482nd Bombardment Group at Alconbury, which was specifically designated as a Pathfinder group.

In the meantime, because supplies of the H2S sets were so limited, the USAAF decided to seek development of a homegrown H2S derivative. It so happened that the Massachusetts Institute of Technology Radiation Laboratory, known as the "Rad Lab," had been doing substantial research on the same technology. It was able to develop an improved variation on the H2S, which it called H2X.

The H2S utilized the S-band microwave frequency between 2 and 4 gigahertz, while the H2X used the X-band frequencies between 8 and 12 gigahertz. The X-band is widely used today for satellite communication and wireless transmission. Because the H2X used a shorter frequency than the H2S, it provided imagery with higher resolution.

By the third week of September 1943, the Rad Lab had installed a dozen H2X sets in a dozen Flying Fortresses, and the aircraft were on their way to England. There, they joined the H2S-equipped bombers in the 482nd Bombardment Group. (See photos on page 171.)

"Although by no means completely successful, the two initial attempts at radar bombing gave room for restrained optimism regarding the new techniques," Arthur Goldberg and Arthur Ferguson wrote in Volume II of *Army Air Forces in World War II*. "Three of the four combat wings that bombed on

These photos of B-17G-15-BO aircraft at Boeing Field in October 1943 illustrate that while the Bendix Chin Turret was standard equipment out of the factory door, the cheek guns were still a modification center item. Note the shrouded Norden Bombsights inside the noses.

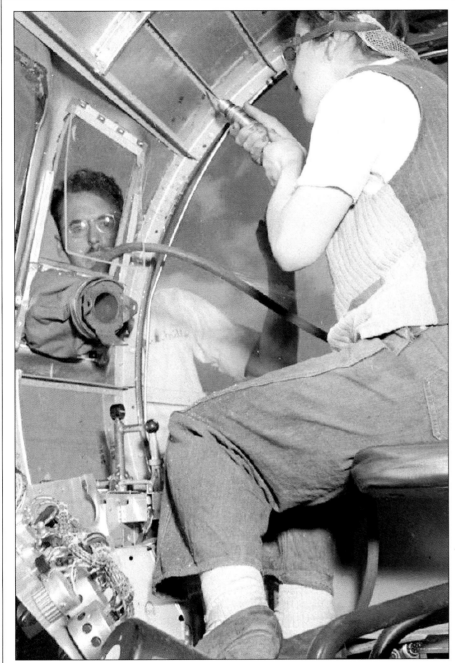

Workers at the Cheyenne Modification Center move components, cut bulk-heads, and prepare for the installation of cheek guns in this B-17G.

an H2S plane achieved the reasonably small average circular error of from one-half to one mile. Difficulty in the fourth sighting resulted in an abnormal error of two to three miles. Results were less encouraging for the combat wing that attempted to bomb on flares dropped by the Pathfinder planes. Confusion at the [beginning of the bomb run] during the first mission and a high wind during the second, which blew the smoke of the markers rapidly from the target area, help to account for an average error of more than five miles. One of the leading combat wings did considerable damage . . . More encouraging than the bombing was the fact that the enemy fighters, since they had to intercept through the overcast, fought at a distinct disadvantage. Overcast bombing was obviously a safer type of bombing than visual."

Promising results were achieved by formations that were led directly by an H2X Pathfinder. Although, it was determined that the smaller the number of bombers led by a Pathfinder, the more condensed and more accurate the bombing pattern would be.

Beginning in 1944, the H2X systems were installed primarily at the modification centers. Between January and May, the Denver Modification Center installed 184 of them for the USAAF and 15 for the Royal Air Force. Thereafter, H2X installation shifted mainly to the Lockheed plant in Dallas, where 300 H2X-equipped B-17Gs were turned out from June through November 1944.

Most of the Flying Fortress work in Dallas during 1944 involved H2X aircraft. Only 59 B-17Gs were built there without it, and these were modified in June and July. The peak of H2X Dallas deliveries came with 94 in July and 65 in August. The last four H2X-equipped B-17Gs rolled out in Dallas in November.

Other modification centers doing small numbers of H2X installations included Cheyenne, which turned out nine such aircraft between August and November 1944, and Tulsa, from which 22 were delivered between July and September 1944.

The H2X (AN/APS-15) was one of the unsung secret weapons of World War II and of the Flying Fortress story.

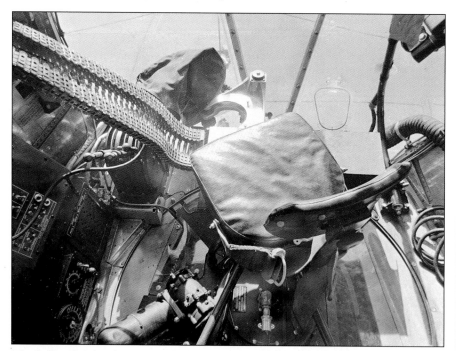

A factory-installed right-side M2 .50-caliber cheek gun is seen in an early B-17G-1-BO (42-31039) in September 1943.

The left-side cheek gun ammunition chute snakes its way through the crowded bombardier's station in a B-17G-1-BO (42-31039) in September 1943. Note the bombardier's chair atop the Bendix Chin Turret. Part of the controller for the latter can be seen at the edge of the photo to the right.

Seattle Plant Expansion: 1943 into 1944

As B-17F production gave way to that of the B-17G in the summer of 1943, the physical evolution of the manufacturing complex at Boeing Field in Seattle continued. However, the trajectory of the evolution had changed. By the fall 1943, the physical plant dedicated to the B-17 had reached the point where floor space was finally adequate for the ongoing tempo of production, which now exceeded 240 aircraft monthly.

In addition to Building 2-40, the huge, expanded high-bay assembly structure, and the adjacent Building 2-41 where fabrication work was done, the Plant 2 campus included Building 2-25, the engineering building, and the warehouse space known as Building 2-31.

Other infrastructure needs arose, and another can of worms was opened—literally on the ground at Boeing Field. On October 9, Lieutenant Colonel M. J. Joyce of the Air Materiel Command's Western Procurement District of the Air Technical Service Command in Santa Monica, California, passed along a request to USAAF headquarters in Washington, DC. Boeing had asked him to approve 75,000 square yards of additional paving at Boeing Field. Existing pavement started to deteriorate and "the possibility of airplanes bogging down in wet weather constituted a serious menace to B-17 production."

The Corps of Engineers estimated a cost of $540,000 for what was soon designated as Project 3G. It called for 7 inches of poured concrete over a 25-inch gravel and aggregate base. As the request worked its way through the wartime bureaucracy, someone at the Western Procurement District suggested that since the paved areas were temporary and would be used only for parking airplanes, a cheaper form of paving ought to be used. With an eye toward saving money, Colonel W. R. Herod of the Resources Control Section at Wright Field recalculated and insisted on October 30 that the job could be done for $284,670.80.

Two weeks later on November 14, Joyce reported that since the rainy season in the Puget Sound area had already commenced, paving operations would be problematic. He suggested steel landing mats such as those being used for aircraft landing fields on South Pacific islands. He said that there was a stock of this matting at the Lathrop Engineer Depot east of San Francisco that could be accessed. The snarl of the bureaucracy was unkind to Project 3G. It turned out that all the matting at Lathrop was already earmarked for overseas use. Thus, the whole affair came full circle, and the Materiel, Maintenance & Distribution (MM&D) office at USAAF headquarters dictated on November 26 that conventional paving must be done.

Through the latter part of 1942 and well into 1943, the focus at Boeing Field had been on a rapid expansion to facilitate Flying Fortress production. By the end of 1943, though, the physical plant at Plant 2 dedicated to the B-17 was essentially complete. The focus of infrastructure projects in the Puget Sound area was now on the needs of the B-29 Superfortress program.

This was not taking place at Plant 2 and Boeing Field. Instead, it took place at Renton, about 5 miles southeast of Boeing Field. The Renton plant, located at the foot of Lake Washington, was originally built for the production of the Boeing PBB-1 Sea Ranger flying boat, but this program had been canceled by the time that the prototype XPBB-1 made its debut flight on July 9, 1942.

At Plant 2, there was virtually no factory floor overlap between the B-17 and B-29 programs when it came to final assembly. Only the three XB-29 Prototypes were built at Boeing Field in Seattle. The YB-29 service test Superfortresses, numbering 14, were built at Boeing's expanding factory complex

A B-17G with the cheek guns installed, circa fall 1943. In March 1944, a redesign came online through the BDV 822 change order that introduced staggered cheek guns, a modification that moved the right-side gun aft.

in Wichita, Kansas, as were 1,620 B-29-BW production aircraft. Boeing also built 1,119 B-29A-BN aircraft at its facility in Renton. An additional 5,000 B-29C-BNs were scheduled to be built at Renton, but these would be canceled in 1945 as the war was ending.

Parenthetically, the Renton facility was on land reclaimed from Lake Washington in 1916 and used by the Pioneer Washington Coal Company, owned by Charles Burnett. When Burnett's wife died, his daughter, Amy, was raised by Mr. and Mrs. Howard Potter, whose own daughter, Bertha, became the wife of William Edward Boeing! After the start of World War II, the land became the property Defense Plant Corporation under Plancor Contract 156.

Although none of the production series Superfortresses were assembled and delivered at Boeing Field in Seattle, components and subassemblies were

A good side view of a B-17G-15-BO in action over Europe with both cheek and chin guns installed. Chow-hound was assigned to the 322nd Bombardment Squadron of the 91st Bombardment Group, based at Bassingbourn, England. Delivered on October 25, 1943, it had completed more than 50 missions when it was shot down on August 8, 1944. (Photo Courtesy USAAF)

An inside view, looking up and forward in the nose section of a B-17G, at the installed cheek gun at the most forward position in the nose. Beginning in March 1944, the gun on the right side of the airplanes would be moved backward to the position of the window visible on the right.

produced there. Air Materiel Command infrastructure Projects 3A-5 and 3A-6 were the last to focus primarily on the needs of Flying Fortress production.

Beginning with Project 3A-7 in May 1944, the focus was directed to the Superfortress, and the paperwork was datelined as "Boeing and Renton." Project 3A-7 specifically noted that the Seattle plant "should build the major subassemblies which would be transported to the Renton plant for final assembly." Also mentioned was "the problem of converting [Plant 2 at Boeing Field] from B-17 to B-29 production," but this idea was never implemented.

Projects 3A-7 and 3A-8 in mid-1944 were concerned with equipment and tooling for the Superfortress program, while Project 3A-10 of January 1945 addressed the physical needs for rapidly expanding B-29 production.

As had been the case with the BDV Committee that produced the B-17F and B-17G, the Air Materiel Command assembled a pool of three manufacturers to produce Superfortresses. In addition to Boeing at Wichita and Renton, both Bell Aircraft and the Glenn L. Martin Company built them. Bell produced 357 B-29-BAs and 310 B-29B-BAs in Atlanta, while Martin produced 204 B-29-MOs in Omaha, Nebraska.

B-17G Blocks of Early 1944

As 1943 ended and 1944 began, and as the combat prowess of the Flying Fortress, especially in the skies over the Third Reich, was becoming the focal point of both headlines and legends, the war stories were rivaled only by the production stories.

The scene at Plant 2 in Seattle was amazing with B-17Gs of several blocks all flowing through the plant like huge parallel aluminum rivers. Blocks 25 and 30 ran concurrently, with respective USAAF first acceptances coming on December 14 and December 6, 1943. Their being out of sequence is attributable to the unusual heavy snow that fell on Seattle that month when finished aircraft backed up in the parking areas and premodification pools waiting for improved flying weather. Many of those that had rolled out later, were actually delivered earlier.

Boeing Blocks 35 and 40 also ran concurrently and were affected by time necessary to sort out the backup in the parking areas. The first B-17G-35-BO was delivered on January 27, 1944, which was three days later than the first B-17G-40-BO. The first Douglas Block 25 B-17G was delivered from Long Beach on November 5, 1943, and the first from Vega in Burbank came on January 13, 1944.

Douglas is noted for adding staggered and enclosed waist gun positions (see page 174) at Block 25 and for adopting the A-2A ball turret at Block 30. Other changes involved a variety of electrical and mechanical components. Douglas delivered its first B-17G-30-DL on December 6, 1943, followed by Boeing's first B-17G-30-BO on December 11—ahead of its first B-17G-25-BO—and Vega's first B-17G-30-VE was handed off on February 10, 1944.

Douglas started Block 35 deliveries on January 17, and Vega began delivering them on March 10.

Big changes for the B-17G as 1944 began included the B-22 high-altitude supercharger, which replaced the existing B-2 type on the R-1820-97 Wright

The H2X (later AN/APS-15) ground scanning radar set was installed in some B-17Gs beginning in early 1944. Operating on a 10-GHz operating frequency, the H2X allowed bombardiers to "see" their targets through cloud cover. (Photo Courtesy USAF)

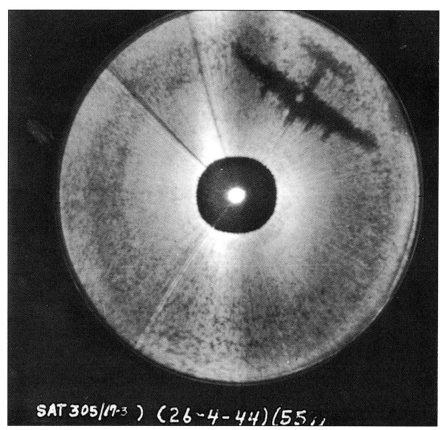

An image of a B-17G is visible here on the radarscope of an H2X (later AN/APS-15) ground scanning radar set. (Photo Courtesy USAF)

Cyclone under the BDV 272 design change designator. As noted at the beginning of this chapter, the manual lists the B-2 with a governed speed of 23,400 rpm and the B-22 with a governed speed of 26,400 rpm.

By early 1944, three companies produced the B-22: General Electric with a monthly output of 6,500 units, Allis-Chalmers with a capacity of 4,500, and Ford, which could turn out 3,500. The B-22s that flowed into the B-17G

The complex task of checking and sorting electrical wiring assemblies is shown at Boeing's Plant 2 in Seattle. (Photo by Andreas Feininger, Library of Congress)

program were built by General Electric as part WW8456556. Mounting provisions for either the B-2 or B-22 were the same, but the oil and return lines had to be revised.

The B-22 was integrated into Vega's assembly line with B-17G-25-VE, which was first delivered on January 13, 1944. Douglas started with its Block 35 deliveries on January 17, and Boeing began with its own Block 35 on January 27.

Other B-17G changes during early 1944 included BDV 809-2, which reinforced the all-synthetic rubber external fittings on the self-sealing fuel and oil tanks. A light fabric patch was cemented around the respective fitting and its base, and a protective coating was applied over the patch. This was introduced in Boeing's Block 30 and the Douglas Block 25.

As had been the case with Boeing's Blocks 25 and 30 at the end of 1943, so too were those of Blocks 35 and 40 transposed. They came on January 27 and 24, respectively. Things were moving quickly in Seattle, and Block 45 deliveries from Plant 2 began on February 15.

The Douglas and Vega Blocks 40 and 45 came several months later. Parenthetically, the Douglas Block 40 aircraft came under a Fiscal Year 1944 order, which meant that these B-17G-40-DLs had the distinction of being the first Flying Fortresses to carry USAAF serial numbers beginning with "44." The first one, 44-6001, was delivered on April 2, although the last Block 30 aircraft (42-107253) had come out the doors at Long Beach only about a week earlier. Douglas delivered its first B-17G-45-DL on May 8.

Vega's Block 40 aircraft were its own final Fiscal Year 1942 Flying Fortresses. Vega's Fiscal Year 1944 deliveries began with Block 45. The first B-17G-40-VE was 42-97936, delivered on April 9, and the first B-17G-45-VE was 44-8001, which was turned over on May 10.

The BDV-specified changes continued during the early months of 1944. For example, BDV 706-2, introduced on Boeing Block 35 and Douglas Block 40, addressed the problem of cracks and dope peeling in the material of the tail gun covers by changing it to 7.9-ounce olive drab duck, which increased the serviceability of the cover. With Boeing Block 30 and Vega Block 10, change BDV 592-20 added a T-30 microphone and HS-33 headset to the fly-away equipment stored in the flyaway stowage box in the bomb bay. Under BDV 592-18, introduced in Boeing and Douglas Block 30 B-17Gs and Vega Block 10s, the SCR-274N command radio transmitter in the radio compartment was changed from a type BC-459A to a type B-457A, which decreased the frequency output of the transmitter.

In February 1944, the BDV Committee made an important reversal to an earlier change. Under BDV 648-1, the multi-engine carbon dioxide fire extinguisher system that had been removed in March 1943 under

Once fabricated, electrical wiring assemblies for Flying Fortresses at Boeing's Plant 2 in Seattle had to be meticulously inspected by dedicated inspection teams. (Photo by Andreas Feininger, Library of Congress)

BDV 648, was now reinstalled. This began with Boeing Block 45 B-17Gs and was incorporated into concurrent Douglas and Vega production. As noted in the February 28, 1944, issue of *Boeing Field Service News*, "Except for minor deviations required in tubing runs to clear structural changes and additional equipment incorporated since deletion of the system, the new installation is fundamentally the same as that used on former B-17F airplanes."

Also in February, the B-17G program reached a milestone reminiscent of the transition to fly-by-wire controls in the 1970s and 1980s. Under BDV 674, "A complete electrical control bomb release system eliminating all former mechanical controls is now installed on production airplanes." This began with aircraft in Boeing's Block 45, Douglas's Block 40, and Vega's Block 45.

Boeing's Final Flying Fortress Order

The historic final order for Flying Fortresses that was placed with the originator of this aircraft type came on February 5, 1944. Supplement 14 to Contract W535 ac-20292 (DA-16) called for a round number of 2,000

As can be seen in these two left-side landing gear detail photos from late 1943, tires for B-17Gs might feature either diamond or herringbone tread.

B-17Gs. The estimated cost was $322,794,788.94 plus a 4-percent fixed fee of $12,911,791.56.

The official Wright Field case study noted that "no additional facilities would be required for the manufacture of these airplanes." However, $2,510,588.94 was budgeted for the purchase of "special tools" and ground handling equipment for the repair of Flying Fortresses manufactured by all the members of the BDV Committee.

Gun Position Changes, Waist, Tail and Cheeks

Throughout the spring of 1944, and into the summer, substantial changes were made to the gun positions within the B-17G. This included the introduction of staggered waist guns and placing the guns behind permanent Plexiglas panels instead of removable hatches. Meanwhile, staggering the waist guns meant that the two gunners could operate more freely because they were not backing into one another. With BDV 517, it was stipulated that staggered waist guns were to be "installed to eliminate interference caused with the former installation when both guns were in action."

This change also necessitated redesigning of the ammunition boxes, armor plating, windows, gun supporting structure, and even the floor. It began for Boeing in February, and first delivered on March 1 with its first B-17G-50-BO series aircraft, but Douglas had introduced the staggered positions in its Block 25 in January. Vega had begun the practice by the time of its Block 50 aircraft in June.

In conjunction with staggering the guns under BDV 517, the subsequent BDV 517-1 decreed that Type K-6 enclosed swivel gun mounts replaced the former fabric enclosed mounts that had been designed by Boeing. This in turn required changing adapters, gun-mount posts, supporting structure, and even the size of the window cutout.

BDV 517-2, hand in hand with the previous changes, called for the removal of the circumferential armor plate used on the former waist gun installation and to replace it with a semicircular plate extending from just below the window to the floor.

BDV 517-3 addressed the problem of ejected cartridge cases and links being scattered throughout the waist gun area. It called for canvas pouches to be installed beneath each gun, attached to the armor plate support angles and "positioned so as not to interfere with the gun at any angle of fire."

On the same note, BDV 517-8 ordered the extending of the plywood floor guard around the top of the ball turret to prevent the expended shells and links from being thrown into the ball turret ring gear and jamming its operation. Both BDV 517-3 and BDV 517-8 first went into effect with the March 31 delivery of Boeing's first Block 60 B-17G (42-102844).

BDV 517-7 was the designation applied to a temporary defrosting system for the enclosed waist gun windows. It involved circulating outside air in through an air scoop with an adjustable damper that regulated the airflow. In 517-10, the waist gun window seal was changed to a cork-impregnated neoprene strip. Neither 517-7 nor 517-10 was actually built into the B-17G until Boeing's Block 70 in May 1944.

The BDV-517-series changes were not without problems. For instance, an Unsatisfactory Report (UR) that appeared in the *Boeing Field Service News* on May 8, 1944, reported that "ammunition chutes pass under the guns and feed from the opposite side, causing excessive drag on the ammunition feed. This necessitates continuous hand charging." Nevertheless, it was stated that "no action was to be taken" at that time.

Other issues with the new waist gun arrangement were noted in the *Boeing Field Service News* of June 19, 1944. One was the cracking of the waist gun windows that occurred when the guns were being removed from their mounts. This was addressed by 517-19 when it was determined that the improper

Detail of the Stinger-type tail turret of a B-17G-10-BO (42-31285) in October 1943.

installation of the elevation stop was the "main contributing factor." A decal describing the proper action was installed in B-17G-75-BOs delivered from May 31, in B-17G-50-VEs after June 6, and in B-17G-50-DLs from July 21.

However, cracking continued to be a nagging problem. In October 1944, BDV 517-14 was introduced to prevent cracking of the waist gun windows due to gun rotation on its longitudinal axis. A small steel block, a half inch on its longest dimension, was designed to fit into a slot cut in the C-19 gun adapter. This block was welded to the barrel sleeve of the K-6A gun mount.

Clearly, this was a nagging problem that was ongoing for months. The *Boeing Field Service News* of December 18, 1944, revisited the 517-14 modifications by recommending that a slightly larger block of 1020 steel be welded to the K-6A mount assembly that would strike "the existing azimuth stop lug on the gun yoke, preventing excessive rotation of the waist guns around their longitudinal axis and the resultant window breakage."

Another concern brought to light in the June 19, 1944, bulletin was the discovery that the K-6 gun mounts required additional adjustment in the field. "Because the K-6 gun mounts on the staggered waist gun are set at the factory to counterbalance the weight of the gun and chute, the spiral springs may need to be readjusted in the field to suit the individual gunner's requirements," the item read. "The two spiral springs incorporated within the mount are adjustable and should be set so that the gun is held approximately horizontal . . . Field adjustment of these springs may become necessary since the effect of ammunition in the chute may change the gun position from that of the factory adjustment. This and other factors change the balance position to one not suited to all gunners."

Adjusting the K-6 mount required removing the fairing enclosing the springs, compressing the springs with a wrench, removing the screws, turning both springs, and reassembling the mechanism.

Meanwhile, tail gun changes were included under the BDV 592 prefix. Specifically, BDV 592-27 of March 27, 1944, summarized the necessary interchange of the Type C-2 adapters "as used on the tail guns with the Type C-3A units used on the side guns to eliminate interference with the C-19 adapters used on the staggered waist guns." The C-2 adapter on the radio compartment gun was to be changed to Type C-3A "to relieve C-2 procurement difficulties."

In March, BDV 798 noted that wiring for the N-8 reflector gunsight for the Browning M2 machine guns in the radio compartment and waist positions would be installed at the factory. However, on April 10, BDV 910-2 announced that the M2 in the upper hatch of the radio compartment was to be deleted and that the breech heater mandated by BDV 781-1 in October 1943 was to be "stowed."

A crowd of workers gathers on December 16, 1943, to commemorate the rollout of the 1,000th Flying Fortress produced by the Douglas Aircraft Company in Long Beach. This aircraft, tail number 42-38113, was a Douglas Block 30 B-17G.

March 1944 also saw changes in the B-17G bomb bay doors. The March 27 issue of the *Boeing Field Service News* noted that the bay door limit switches had previously been actuated by "a slider operating on a threaded portion of the fore and aft torque rod of the bomb bay door motor." Later, it added "because wear of the threads on the torque rod and slider made correct setting of the limit switches difficult, this system was changed to an arrangement wherein the switches were mounted on a sheet metal bracket attached to the bevel gear drive housing of the left rear door retracting screw. Strikers attached to each end of the retracting screw actuated the new switches. However, deflection of the sheet metal bracket and the short travel available on the strikers also made correct adjustment of these switches extremely difficult."

In March, "to correct these troublesome conditions, once and for all, an entirely new type bomb door limit switch is now being installed on the B-17G. The switch incorporates two micro-switches, one each for the up and down positions, located inside a cast housing mounted on the bomb bay catwalk truss. The switches are actuated by two circular cams driven by a worm gear connected to the fore and aft retracting motor torque rod."

The lessons from the increasing tempo of the strategic air assault against the Third Reich continued to result in changes that enhanced the "fortress" character of the Flying Fortress. With Vega's Block 35 B-17Gs, first delivered on March 10, 1944, these changes included staggered cheek guns under the BDV 822 change order.

The cheek guns, located in small enclosures protruding from the sides of the nose to provide better forward visibility for the gunner, had first appeared in the B-17F-115-BO (42-30631) on July 31, 1943. In the March 1944 "staggered cheek" project, gun assemblies identified as 15-13839-4 on the left and 15-13843-9 on the right (each containing a .50-caliber Browning M2 machine gun) were installed. The assembly also included a K-9 gun mount, a doubler, a sighting window, a scanning window, and a larger pickup window.

As noted on page 147, the metal enclosure for the cheek gun was invented by W. W. Erickson of United Air Lines, who was at the Cheyenne Modification Center where the B-17Fs and B-17Gs were going for modification. It was of a monocoque design, meaning that like a single-hull boat or certain aircraft fuselages, its structural load was carried by its skin, rather than an internal frame.

Spray-painting the national insignia on the side of a B-17G adjacent to the panel that covered the waist gunner's position.

The wings and tail have been mated, but there are still details to be attended to here at Boeing's Plant 2 in December 1943. The top turret cover of this Block 30 B-17G has been pulled and is lying on the right wing.

A stabilizer shock cowl attachment assembly, designated as 3-19996, was installed for each gun. All of the existing equipment in the nose that had to interface with these assemblies had to be moved around and relocated to provide for the change.

Following the debut of the staggered cheek guns with Vega B-17G-35-VE (42-97836) on March 10, they first appeared in Seattle with the first B-17G-60-BO (42-102944) on March 31. Douglas delivered its first cheek guns with its first B-17G-40-DL (44-6001) on April 2. In October, the B-13 gunsight rings on the cheek guns were beginning to be superseded by N-8A reflector sights.

The Cheyenne Tail Turret

The development of the first generation of powered aircraft gun turrets for the Flying Fortress in 1941 was discussed in Chapter 6, and that of the Bendix Chin Turret is discussed at the beginning of the present chapter. Each of these represented the work of major American engineering firms. This was in contrast with the design and implementation of the famous Cheyenne Tail Turret, a distinctive turret that came about as an after-production retrofit at the Cheyenne Modification Center in Wyoming. View photos of the Cheyenne Trail Turret on pages 207-211.

The United Air Lines facility in Cheyenne, Wyoming, was the most important of the half-dozen modification centers that handled Flying Fortresses during World War II. Indeed, 47 percent of all Flying Fortresses, a total of 5,736 aircraft, passed through Cheyenne. This included the vast majority of those built by Boeing in Seattle that were sent for modification, as well as a sizable number of Vega and Douglas-built Flying Fortresses.

Cheyenne's importance to the Flying Fortress can be traced to Boeing's long-standing relationship with United Air Lines that went back to their having been sister companies prior to 1934. The airport at Cheyenne was a key part of United's original route map. It was established in 1920 as a refueling stop for transcontinental air mail flights. It quickly became one vital to the route leading from New York to Chicago and on to San Francisco. Indeed, Cheyenne and Chicago were the two principal inland locations on the Transcontinental Air Mail Lighted Route inaugurated in 1924.

In the distance, completed inside wing sections are being assembled, while in the foreground, workers at Boeing's Plant 2 are working toward finishing touches on these B-17Gs in late December 1943.

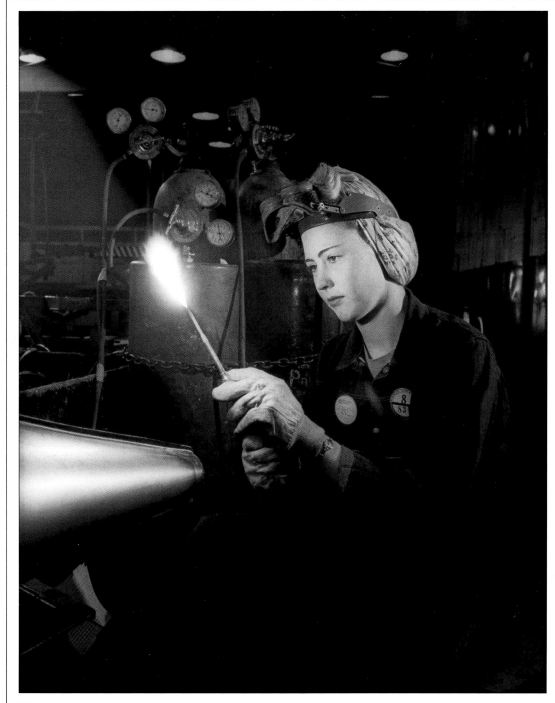

An electric spot welder is used on sheet metal wing panels for a Flying Fortress at Boeing's Plant 2 in Seattle. (Photo by Andreas Feininger, Library of Congress)

An acetylene welding torch is lit at the Vega Aircraft Company facility in Burbank in 1943.

In this scene at Boeing's Plant 2 in November 1943, "Rosie the Riveter" is fastening sheet metal panels with an automatic riveting machine.

An acetylene torch is used to weld smaller components at the Vega Aircraft plant in Burbank.

Cheyenne became an important base for Boeing Air Transport (BAT), which became part of a consortium of Boeing-owned carriers organized as United Air Lines in 1931 and divested by Boeing in 1934. Cheyenne also hosted operations of Plains Airways and Western Air Transport.

The importance of Cheyenne as a prewar maintenance facility was underscored by a 1935 article in *Popular Mechanics* magazine, where it is described as "the largest airplane overhaul and repair base in the world with around 500 employees."

Michael Kassel, a Cheyenne-based historian, recalled that "the mechanics of this time were amazing. These guys could strip a Boeing 247 down to its basic frame, rebuild and repair all its systems, and have the aircraft ready to fly in four days."

The key man for the United Air Lines operation at Cheyenne was Ralph S. Johnson, who had a stellar reputation in the industry. When the Cheyenne Modification Center was created in 1942, it was Johnson who took over as manager. At its peak, the Cheyenne Modification Center had a staff of around 3,600 men and women.

The Cheyenne Turret was an improvement on the conventional Stinger turret that had been standard on all Flying Fortresses since the first B-17E in October 1941. It was a better environment for the gunner, as he was moved closer to the paired Browning M2 .50-caliber machine guns for better control. The former "post and bead" gunsight was replaced with an N-8 reflector sight for enhanced accuracy. Instead of peering through small windows, the gunner was now in a sort of greenhouse enclosure. This afforded a much better field of view, although it did impart the feeling of being more exposed to enemy interceptor fire. Best of all, perhaps, instead of being on his knees while operating the guns, he was now moved to a bicycle seat.

The Cheyenne Tail Turret first appeared in May 1944 in Vega Block 30 B-17Gs, and by June it was in Boeing Block 80 B-17Gs. According to William Wolf in *US Aerial Armament in World War II*, Cheyenne Tail Turrets were incorporated by Douglas in its Block 45. In *The B-17 Flying Fortress Story*, William Freeman mentioned that Douglas and Vega added the N-8 gunsight in its Block 50 and Block 55, respectively.

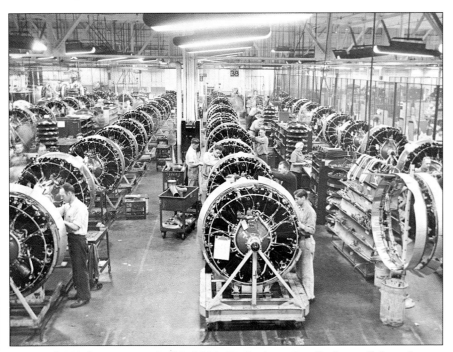

Rows of Wright Aeronautical R-1820-97 Cyclone 9-cylinder radial engines lined up on the factory floor in December 1943 are prepared for installation into rows of B-17Gs.

In this view from the floor within Building 2-40 of the Boeing Plant 2 complex in December 1943, we get a closer look at the engine work on the B-17G inner wing sections, while aircraft closer to completion are seen in the distance inside this vast high-bay building.

The Cheyenne Tail Turret retrofit was associated with the Boeing-Douglas-Vega Committee Modification Change number BDV M930, as well as BDV M930-1. The latter appeared in September 1944 and involved an aluminum swivel ball mounting for the pair of guns.

The "cone" of defensive fire afforded by the Cheyenne Tail Turret was considerably larger than that of the Stinger Turret. With the latter, the gunner could elevate the guns 30 degrees and depress them 15 degrees. This compared to 70 degrees and 40 degrees, respectively, in the Cheyenne Tail Turret. The Stinger gunner could traverse his guns 30 degrees to the right or left, while the Cheyenne gunner could traverse them 80 degrees either way—almost a full right angle!

It is reckoned that about 1,550 Vega B-17Gs received the Cheyenne Tail Turret in Cheyenne along with 1,435 Boeing aircraft and 1,525 from Douglas for a total of around 4,410. Additional aircraft received the turret at field modification centers in the United Kingdom, so the exact number is unknown. Just over half of all B-17Gs were retrofitted with a Cheyenne Tail Turret.

Subtle Variations and the B-17G Blocks of Mid-1944

As we have seen, the three members of the BDV Committee did not introduce all changes simultaneously, and they did not do so in corresponding block numbers. Note that many changes did not occur with all members of the BDV Committee.

In its Block 50 B-17G, which was introduced on June 15, 1944, Douglas incorporated the life raft compartment modifications and the five upgraded oxygen regulators that Boeing incorporated into its Block 65 and 70 B-17Gs in April and May.

Vega first delivered its Block 55 and Block 60 B-17Gs on July 7 and August 3, respectively. Douglas launched these blocks on August 22 and September 25. By this time, some aircraft from all three BDV Committee members were receiving Cheyenne tail modifications at the depots, and the updated AN-prefix electronics were becoming available and were being installed.

Many of the changes seen in mid-1944 were what one might regard as

A routing machine is used to cut ribs for the tail surfaces of a Flying Fortress at Boeing's Plant 2 in Seattle. (Photo by Andreas Feininger, Library of Congress)

minor. In its Block 65 B-17Gs, first delivered on April 25, Boeing made subtle changes to the starter gearbox and the life raft compartment.

Also in Boeing Block 65, a new upper turret rain seal was required equipment under BDV 579-1. Previously, the seal used had been a dural extrusion seal, one made of "duralumin," a copper-aluminum alloy. To "maintain a better seal against the infiltration of sand, dust and moisture," this type was replaced with a Kirkhill Rubber Company G-1556 Neoprene Extrusion. It was attached to the turret well wall with wing fabric fasteners and was not interchangeable with the dural-type seal. Vega incorporated the Kirkhill seal

The finishing touches for the deicer boot are brushed on the vertical stabilizer of a Vega-built B-17G-30-VE (42-97825) in January 1944.

into its Block 45 B-17Gs as of May 10, but Douglas did make the upgrade until its Block 55 B-17G was delivered on August 22.

Beginning on May 10, 1944, Boeing Block 70 B-17Gs added five extra upgraded oxygen regulators, an oil reserve for the propeller feathering system, and a radio compass antenna.

Directed by BDV 827 in June, the propeller feathering pump feed line system was changed so that an oil reserve would remain in the engine oil tank for prop feathering even after the engine oil supply was gone. This was accomplished by running a separate line from the feathering pump directly to the bottom of the engine oil tank pump. The standpipe for the engine oil supply in the tank was 2.5 inches higher than the feathering pump supply outlet, so this permitted several gallons of oil reserve for emergency feathering.

This oil system had become standard on the Douglas B-17G-40-DL with the April 2 delivery, and on the Vega B-17G-40-VE as of its first delivery on April 9.

Mandated by BDV 728, the radio compass antenna that reached B-17Gs with Boeing's Block 70 debut on May 10, 1944, became standard on the first Block 45 Vega B-17G, which was delivered on the same day. Hoverer, it had been standard on Douglas B-17Gs since the first delivery of the first B-17G-15-DL back on September 6, 1943. The antenna, with two 6-188224 radio masts, was located on the right lower side of the center fuselage. Two government-furnished IN-88 strain insulators and an IN-79 lead-in insulator were also installed.

Through 1944, as in much of 1943, there was no parallel between the Vega and Douglas production blocks and those of Boeing. Introductions of Vega and Douglas Block 50 through 75 aircraft came much later in the year. In fact, Douglas's Block 75 deliveries began in January 1945. Although major upgrades did appear close to the same time in Seattle, Burbank, and Long Beach, the respective block numbers were not aligned.

Highlights of 1944 B-17G Electronics Systems

It is axiomatic that World War II saw rapid leaps in technology. While the basic Flying Fortress airframe was dated—certainly compared to the magnificent B-29 Superfortress that was entering service by 1944—the electronics that started filling the Flying Fortress production blocks in mid-1944 would have been unimaginable to most people before the war. Electronics changes and upgrades that were introduced into these blocks from the spring of 1944 through early 1945 were numerous.

Fuselage sections are fabricated in the foreground at the at the Vega Aircraft plant in Burbank, while final assembly of B-17Gs takes place in the distance. By the latter half of 1943, B-17Gs were being delivered unpainted.

A line inspector at the Vega Aircraft plant in Burbank carefully examines some electrical wiring. (Photo by Alfred Palmer, Library of Congress)

The designations were now standardized under the Army-Navy (AN) nomenclature system and the basic B-17 communications receiver (the BC-348 radio) was officially redesignated as AN/ARR-11. Despite the official redesignations of this and other equipment, the previous designations continued to be used operationally as manuals and equipment markings remained in place.

As noted previously, the B-17Gs were equipped with SCR-274N AM radios that had become standard in the B-17F early in 1943. These provided two-way continuous wave (CW), modulated continuous wave (MCW), and Morse code capability. These were positioned on shelves or racks high on the wall of Bulkhead 5 on the right side of the radio operator's compartment opposite the radio operator's desk where the BC-348 radio receiver was.

Pairs of SCR-274N radios were typically installed in B-17Fs, and this carried over into the B-17G—although with variations. For example, early April 1944 found Vega adding space for extra SCR-274N radios in its Block 40, but Douglas was deleting it in Block 45 a month later. Boeing had also made changes to the SCR-274N installation in its own Block 45 in

February and began deleting space for extra SCR-274N radios in March. Under BDV 592-18 in January 1944, the SCR-274N radios were earmarked to be superseded by the Western Electric type BC-457-A, which decreased frequency output.

The radio antenna, meanwhile, was contained within a 25-inch LP-21 series (LP-21-A, LP-21-LM, etc.) radio antenna loop mounted beneath the aircraft under the radio operator's compartment.

Other Army-Navy electronics systems in use in the B-17G ranged from the AN/AIC-2 interphone system to the AN/APQ-9 High Power Barrage Jamming Transmitter, a 475 to 585 MHz unit developed by the Delco Electronics, which was founded as Dayton Engineering Laboratories in 1909 and acquired by General Motors in 1918.

Of course, not to be overlooked when discussing "AN" electronic systems is the highly consequential AN/APS-15 (H2X) airborne, ground-scanning radar (discussed earlier in this chapter under the heading "H2X (AN/APS-15) Radar"). Having been first deployed operationally in September 1943, the AN/APS-15 was a key installation in B-17Gs through 1944 and into 1945.

 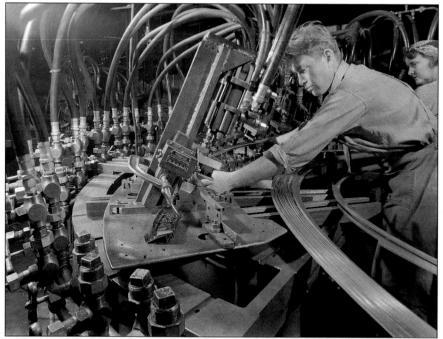

Best known by its nickname "Octopus," the Boeing-designed Circumferential Hydropunch was a punching machine used for working on parts for the Flying Fortress. In a single operation, it punched a series of holes and trimmed the ends of circumferential stiffeners for fuselages. With the Octopus, one employee could turn out in one day what it previously took a month to do. (Photo by Andreas Feininger, Library of Congress)

Significant among other Flying Fortress electronic components of 1944 and 1945 was the "Carpet" series of jamming transmitters. These were developed by Delco. The original AN/APT-2 Carpet system was a 450 to 720 MHz L-Band transmitter that was made by both Delco and Hudson American and used in both the B-17 and B-24. Delco's AN/APQ-9 High Power Barrage Jamming Transmitter was known as Carpet III.

The AN/APT-5 Carpet IV was a 350- to 1,200-MHz L-Band Semibarrage Jamming Radar Transmitter designed to replace the AN/APT-2 with a more powerful unit. It was manufactured by Delco, as well as by Aircraft Accessories Corporation (later Aireon Manufacturing). The AN/APT-5 was used in both the B-17 and B-24 during the war but was still a component of the electronics suite in the B-47A, B-47B, and RB-47K jet bomber family through the 1950s.

Dating to early 1944, the AN/ARN-2 and AN/ARN-5 Direction Finding Receivers worked with the AN/CRN-2 Glide Path Transmitter, which evolved from the earlier SCR-592. As noted in the Air Technical Service Command

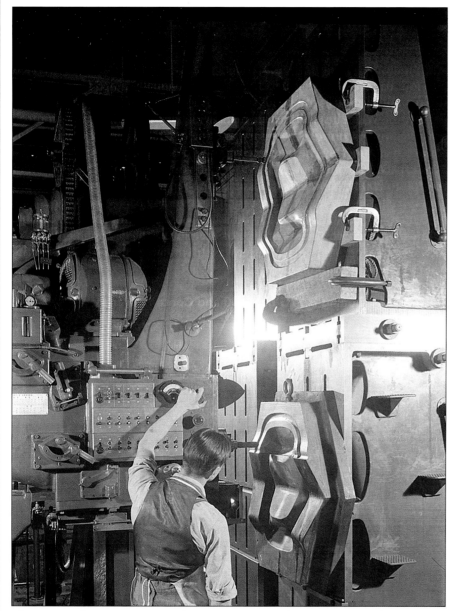

This piece of equipment seen here at Boeing's Plant 2 was used for duplicating dies, especially those for use in ductwork in the Flying Fortress's turbo superchargers. Known as a "Kellar Machine," it was made by the Kellar Machine Company of Buffalo, New York, a company that still exists as Kellar Technology Corporation. (Photo by Andreas Feininger, Library of Congress)

These plaster casts would form the patterns for supercharger ductwork for R-1820-97 Cyclone engines that would in turn be reproduced on a Kellar Machine. (Photo by Andreas Feininger, Library of Congress)

(ATSC) description, "Signals from the transmitter are received by the pilot of the aircraft over the AN/ARN-5 receiving equipment, which provides visual indication of the proper course of descent in the vertical plane during instrument landing operation. At an altitude of 3,000 feet, it provides a straight-line glide path course with good definition from a minimum distance of 15 miles from the point of landing contact with the ground. The angle indicated between the horizontal and the glide path is readily adjustable between 2 and 5 degrees."

As mentioned in Chapter 7, the B-17G's AN/ARN-7 Radio Compass of 1944 evolved from the SCR-269G Radio Compass installed in B-17F aircraft two years earlier. It was under BDV 487-1 that the SCR-269G was formally superseded with the AN/ARN-7 "to meet latest AAF requirements." The AN/ARN-7 was first officially delivered in production B-17G aircraft with the beginning of Boeing's Block 80 on June 22, 1944.

The ATSC overview of the AN/ARN-7 noted that it employed all the components of the earlier SCR-269G system except the BC-433G Radio Compass Unit and BC-434A Radio Control Box.

According to the ATSC summary, the AN/ARN-7 was "an automatic bearing-indicating radio compass operating from a 400-cycle, 115-volt power supply. It provides aural reception of modulated radio signals as an ordinary 100 to 1750 kc, radio receiver and automatic loop orientation and loop azimuth indication in degrees . . . Frequency range of the AN/ARN-7 is divided into four bands covering 100 to 1750 kc. It is manually tuned from either of two remote positions, with bands switched electrically from the position having control. When installations are made which use only one remote control, no switching of Control is necessary, and the one radio control box used has control at all times. . . The new receiver, R-5/ARN-7, is a 15-tube superheterodyne capable of [continuous wave] tone and voice reception. The addition of the 100 to 200 kc band makes possible long-range operation in connection with established low-frequency transmitters in many parts of the world."

The AN/ARN-7 was originally designed as an interim compass, capable of low-frequency reception, pending completion of the development of AN/ARN-6 Radio Compass, but the latter was still in development in 1945 as the war in Europe was winding down.

Boeing B-17G Block 80 and Contemporaries

G. H. Knight and A. Johnson prepare the base for a plastic pattern for Flying Fortress parts at the Boeing plant at Seattle. These patterns were to be reproduced on the Kellar machine. (Photo by Andreas Feininger, Library of Congress)

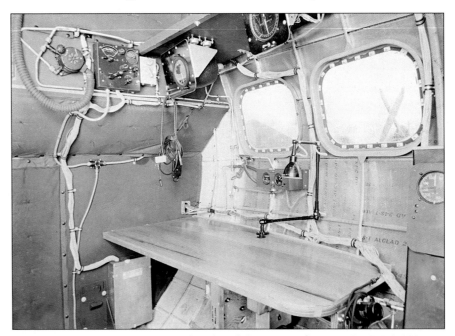

The navigator's table on the left side of the nose of a B-17G-45-BO (42-97183) in February 1944. Assigned to the 2nd Bomb Group in the Mediterranean, this aircraft was shot down five months later.

For Boeing, a sizable number of changes entered the stream with the debut of its Block 80 B-17G, which was first delivered on June 22, 1943. In looking at the Boeing Block 80 changes, we find them aligning with Blocks 50 to 60 for Vega and Blocks 50 to 55 for Douglas. At that time, Boeing was a full half year out of synch with the California planemakers, for which Block 80 came on November 29 for Vega and lagged to February 11, 1945, for Douglas.

Among the changes introduced during the summer of 1944 in B-17G-80-BO aircraft, as well as in B-17G-50-DL and B-17G-60-VE Flying Fortresses, were BDV 674-6 and 674-8. It will be recalled that the original BDV 674 in February 1944 had brought in a complete electrical control bomb release system, eliminating all former mechanical controls. Half a year later, this electrical system was showing its vulnerability to gunfire. Therefore, additional wiring was run from the bomb bay fuel tank switch to the outboard bomb racks. Revisions were also made to the electrical bomb control system for a separate bomb door safety switch for each rack selector circuit.

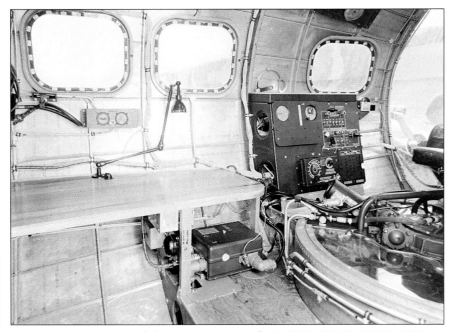

The left front corner of the nose section of a B-17G-45-BO (42-97183) in February 1944. The navigator's table is on the left; the bombardier's area is on the right. Note the top of the Bendix Chin Turret below the bombardier's panel. This area would be further crowded if cheek guns were later installed.

This winding line of unpainted, natural-metal B-17Gs leading from the ramp at Plant 2 to Boeing Field has the feel of motion. By 1944, Boeing had achieved monthly totals of more than 360 B-17Gs and actually had days when as many as 16 finished aircraft traveled the route pictured here. Also by 1944, camouflage paint was no longer required by the USAAF.

Electrical bomb release systems revised under BDV 674-6 and 674-8 were first delivered in the previously mentioned production blocks from Long Beach on June 15, from Seattle on June 22, and from Burbank on August 3.

At the same time, the change designated as BDV 674-5 addressed the issue of inadvertent damage to the bomb release boxes by flight personnel passing through the bomb bay on the catwalk. The resolution involved half-inch angle guards installed on the shear plate of the inboard bomb racks to cover the release boxes nearest to the catwalk.

As discussed earlier in this chapter under the heading "Highlights of 1944 B-17G Electronics Systems," it was also in its Block 80 B-17G that Boeing began installing the AN/ARN-7 Radio Compass and the AN/ARN-5 Glide Path Receiver.

Another major alteration to the B-17G that came in June 1944 with Boeing's Block 80 was a new hot air cabin heating system. This was also introduced the same month in Douglas Block 50 and Vega Block 50 B-17Gs.

As summarized in the *Boeing Field Service News* of July 17, the idea was to "ensure more adequate heating and defrosting in all compartments of the B-17" through the installation of "a new engine exhaust, hot-air cabin heating system." It was noted in what seemed almost like a sales pitch that "combat crews who fly in B-17G airplanes equipped with the new system will perform their duties more efficiently because the necessity for bulky clothing will be practically eliminated. Ground crews will welcome the system's straightforward, simple maintenance requirements."

In the new system, primary heat exchangers replaced the straight section of the inboard exhaust stacks and were covered by scoops that provided a positive airflow over the exchanger. Outside air passed over these exchangers, was heated, and then passed through steel ducting to flapper valves in the trailing edge of each inboard wing. The valves, controlled individually from the radio room, either diverted the hot air through openings in the upper surface or sent it to secondary heat exchangers in the trailing edge of each inboard wing before discharging it overboard.

In this view, we are looking aft through the waist of the aircraft with the top of the Sperry Ball Turret on the floor in the foreground. Until early 1944, the windows for the two waist guns in the B-17G were directly across from one another, as had been the case in earlier variants. After that, they were staggered.

This photo of a pair of gunners manning their M2 .50-caliber waist guns illustrates how having the two gunners back to back was unwieldy. They often backed into one another while they were working! Also seen here are metal ammunition boxes rather than the larger-capacity plywood boxes.

The hot air for the cabin was taken from each inboard carburetor air scoop and ducted to valves interconnected with the hot-air valves. When the cold-air valves were closed, no air passed into the cabin ducting. When the valves were opened, the cold air passed through the secondary heat exchangers to be heated and then passed into the cabin. Two control handles in the radio compartment included one for the No. 2 nacelle heating system, and another for the No. 3 nacelle system.

It was noted that 50-hour inspections should be conducted and that cracked heat exchangers should be replaced rather than repaired in the field.

Into the Fall of 1944

Boeing's Block 85 and 90 B-17Gs, delivered on July 15 and August 7, saw a number of changes that were relatively minor in comparison to those that took place in Boeing's Block 80 and the contemporary California B-17G blocks.

The staggered waist guns inside the fifth B-17G-50-BO (42-102383) on February 23, 1944. Block 50 marked the debut of the staggered waist guns for Boeing. The one-piece Plexiglas panel was one of several fixed window configurations seen in 1944 deliveries. This window, while it seemed like it had been a good idea, was prone to cracking when the gun was in use and to frosting over at high altitude.

The waist section of a B-17G, looking forward, shows the staggered waist gun positions that became standard with Vega in January 1944, with Boeing by March and at Douglas a bit later. Note the wall-mounted plywood ammunition boxes forward of each gun, and the canvas pouches below to catch expended cartridge cases.

With Block 85, the radio compartment was revised under BDV 823A to incorporate an enclosed gun with the K-6A gun mount installed in a new "T" type magnesium gun support. This change was an alteration that had been previously executed at modification centers. Supporting the gun mount assembly, which was designated as 9-8973, was two angle fittings located at the rear of the fairing and attached to the fairing plate. The gun support was installed with three identical mounting pins with a cutout provided in the window to accommodate the gun. The manner of this installation sealed the compartment against loss of heat while mounting the gun in the firing position.

It was noted in the specifications that "the gun can be quickly jettisoned by pulling the pins. Ditching procedure is unchanged because the hatch is still quickly removable."

Hand in hand with BDV 823A came BDV 823A-2, which addressed the necessity of cleaning the exterior of the radio compartment gun window during flight. A circular Plexiglas door, 6 inches in diameter, was installed in the win-

In early 1944, staggering the placement of the waist guns was accompanied by the addition of the more permanent three-panel window, which was used rather than a removable hatch or a single-piece Plexiglas window.

A look behind the three-panel window originally developed by Vega. Having a more-permanent window allowed for a warmer environment for the gunners at high altitude, where temperatures were far below freezing.

dow forward of the gun mount. A handle and spring on the door secured it when closed, and a cotton webbing strap held the door in the open position.

Also in Boeing Block 85 B-17Gs came BDV 357-8, which was, according to the *Boeing Field Service News*, a reaction to "numerous unsatisfactory reports . . . received on the failure of the outboard nacelle carburetor air filter frame support brackets." The issue was resolved with a heavier bracket.

In the same block, Boeing revised the engine ring cowling under BDV 832 by rotating it 42 degrees "to improve accessibility." The change included an access door for the engine oil sump drain with quick-acting, flush-type latch. The cowling was equipped with a new turnbuckle-type latch mechanism that was actuated by applying a wrench to the turnbuckle. The two forward latches were accessible from the inside, while the rear one had a slot provided for outside accessibility.

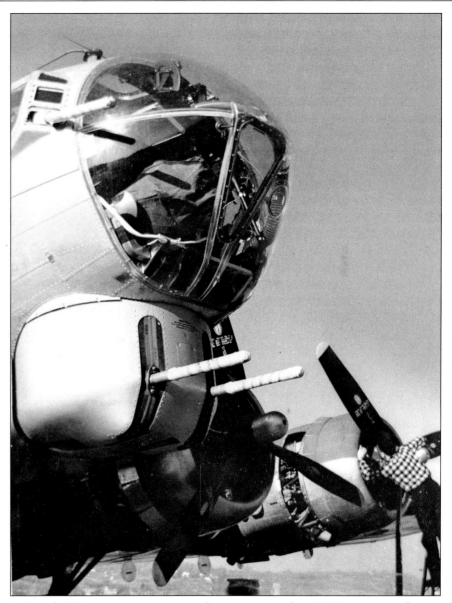

In March 1944, as moves were underway across the BDV Committee factories to begin staggering waist guns, the idea of installing staggered guns in the cheek positions also came to the fore. The gun on the left side of the airplane (right in the picture) remained as far forward as possible, while the one on the other side was moved one window panel back from where it is seen here.

An interior view of the left side M2 .50-caliber waist gun with the plywood ammunition box on the wall to the right. A defrosting system for the window was not fully refined until May 1944.

For its Block 90 B-17G, first delivered on August 7, 1944, Boeing introduced a new Plexiglas nose with what was described in the *Boeing Field Service News* as "a radical change in contour." Although, to the untrained eye, the "radical" nature of the profile change was not readily apparent. Under BDV 725-3, the existing Plexiglas nose, designated as 15-11406-21, was superseded on the production line by 15-11406-28, which was said to possess "better optical qualities."

In turn, the location of the thermometer within the Plexiglas was moved to a position 2.5 inches below the horizontal centerline and 10 inches outboard of the vertical centerline. Alterations were also made to the supporting brackets of the nose defrosting outlets to fit the shape of 15-11406-28.

Meanwhile, nose cover 15-10614-86 was replaced by a new cover designated as 15-10614-87.

Boeing's Block 90 B-17G also saw the tail wheel stub axle amended to incorporate two sets of cotter-pin holes for finer adjustment of the retaining nut, minimizing the possibility of having the nut too tight or too loose.

As outlined in BDV 913P-2 Technical Order 01-20EF-2, the nut was to be tightened until the wheel drags, then loosened until the drag is just relieved. The location of the existing cotter-pin hole is rotated 450 degrees and one hole is added, spaced at 90 degrees to the rotated position.

The BDV 913P-2 change was incorporated into Vega's Block 60 B-17Gs, which were first delivered on August 3, four days ahead of Boeing's first Block

In staggering the cheek guns in 1944, the gun on the left side of the aircraft was placed as cheek guns had been installed going back to 1943. The one on the right was moved aft to the next window position.

90. It flowed into the Long Beach production line on October 8 at the middle of the Douglas Block 50 run.

On the B-17G-90-BO assembly line, Boeing also introduced changes to recently adopted modifications. The "complete electrical control bomb release system," which was introduced in Boeing Block 45 in February under BDV 674 and modified several times through the summer, now had its bomb release circuit revised under BDV 674-12. Specifically, the bomb rack wiring was changed "in accordance with AAF drawing H43G1O999" so that the external racks would release prior to the release of any internal racks when all rack selector switches were in the "on" position.

A B-17G arrives from the factory at the Cheyenne Modification Center ready to have cheek turrets grafted onto its nose.

The B-17G-90-BO line also found changes being introduced to the cheek gun installations that had become standard equipment in March and April under BDV 822. Beginning in August, under BDV 798-2, the Boeing Block 90 B-17G cheek guns were now equipped with necessary wiring so that the B-13 gunsight rings could be replaced by either N-8 or N-8A reflector gunsights, which were also used in the tail guns and waist guns.

For these sights, an O-1C rheostat for current control was installed on each side of the nose: the right side one near the navigator's compartment and the other near the Bombardier's Control Panel Assembly. The actual installations of N-8A sights began under BDV 798-5 during Boeing's Block 100 in October. BDV 798-5 also provided for an A-11 gun post sight assembly.

Minor Boeing Block 90 changes (applied to Douglas Block 55 B-17Gs and those of Vega's Block 95) included BDV 907, which installed a new oil separator to limit the maximum air pressure at the deicer boots. It provided an adequate airflow through the relief valve without exceeding the 8-psi maximum pressure. Meanwhile, BVD 964 reversed the positions of the deicer gauge and the hydraulic pressure gauge. This was done to separate the oxygen and hydraulic oil lines on the pilot's instrument panel to reduce fire hazard.

As happened often in the course of the BDV-designated changes, there were some that occurred more or less simultaneously and others that were introduced at widely separated times. BDV 858-1, the new AiResearch 2R6697 engine oil cooler, is a case in point. This device reached Boeing's B-17Gs at its Block 90 with aircraft 43-38471 on August 7, but it had been installed at Douglas with its B-17G-45-DL number 44-6128 on May 8, and it would not reach the Vega production line until its B-17G-95 VE number 44-85492, which was delivered on February 26, 1945.

Made by the AiResearch subsidiary of the Garrett Corporation, this 11-inch-diameter engine oil cooler was designated as Type 6-16812 by the USAAF. Equipped with standard copper tubing, it was a low-back-pressure type with a surge-protection valve and automatic full-closing shutters. Since it was physically interchangeable with the former type, the existing cradle support and drain could be used.

On September 21, under BDV 858-2, a drain pan was installed to provide a means of directing expended oil from the oil cooler through the present drain access door. This first appeared in Boeing's Block 95 B-17G number 43-38794.

For its Blocks 95, 100, and 105 B-17Gs (which were handed off on August 7, October 2, and November 24), Boeing's changes were minimal. Aside from the gradual introductions of electronics, these saw relatively few changes. These coincided with Blocks 65, 70, and 75 from both California manufacturers. Vega's initial deliveries of the three blocks came on September 3, September 30, and October 20, respectively. For Douglas, they came on November 11, December 9, and on January 8, 1945, respectively.

At this point, Boeing made internal changes at Plant 2 that were not applied as BDV changes. Announced in the *Boeing Field Service News* on September 25, 1944, these were based on modification center technical drawings and carried "M" prefixes. Applied on some aircraft going back to the middle of Block 85, M1O16 allowed for manual lowering of the main landing gear when bomb bay tanks were installed. Beginning in mid-Block 90, M517-12 and M517-15 added a waist gun window clean-off door and door latch.

Some of the specific BDV-designated factory modifications taking place in the blocks from the three manufacturers during the fall of 1944 included BDV 648-4 and BDV 945. BDV 648-4 required that all of the aluminum alloy tubing in the engine fire extinguisher system forward of the firewall (except discharge tubing and the discharge tubing plug) be replaced with corrosion-resistant steel tubing. BDV 945 mandated that shims should be installed to "prevent installing the bomb shackles backwards."

To prevent erratic operation and premature failure as a result of vibration, BDV 1028 called for shock mounts consisting of neoprene spacers to be installed for the suction-relief valves in the vacuum system. To support the propeller feathering line, BDV 947 attached a bracket to the propeller governor housing.

On October 25, during Boeing Block 100 B-17G production, the *Boeing Field Service News* described BDV 953, which made a number of revisions on the flight deck to "provide sufficient clearance for the operation and service installation of the C-1 autopilot Formation Stick." These included straightening and shortening the hand pump handle and "reworking" the elevator control column.

The Formation Stick (see information under the heading "The Honeywell C-1 Autopilot" in Chapter 7) was provided for under BDV 953 and

An example of a staggered cheek gun installation done at the factory rather than at a modification center. Here we see a B-17G-60-BO (42-102955) at Boeing Field on April 20, 1944. Note the shrouded Norden Bombsight inside the nose.

installed at the modification centers, but it was factory installed under BDV 953-1. For Vega, this came with Block 80 B-17Gs in November 1944, but for the other manufacturers, it would not come until January 1945 under Boeing Block 105 and Douglas Block 70.

There were other changes taking place in October 1944 that effected Boeing's Block 100 B-17Gs as well as its California contemporaries. Under BDV 581A-7, the D-5 fuel valves for the outboard tanks were relocated to improve accessibility for servicing, while BDV 827-4 added provisions for draining the 1-inch propeller feathering oil line through adding drain

Betty Lou Wise, a worker at Boeing's Plant 2, carefully installs an M2 .50-caliber machine gun in the right cheek position of a B-17G-65-BO. Note the pair of plywood ammunition boxes.

plugs in the lines forward of the outboard firewalls and at each tank sump. BDV 910-3 eliminated the gun rails and wind deflector for the radio compartment gun, replacing it with a web-type bulkhead running fore and aft on each side of the gun well. To increase the load-carrying capacity of the bomb door, BDV 909 ordered the strengthening of the control gear shank.

BDV 954 dictated substantial changes to the portable oxygen systems within the B-17G cabin. The A-4 portable oxygen bottles were replaced with D-2 bottles, and stowage brackets for the 13 bottles were redesigned to also accommodate either D-12 or A-6 type bottles at the existing locations. The *Boeing Field Service News* of October 23, 1944, noted that this provided larger-capacity "walk-around oxygen equipment," although the "control box for the trailing antenna in the radio compartment and the signal light box aft of the pilot's seat" had to be moved to make room.

Most of the issues related to the staggered waist gun arrangement introduced earlier in the year were addressed under BDV changes numbered in the 517 series. However, changes to the waist gunner's headset cord that were first seen on Boeing's B-17G-100-BO number 43-38974, which were delivered on October 26, and on Vega's B-17G-85 VE number 44-8801, which were delivered on December 31, were dealt with under BDV 1017. This change was initiated to prevent tangling the waist gunners' cords formerly connected to the waist gunner's panel located forward of the window or at the top of the fuselage.

The problem was fixed by the headphone extensions and assemblies being connected to the jack box and attached to their respective gun adapters with spring clips. When not attached to the gunner's headset, the cords were now configured so that they could be coiled and stowed at the end of each gun.

The Final B-17G Blocks of 1944

In Seattle, Boeing's Block 105 deliveries began on November 24, 1944, while Vega's first B-17G-80-VE was delivered from Burbank on November 29. At Long Beach, Douglas handed over its first Block 70 B-17G on December 9. Each of these production blocks continued into the first month of the new year.

One change that was made in late 1944 at the time of Boeing's Block 105 was so obvious that it is hard to imagine it was not made sooner—bulletproof glass for flight deck windshields! Under BDV 880A, bulletproof glass made its debut with Vega's B-17G-75-VE number 44-8698 on November 22. Boeing made its own first installation with B-17G-105-BO number

A look inside the nose of a B-17G-85-DL shows the same area where Betty Lou Wise was working on page 197. In this wide-angle view, we also see the bombardier's chair and the Bendix Chin Turret controller in the forward area. Note the pair of plywood ammunition boxes and the oxygen bottle on the right. The Norden Bombsight is visible in the center of the nose. In the wartime photos elsewhere in this book, it is shrouded for the sake of secrecy. Here, it is uncovered. (See page 237 for a detailed view of the Norden Bombsight.) (Photo by Bill Yenne)

43-39117, which were delivered on December 8, and Douglas followed with B-17G-70-DL number 44-6876 on the following day.

As described in the *Boeing Field Service News* (but curiously not until January 29, 1945), the "windshield and knock-out panels are replaced by bulletproof windshield assemblies. The assembly consists of a 1.5-inch bulletproof pane, a 0.28-inch-thick laminated pane on the inside and a 0.25-inch air space between . . . The hot-air defrosting outlets are revised to accommodate the thicker windshield; otherwise, the new windshields are interchangeable with the old. Windshield wipers are reinstalled thus necessitating some rework to the shelf below the windshields."

Minor changes to Block 105 Boeing B-17Gs during the last weeks of 1944 were many. For example, with the delivery of 43-39174 on December 23, engine control cable adjustments were implemented under BDV 1004. As noted at the time, "to facilitate field adjustments of the engine controls, the existing eye terminals at the wing-fuselage junction are replaced by turnbuckles. This allows adjustment of cable tension through the battery access door." Vega already began making this change as of November 29 with its Block 80 B-17G numbered 44-8701.

It was also in Boeing's Block 105 that further modifications were made to the engine oil cooler system installed under BDV 858-1 that had reached Boeing's Plant 2 in August with Block 90 B-17Gs. Under change number BDV 858-4, first delivered on December 30 with B-17G-105-BO number 43-39196, arrangements were introduced to facilitate the easy installation and removal of the cooler for maintenance.

One of the final significant and easily noticeable B-17G alterations of 1944 came with the delivery of Vega's B-17G-80-VE number 44-8765 on December 20 and Boeing's B-17G-105-BO number 43-39169 on the day after Christmas. Under BDV 716-13, the cloth gun slot enclosures with zippers that were used in the chin turrets were replaced with metal slot enclosures that the *Boeing Field Service News* called "more satisfactory." These had steel strips attached to the gun barrels that moved in elevation with the guns. They were similar to those already being used in the upper turret.

The Modification Centers in 1944

At the beginning of 1943, Colonel Bryant Boatner, head of the Modifi-

These are above and below images of the right-side cheek gun in the staggered configuration, circa March 1944. Note the shrouded Norden Bombsight inside the nose.

cation Section of the Materiel Command, had been an outspoken advocate of shifting the primary responsibility for modification from the modification centers back to the factories of the manufacturers. This had been impossible in 1943 and early 1944, but in April 1944, a new contracting policy was adopted in which the manufacturers took over responsibility for most of the modification centers.

As Virginia Toole explained in her history of the program, *The Modification of Army Aircraft in the United States*, "The manufacturers undertook both the engineering of [production changes] in the modification center or centers processing their aircraft and also the direct management of the modification centers themselves. In other words, modification was done under the production contract with the prime contractor rather than under a separate open contract arrangement."

She goes on to say that effective on June 6, 1944, "the old plan of dual acceptance gave way to a single acceptance plan."

An important change in the new system was that the USAAF now no longer accepted each aircraft at the factory prior to its being flown to the modification center. Most aircraft would not now become government property until after they had been processed by a center. One exception to this new pattern was at the Cheyenne Modification Center in Wyoming that was operated by United Air Lines (Center No. 10), where most B-17Gs were going. It remained as an open contract center to allow it to accept spillover

The left-side cheek gun, seen here circa March 1944, was generally unchanged in position from the unstaggered to staggered configurations. Note the shrouded Norden Bombsight inside the nose.

In April 1944 as the cheek and waist gun staggering project was moving into full swing, the BDV 910-2 change order directed that the lone, rearward-pointing M2 .50-caliber machine gun in the upper hatch of the radio operator's compartment was no longer to be installed. This is probably one of the last ones.

from other centers that might get backed up, although, in practice, it modified few other aircraft types.

In the meantime, the USAAF had been striving since 1942 to move the additional modification work done at its own depots into the modification centers. Indeed, USAAF Commanding General Hap Arnold issued a directive to this effect on March 16, 1944. However, it was determined that transferring this work would result in so much lost motion that Arnold rescinded his order. The 12 major USAAF air depots did work primarily on aircraft that had already been in service, but they continued to supplement the work of the modification centers throughout the war.

Clearly, the mighty engine of the manufacturing and modification system had developed a momentum of its own, and the USAAF realized that it was in the best interests of the war effort to fine-tune it only as necessary to keep that momentum. One issue had been the parallel bureaucracies of the Materiel Command and Air Service Command, and these two were formally merged on September 1, 1944, as the Air Technical Service Command (ATSC).

The Cheyenne Modification Center maintained a monthly average of just under 300 B-17Gs through August but handled just 68 in September and just one in December. Cheyenne's biggest month ever had been 312 in February 1944, although it did reach 307 aircraft in August. Cheyenne's total for 1944 (essentially nine months of deliveries) was 2,398, which included 134 H2X-equipped B-17Gs and nine F-9 reconnaissance variants of the B-17G. This total for 1944 was compared to 2,372 aircraft that passed through Cheyenne in 1943.

The story at the Denver Modification Center managed by Continental Airlines (Center No. 13) was similar to that in Cheyenne. A total of 523 Flying Fortresses were processed through June, and the peak was 70 in January. Thereafter, the numbers tapered off to just 14 in June. In 1943, Denver had modified 1,431 Flying Fortresses, which was up from 203 in 1942.

The Tulsa Modification Center operated by Douglas Aircraft (Center No. 16), which had modified 51 Flying Fortresses in 1943, increased its Flying Fortress output in 1944 with 505 aircraft passing through between February and October. Its peak month was May with 125. In June 1944, the Douglas Aircraft main Flying Fortress plat at Long Beach modified 66 B-17Gs.

The Lockheed Aircraft Company's Dallas Modification Center at Love Field (Center No. 3) processed 359 Flying Fortresses between June and October, which was up from 218 in 1943.

By the end of 1944, many Flying Fortresses, especially those built by Douglas, were bypassing modification and going directly to USAAF training and overseas crew processing bases at places such as Lincoln Field and Kearney Field in Nebraska as well as to Hunter Field in Georgia.

Although there was a slowing pace at the end of the year, 1944 was the peak year for modification. The total of all aircraft of all USAAF types mod-

On the subject of turrets, circa early 1944, this photo from February of that year depicts a Royal Air Force Fortress IIA with a very unconventional chin turret. This is a British-designed and -installed Bristol B.16 turret that was part of an experimental program looking at methods for shooting up surfaced German U-Boats. The RAF assigned its Fortress aircraft to its Coastal Command for antisubmarine work. The B.16 contained a 40-mm Vickers Type S gun and was remotely controlled from beneath the turret. This aircraft, which carried RAF serial FK185, was originally ordered by the USAAF as a B-17E.

Two men use Kirksite dies for the forming of parts of a Flying Fortress. Kirksite is an alloy comprised primarily of zinc with aluminum and copper additives. The key advantage of using Kirksite to make a die is a low melting temperature of 750 degrees. (Photo by Andreas Feininger, Library of Congress)

The F-9 "Foto" Flying Fortress

During World War II, the USAAF modified a number of examples of various combat aircraft types as photoreconnaissance aircraft by installing aerial cameras and deleting some or all armament. These were then redesignated with the letter "F" for "Fotographic." This designator is not, of course, to be confused with the postwar "F" for "Fighter" designator that superseded the earlier "P" for "Pursuit" designator. The latter is the reason that a "P" for "Photographic" designation was not used.

In addition to conversions from existing types, some aircraft, such as the infamous Hughes XF-11A and the Republic XF-12A Rainbow, were designed from the ground up as reconnaissance aircraft. There were also variants of combat types that came off the assembly line as reconnaissance aircraft. The most common of the latter were the Lockheed F-4 and F-5 Lightnings, which were variants of the P-38. Lockheed built 119 F-4s (based on the P-38E and P-38F) as well as 381 F-5s (based on the P-38G and P-38H)—and then converted more than 800 P-38s into F-5s.

The reconnaissance designation for the Flying Fortress was F-9. None were built at the factories as F-9s but were retrofitted at modification centers or at USAAF depots. The initial batch, designated as F-9 without a suffix, were all B-17Fs, one each from Douglas and Vega, and 14 from Boeing. The camera installations were in the nose, bomb bay, and aft fuselage.

The F-9A conversions included 10 Boeing B-17Fs and 14 from Vega. It seems that they differed from the F-9s in that they had cameras installed only in their bomb bays. The F-9B designation applied to 25 of the previous B-17F conversions in which the camera configurations were altered.

The F-9C designations went to nine Boeing B-17Gs and a Douglas B-17G that were converted. At least one of these had a horizon-to-horizon tri-metrogen mapping camera, probably a K-17-type camera, installed in its chin turret. The K-17's A-5 film magazine could provide 200 9x9-inch negatives. Other cameras included the K-18 high-altitude camera that yielded very high-resolution 9x19-inch negatives.

According to Captain Robert Ackerman of the USAAF Historical Office, who compiled the data for Virginia Toole's *The Modification of Army Aircraft in the United States* (1947), the nine Boeing F-9C conversions took place at Cheyenne between August and November 1944. Other conversations apparently took place at depots or in the field.

Operationally, the USAAF favored the Consolidated Liberator over the

An electric spot welding device is used to complete components for installation in Flying Fortresses. (Andreas Feininger, Library of Congress)

Flying Fortress as a photoreconnaissance platform. After 4 B-24Ds became F-7s, 86 B-24Js were converted as F-7As, and 125 F-7Bs were derived from B-24Js, B-24Ls, and B-24Ms.

After the war, the surviving F-9 variants were briefly redesignated as FB-17F and FB-17G before becoming RB-17Fs and RB-17Gs in 1948.

Early 1945 B-17G Blocks

The remarkable miracle of American wartime aircraft production was certainly manifest in Boeing-designed bombers as the world entered its final calendar year of World War II. It was noted officially by the Air Materiel Command that in 1944 alone, Boeing alone had produced in Seattle and Renton 3,148 B-17 and B-29 bombers, amounting to 77.4 million pounds of airframe valued at $387 million ($5.6 billion in today's valuation).

As 1945 started, the BDV Committee changes continued to affect the work being done on the three B-17G assembly lines. One of the first such modifications to be seen involved the C-1 Autopilot and the Formation Stick, the control system that was used to easily maneuver a B-17G while it was flying in formation with other aircraft.

As noted previously, the Formation Sticks had been installed at the modification centers, but BDV 953 of October 1944 stipulated that subtle alterations should be made to the flight deck configuration so that they could be installed at the three BDV Committee factories.

According to the *Boeing Field Service News*, the actual factory installation, covered under BDV 953-1, began with Vega's B-17G-80-VE aircraft, which were first delivered on November 29, 1944, but did not reach Seattle and Long Beach until January 1945. BDV 953-1 was implemented with the first B-17G-70-DL (44-6876), delivered on January 5 and a mid-block B-17G-105-BO (43-39209) delivered two days later.

As BDV 953-1 was being implemented by Douglas and Boeing, it was being done with BDV 953-2 already crowding it in the queue. The latter was a wiring change to the Formation Stick which had been specified by Technical Order 11-60AA-12 of December 28, 1944. The purpose was to limit violent maneuvers that had formerly been possible with the Formation Stick. It is indicative of the flow of work at Boeing's Plant 2 that BDV 953-2 finally reached Block 105 aircraft with number 43-39288, which was delivered 3 weeks and 79 aircraft later

Forward fuselages for B-17Gs on the floor in Building 2-40, the big high-bay assembly building that was the centerpiece and dominant fixture at the Boeing Plant 2 complex.

than BDV 953-1. As usual, the slack was taken up at the modification centers.

It was in B-17G-105-BO number 43-39209, the same Boeing aircraft first affected by BDV 953-1, that revisions were made in the lighting for the Automatic Flight Control Equipment (AFCE). This system had previously been upgraded in the B-17F under by BDV 685 in April 1943. Nine months later, under BDV 1003, the AFCE tell-tale lights were relocated under the remote compass, and the Pilot Direction Indicator (PDI) was relocated on the pilot's instrument panel. As noted in the *Boeing Field Service News* at the time, "This places them directly in the pilot's line of vision. The change necessitated moving the bomb release indicator light to a position between the voltmeter and the deicer pressure gauge."

On January 17, 1945, another Boeing B-17G from later in Block 105 (43-39249) was the first to be delivered with its inboard superchargers sealed. Initiated under BDV 914-3, the idea was to decrease the fire hazard if fuel vapors leaked into the inboard superchargers. A hood was installed to seal them from the inside of the wing. BDV-914-3 was implemented by Vega in Burbank with 44-85492, a Block 95 B-17G, in late February.

While almost none of the changes reached the three factories at exactly the same time, it was now routine for some BDV-designated changes to reach the different production lines on very widely separated dates. For example, take the C-3A bomb hoist. Mandated by BDV 1038, it was first delivered from

A team of workers at Boeing's Plant 2 bend and cut metal tubing and conduits into specified shapes and lengths for various applications inside the Flying Fortress. (Photo by Andreas Feininger, Library of Congress)

Workers pour a lead die that will be used in the production of parts for Flying Fortresses at Boeing's Plant 2. (Photo by Andreas Feininger, Library of Congress)

A worker at Boeing's Plant 2 uses a metal template as a guide to make wood patterns on a heavy-duty routing machine, a stage in the final production of subcomponents for a Flying Fortress. (Photo by Andreas Feininger, Library of Congress)

Seattle on December 9, 1944, in aircraft number 43-39124, a B-17G-105-BO. The first Vega aircraft with the C-3A was a B-17G-100-VE, number 44-85642, which was not delivered until April 14, 1945.

A number of additional minor BDV-designated changes, linked to Boeing Block 105 B-17Gs, entered into the production lines in early 1945. On January 7, Boeing delivered B-17G-105-BO number 43-39209, the first with a new bomb bay door indicator light added to both the pilot's and bombardier's control panel. As stipulated by BDV 674-11A, the light flashed the message "BOMB DOOR CLOSED," while the single-pole, single-throw bomb bay door "UP" limit switch (WZRQ41) was replaced by a single-pole, double-throw switch (BZ-RQ41). The "DOWN" limit switch was also changed from WZ-RQ41 to BZ-RQ41 to permit interchangeability. Obviously, the "BOMB DOOR CLOSED" indicator light illuminated only when the bomb bay door control switch was in the "UP" position. BDV 674-11A was seen on the Vega delivery aprons in Long Beach on January 8 and in Burbank on February 3. The respective Douglas and Vega Blocks were 75 and 90.

The first B-17G-80-DL, delivered from Long Beach on February 11, 1945, saw the flight deck armor being superseded by flak curtains, and Boeing had begun doing so in October 1944. Vega was doing the same by its Block 90, which was first delivered on January 29.

Boeing B-17G Block 110

Boeing delivered the first B-17G of Block 110, its final Flying Fortress production block, on January 28, 1945. This coincided almost exactly with Vega's first Block 90, which was delivered the following day. Vega would not deliver the first of its own final block, also Block 110, until June.

It was in this same first Block 110 aircraft, number 43-39274, that Boeing first installed the Sperry K-13 computing gunsight on the waist guns. The K-13 was a pneumatically powered compensating gunsight designed to account for altitude and air speed. Therefore, it calculated bullet trajectories and fall, which improved accuracy.

The K-13 superseded the N-8A gunsight, which had replaced the old B-13 gunsight rings only three months earlier in October 1944. The K-13 used the same K-7 gun mount as the N-8A, but the K-7 was modified to provide an azimuth stop to protect the sight. The beam assemblies on the modified K-7 mount were replaced by flanged web installations and other minor revisions.

US Navy Flying Fortresses

During World War II, the USAAF and the US Navy almost always acquired

aircraft types exclusive of one another with little overlap. There were exceptions, however, when it came to trainers and transports. For example, the US Navy operated more than 1,900 North American Aviation Texan trainers and around 500 Douglas Skytrain transports. The USAAF designated its Texans as AT-6 and its Skytrains as C-47 and C-53, while the Navy used the respective designations SNJ and R4D. The majority of these were acquired under USAAF contracts, given USAAF tail numbers, transferred directly to the Navy, and renumbered with Bureau of Aeronautics tail numbers.

Late in the war, the US Navy operated around 40 Flying Fortresses with the PB (Patrol, Boeing) designation prefix. The first was a lone B-17F-75-DL (42-3521) that was originally delivered on March 20, 1943, and flown in combat with the USAAF over Europe. It was returned to the United States in March 1945, transferred to the Navy, redesignated as a PB-1, and renumbered with the Bureau of Aeronautics tail number Bu34106. Retrofitted to B-17G standard with a chin turret, it served as a prototype for future Flying Fortress long-range naval patrol bombers.

However, the Navy decided instead to use the Flying Fortress as a radar-equipped long-range reconnaissance aircraft. Designated as PB-1W, they were intended to support Navy and Marine Corps operations during the invasion of Japan, scheduled to begin in November 1945, and during the ensuing ground

This installation of a rear ball turret in a B-17G-90-BO (42-38660) is an early precursor to the Cheyenne Tail Turret. This modification was made in September 1944 under BDV change order M930-1. (Boeing Photo Courtesy of Mike Lombardi)

campaign that was expected to last through much of 1946 and possibly beyond. The "W" suffix in Navy nomenclature has been used to describe a variety of radar-intensive missions from weather reconnaissance to airborne early warning.

In June 1945, the US Navy started receiving B-17G Flying Fortresses direct from the Douglas and Vega factories, although each of these was part of a USAAF order and had a USAAF tail number. They were each delivered to the Naval Aircraft Modification Unit (NAMU) at Naval Air Station Johnsville in Pennsylvania.

The first PB-1W was a Flying Fortress (44-83538) that had been delivered to the USAAF in March 1945 but reassigned to NAMU on June 4 and renumbered as Bu34114.

On July 11, four unique aircraft flew into Johnsville. These were the only four Douglas Block 97 B-17Gs, and each one of them were earmarked to become a Navy PB-1W. Thereafter, The Navy received at least 17 B-17Gs from the Douglas Block 95, including the last four Flying Fortresses that Douglas built. The Navy also received 15 of the last 30 Block 110 B-17Gs that were built by Vega. These B-17G-110-VE aircraft, along with at least one of the B-17G-95-DLs, were transferred to the US Coast Guard under the PB-1G designation. In turn, they were modified to carry a large lifeboat and were used as air-sea rescue aircraft.

The B-17H and Other Variants

Having just mentioned the Coast Guard's PB-1G air-sea rescue conversion of Douglas and Vega B-17Gs, it will be of interest to also mention the lifeboat-equipped B-17H. This was not a separate Flying Fortress variant but a conversion of around a dozen existing B-17Gs by the USAAF in 1945.

On April 8, 1944, B-17G-30-VE (42-97825) was completed at the Vega Aircraft factory in Burbank, having been equipped with the conventional Stinger Turret seen here. On May 1, 1944, this aircraft arrived at the Cheyenne Modification Center in Wyoming by way of Denver, and on May 16, it departed from Wyoming equipped with this Cheyenne Tail Turret.

The inside of a Cheyenne Tail Turret in a B-17G-110-BO, looking aft, in a January 1945 photo. Note the ammunition feeds on either side of the gunner's bicycle-type seat. The twin M2 .50-caliber guns are installed.

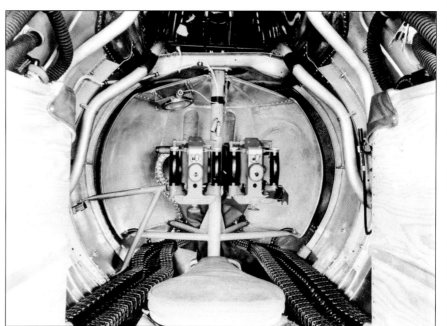

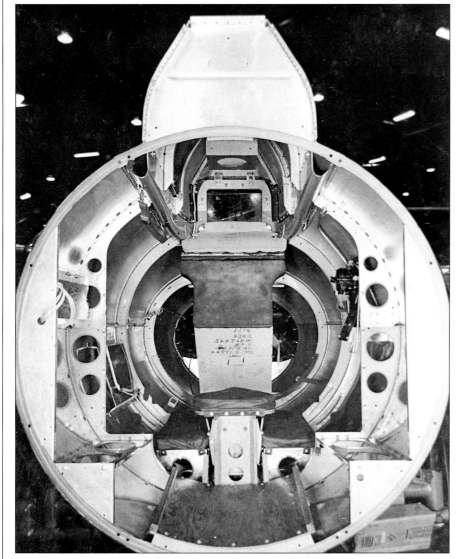

The inside of a standard Stinger Tail Turret (without guns) in a B-17G-10-BO, looking aft, in a June 1943 photo.

The gunner's view, looking up and aft, from inside a B-17G Cheyenne Tail Turret.

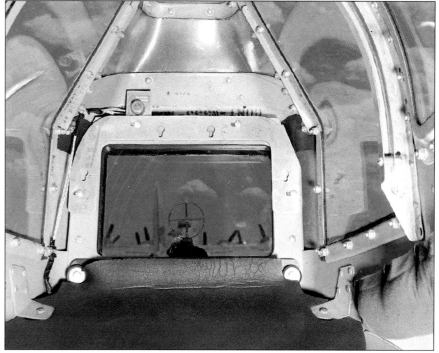

As an aircraft that was not factory originated and developed, it is beyond the scope of this book, but it is mentioned because in the interest of completeness and because of the use of the variant sequence letter "H," which would have been the next variant beyond the B-17G if the Flying Fortress had continued to evolve. (See photo on page 227).

In 1948, the existing B-17H aircraft were redesignated as SB-17G ("S" for Search and Rescue).

Unlike the Consolidated C-87 Liberator Express, which was a factory-built transport variant of the B-24 Liberator, there were no USAAF transport variants of the Flying Fortress that were produced in a factory. However, at least two B-17Es and two B-17Fs were field converted to transport configuration and officially redesignated as C-108, C-108A and C-108B. One of these, named "Bataan," was General Douglas MacArthur's executive transport. After the war, there were some postwar CB-17G and VB-17G transport conversions.

The postwar USAAF and US Air Force also operated target drone conversions that included the QB-17G (later BQ-7), QB-17L, QB-17N, and QB-17P as well as some DB-17F and DB-17G drone director conversions.

Winding Down the Modification Centers in 1945

As 1945 began, Flying Fortresses on order continued to be produced, although no new orders were placed or planned. The end was in sight. As this winding down was underway, the archipelago of modification centers continued to function, but the urgency was beginning to diminish. The cen-

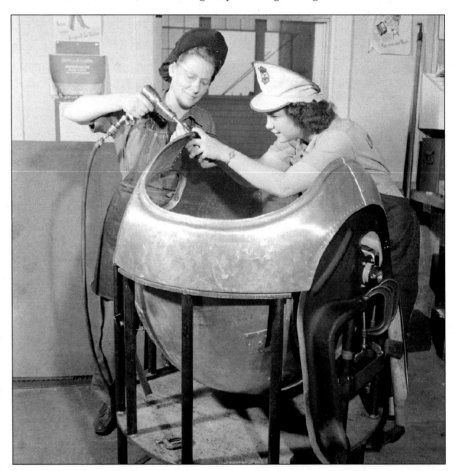

United Air Lines staffers wear interesting headgear at the Cheyenne Modification Center as they and work on the cowling for a B-17G Cheyenne Tail Turret.

Men work inside a Cheyenne Tail Turret in a B-17G.

ters had experienced an ever-increasing tempo through the middle of 1944, but the volume had gradually begun to slack off by the autumn. Overall, the total number of aircraft being processed at the start of 1945 was less than a quarter of the volume of June 1944.

At the Cheyenne Modification Center in Wyoming (Center No. 10), where a monthly average of around 300 aircraft had been the norm at the start of 1944, only a single Flying Fortress rolled though during the last four months of that year. Activates resumed at the start of 1945 with 77 and 74 aircraft passing though in January and March, respectively, but thereafter the average dipped to just below 40 until all work ended in August. The 1945 total for Cheyenne was 358, compared to 2,398 for the 9 months that the center was active in 1944.

The Denver Modification Center (Center No. 13), traditionally the number two Flying Fortress center, processed none in 1945. The Tulsa Modifi-cation Center (Center No. 16), which had modified 505 Flying Fortresses in 1944, worked on just seven in 1945. The Lockheed Aircraft Company's Dallas Modification Center at Love Field (Center No. 3) processed 359 Flying Fortresses in 5 months of 1944 and then handled just 171 in 1945.

The Louisville Modification Center in Kentucky (Center No. 9), which had spent most of the war modifying A-31s, A-36s, and B-24s, wound down virtually all of its activities at the start of 1945 but processed 194 of the last B-17Gs between March and July.

For the USAAF, much of the emphasis was shifting from modification of

The outside cowling is fit onto a Cheyenne Tail Turret in the tail of a B-17G.

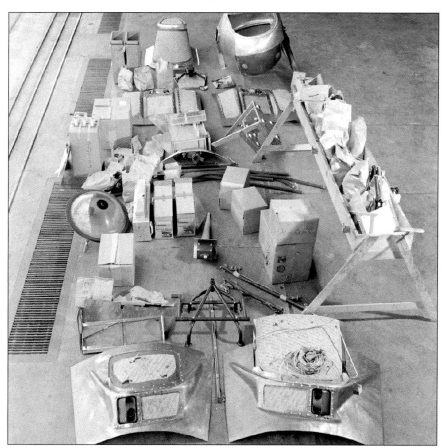

This kit was supplied for each B-17G modified at the Cheyenne Modification Center. It included boxes of components, such as electronics and other parts, as well as miscellaneous hardware. In the foreground are the Erickson cheek gun enclosures, and in the back is a Cheyenne Tail Turret cowling.

The control panel of the fifth B-17G-10-BO (42-31236) in September 1943. (Please refer to the control panel diagram in Appendix I.)

newly-produced aircraft to preparing existing veteran aircraft from the European Theater for new operations in the Pacific.

By the beginning of 1945, the vise was closing on Germany and the final demise of the Third Reich was within sight. However, even by most optimistic estimates, the defeat of the tenacious Empire of Japan was something that was unlikely until the Operation Downfall invasions of the Japanese home islands in late 1945 and early 1946. In the Pacific, GIs used the phrase "hell to heaven in forty-seven," or the cynical "Golden Gate by forty-eight."

In anticipation of Downfall, the Air Technical Service Command was making plans to bring aircraft home from Europe and readying them for the Pacific at its own large air depots, especially those in Sacramento and San Bernardino, California.

The 1945 monthly average for all the traditional modification centers was nearly a thousand aircraft of all types through

The control panel of a B-17G-45-BO in February 1944. (Please refer to the control panel diagram in Appendix I.)

The control panel of a B-17G-85-DL that was delivered in April 1945. This panel is inside a restored aircraft in May 2019. (Please refer to the control panel diagram in Appendix I.) (Photo by Bill Yenne)

This photograph of the left, or Command Pilot's, seat and the left-side instruments in a restored B-17G-85-DL was taken in 2019. (Please refer to the control panel diagrams in Appendix I.) (Photo by Bill Yenne)

Here, we look right on the fight deck of a restored B-17G-85-DL toward the copilot's seat and right-side instruments. (Please refer to the control panel diagrams in Appendix I.) (Photo by Bill Yenne)

June. This fell when the war ended, but it was still at 267 in September. The official records indicate that the modification program ended with a dozen aircraft in November. One was a Curtiss P-40 Warhawk, and the rest were Lockheed P-80 Shooting Star jet fighters modified at Love Field.

The total of all USAAF aircraft of all types modified by all the USAAF modification centers during the war stood at 58,878. In 1945, the total was 7,355; compared to 25,478 in 1944; 22,007 in 1943; and 4,038 in 1942. The modification center program formally ended in November 1945, and the centers were officially closed. All modification work reverted back to the USAAF's own air depots where it had been prior to 1942.

A detailed view is shown of the four fuel mixture controls, one for each engine, on the control pedestal in the center console between the pilot's and copilot's seat in a restored B-17G-85-DL. To the immediate left of these is the turbocharger and mixture control lock. (Photo by Bill Yenne)

A detailed view of the Automatic Flight Control Equipment (AFCE) panel is shown in a restored B-17G-85-DL. The panel was located below the flight control pedestal and between the pilot and copilot seats on the flight deck. (Photo by Bill Yenne)

Final B-17G Blocks and Concluding Deliveries

For most of the B-17G production blocks delivered from the BDV Committee plants in the spring of 1945, the factory changes were scant. Vega's Blocks 100, 105, and 110, which were first delivered on April 24, April 30, and June 16, respectively, were essentially identical. The same was true for Douglas, which first delivered its Blocks 85, 90, and 95 on March 15, April 12, and May 4, respectively.

An anomaly occurred toward the end of the Douglas Block 95 aircraft with four Block 97 B-17Gs. Discussed earlier in this chapter under the heading "US Navy Flying Fortresses," these were B-17Gs ordered under USAAF contract with USAAF tail numbers, but they were built explicitly for transfer to the US Navy and redesignated as PB-1W. They were delivered to the

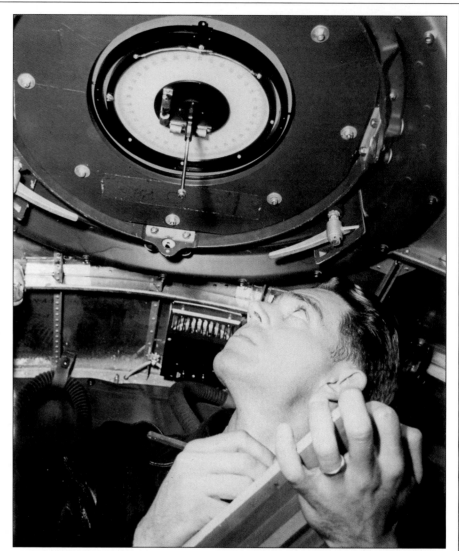

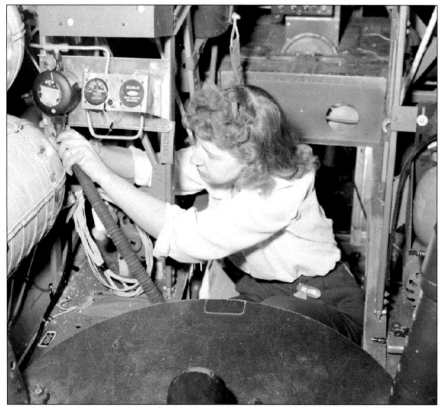

A worker adjusts the oxygen system directly behind the pilot's seat in a B-17G. The Automatic Flight Control Equipment (AFCE) is visible directly above her head.

Carlyle Crecelius takes a reading from a Boeing-developed shadow compass on June 14, 1944. Installed in the astrodome of this B-17G-75-BO, the shadow compass was used to check variations of airplane compasses. "No outside influences affect the shadow compass," read a Boeing press release of the time. It also mentioned that during World War II, scientists had made greater improvements in magnetic compass technology than at any time in the preceding 4,000 years. Crecelius was a noted engineer and inventor, whose name appears on a number of patents for meters and measuring devices through the ensuing decades.

High over the snow-capped Sierras, a B-17G-40-VE heads out from the Vega Aircraft factory in Burbank on its April 26, 1944 delivery flight. Serving with the 305th Bomb Group, it was shot down over Germany four months later.

USAAF on July 2, 1945, and passed on to the Naval Aircraft Modification Unit (NAMU) at Johnsville, Pennsylvania, nine days later and given Navy tail numbers.

These four Block 97 aircraft were interspersed within the Block 95 deliveries. Indeed, there were 25 Block 95 aircraft with higher tail numbers than the Block 97 ones. The Block 95/97 aircraft marked the end of production for Douglas, while both Boeing and Vega ran production through their respective Blocks 110. These were first delivered 5 months apart on January 28 and June 16, 1945.

Boeing staged a festive rollout for its 4,035th and final B-17G (B-17G-110-BO, serial number 43-39508) on April 9, 1945. It was the 6,981st Model 299 to have been built at Plant 2.

The last Vega B-17G-110-VE (44-85841) was delivered on August 4, 1945, with only days left in World War II. Vega had produced 500 B-17Fs and 2,250 B-17Gs.

By sequence numbers, the final three Douglas B-17G-95-DLs were those built with USAAF B-17G serial numbers 44-83883 though 44-83885—then delivered to the US Navy in June and July under the designation PB-1W. Chronologically, however, the final three Douglas B-17Gs were 44-83880 through 44-83882, which were all delivered on August 29, 1945, two weeks after Emperor Hirohito ordered Imperial Japanese forces to stand down. These three brought the Douglas total of Flying Fortress production to 605 B-17Fs and 2,395 B-17Gs.

According to the *USAAF Statistical Digest*, the number of Flying Fortresses on hand in the United States at the end of August 1945 was 2,405, and the number for the peak month (July 1945) was 2,449. The number of Flying Fortresses on hand overseas at the end of August 1945 was 1,272, and the number for the peak operational month (March 1945) was 3,006.

The total number of Flying Fortresses produced was 12,731. Of this total, 55 percent were built by Boeing, 24 percent by Douglas, and 21 percent by Vega. Of these 12,731, 68 percent were B-17Gs, 27 percent were B-17Fs, and 4 percent were B-17Es. The remainder being the earlier variants.

Inside a B-17G-85-BO radio operator's station, just aft of Bulkhead 5, in July 1944. The Belmont BC-348-H radio receiver is on the radio operator's desk at the left. On the high racks on the right are the SCR-274N two-way radios, of which at least two were typically installed.

Inside the radio operator's station of a restored B-17G-85-DL that was delivered in April 1945. The Belmont BC-348-H radio receiver is in its usual place on the radio operator's desk at the left. The fixed seat of the radio operator came and went. It was present in early B-17Fs and mid-production B-17Gs, but here, as in late production B-17Fs, it is replaced by a chair. (Photo by Bill Yenne)

In this area of the Vega Aircraft factory in Burbank where small subcomponents were assembled, small parts such as screws and specialized connectors were kept in row upon row of small bins.

A sheet metal worker at Boeing's Plant 2 handles some raw sheets that will soon be cut and formed into wings, tails, or parts of a Flying Fortress fuselage. (Photo by Andreas Feininger, Library of Congress)

At work inside the aft fuselage of a B-17G. The sheet metal has already been riveted to the vertical tail surfaces.

Ranks of tailed B-17G aft fuselages lined up at Boeing's Plant 2, awaiting the moment they will join completed forward fuselages.

A crowd gathers as the 5,000th Flying Fortress built at Boeing's Plant 2 rolls out for its May 5, 1944, delivery flight to Cheyenne. It carries the signatures of hundreds of Boeing workers. Appropriately named "5 Grand," this B-17G-70-BO (43-37716) was assigned to the 338th Bomb Squadron of the Eighth Air Force's 96th Bomb Group. It came back to the States for a war bond tour in June 1945 after 78 missions.

The 3,971st B-17G passed through the Cheyenne Modification Center in May 1945. The center was operated by United Air Lines.

In May 1944, Hollywood movie star Frances Langford, whose favorite charity was the March of Dimes, made the short trip out to the Vega Aircraft factory in Burbank for a publicity photo op with this B-17G-70-VE (44-8028).

From Arsenal of Democracy to Desert Boneyards

This book about the development and manufacturing of the Flying Fortress certainly begs the question of what happened to those that survived World War II. Many veterans were flown home by their final crews and parked at army airfields across the nation. In turn, these were sent to disposal sites where they were joined by hundreds of factory-fresh B-17Gs that had never flown in foreign air space.

They were joined by thousands of other military surplus aircraft. The American aircraft industry had built around 294,000 aircraft during World War II. Of these, about 44,000 were lost in combat and other overseas operations, and about 22,000 were written off in accidents before going overseas or in training mishaps. The balance were scrapped overseas or never left the United States.

Plans were being made as early as 1944 for scrapping surplus aircraft at

home. In the months following VJ Day, an estimated 117,000 aircraft were moved into about two dozen sites that had been identified by the Air Technical Service Command as disposal locations where the War Assets Administration and the Reconstruction Finance Corporation (RFC) handled their disposal.

Some were sold to private parties or retained by the USAAF for later transfer to Allied governments. Relatively small numbers were mothballed, especially in the desert Southwest, for possible future use. General Hap

The right-side waist gun installation on a B-17G-110-BO as seen in late January 1945. The small label on the plywood ammunition box in the background reads "Load Points Outward"—just in case you thought otherwise!

This view inside a B-17G bomb bay on April 26, 1945, shows a 2,000-pound bomb being hoisted aboard.

Arnold, the commanding general of the USAAF thought that selling off large numbers of surplus aircraft would have an adverse effect on the American aircraft industry after the war, so most were earmarked to be cut up for scrap and melted into aluminum ingots.

Kingman Army Air Field in Arizona, with a 6,800-foot main runway surrounded by vast open spaces was chosen to receive B-17 and B-24 heavy bombers. By early 1946, nearly 5,500 aircraft, most of them heavy bombers, had been brought there. Engines, life rafts, fire extinguishers, radios, oxygen equipment, and other components, notably Norden bombsights, were pulled out. Under an 18-month, $2.78-million contract, the Wunderlich Contracting Company of Jefferson City, Missouri, chopped the airframes into pieces with a giant guillotine and turned these complex flying machines into 28,500 tons of aluminum ingots and 10,000 tons of scrap steel. By the summer of 1948, the airplanes were gone.

From Factory Expansion to Disposition of Facilities

From 1940 to 1944, there had been a great deal of attention given by the Air Materiel Command, especially by its Industrial Planning Section at Wright Field, to the construction of aircraft factories and the expansion of existing facilities. Throughout this book, we have looked at the case study of the Flying Fortress facilities at Boeing's Plant 2 in Seattle and the adjacent Boeing Field (King County Airport), as a microcosm of what was taking place

Looking forward through the bomb bay of a restored B-17G, we see three inert 500-pound bombs on the rack.

An exterior view of a B-17G top turret with its paired M2 .50-caliber machine guns pointed skyward.

throughout the United States.

Of the Project 3A series that we have monitored throughout this book, Projects 3A through 3A-6 (1940 to 1943) dealt with the infrastructure needs of the ongoing Flying Fortress program and the required rapid acceleration of production. With Projects 3A-7 through 3A-10, the emphasis shifted to

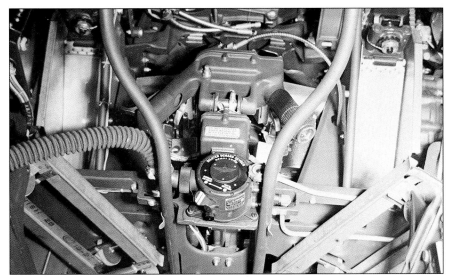

Looking up through the complex web of components into the top turret of a B-17G-110-BO in February 1945.

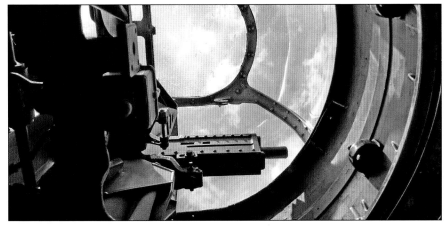

Looking up into the top turret of a restored B-17G-85-DL that was delivered in April 1945. In this photo, taken in tight confines, only the right-side machine gun is visible. (Photo by Bill Yenne)

Looking forward at the Sperry Ball Turret of a restored B-17G-85-DL that was delivered in April 1945. The open bomb bay doors are seen behind the turret. (Photo by Bill Yenne)

Boeing's B-29 Superfortress.

In keeping with the case study, it was officially noted by the Air Materiel Command that as of April 1945, Boeing had invested $24,758,003.35 ($350 million in current valuation) in its three major plants while operating eight branch plants and having 5 Seattle office buildings and 15 warehouses under lease. The federal government, mainly through the Defense Plant Corporation, had invested $8.8 million at Boeing Field in Seattle alone.

In the early days, money was no object, but by May 1945, with Project 3A-11 (a revision of 3A-8), the Air Materiel Command and the Resources Division of the USAAF were much more uncompromising in their questioning of the needs itemized in funding requests. In 1945, the focus turned first to curtailing expansion and ultimately to the disposition of the facilities that had been built with great urgency just a few years before.

On August 13, a few days after two nuclear strikes were made against Japan, Captain W. M. Howell, the Air Materiel's Contract Officer at Wright Field, officially notified Boeing of the immediate cancellation of two major Emergency Plant Facility (EPF) program infrastructure initiatives that had transformed the face of Boeing Field and Plant 2. These included Defense Aid

A technician works on a stamping machine during Flying Fortress production at Boeing's Plant 2 in Seattle. (Photo by Andreas Feininger, Library of Congress)

Barbara Scott is at work on a Wright R-1820-97 radial engine for a B-17G at the Vega Aircraft plant in Burbank.

Contract DA W535 ac-196 of 1941 as well as EPF Contract W535 ac-26185 of 1942, which covered leasehold improvements new buildings.

Two days later, Emperor Hirohito issued his reluctant command to all his Imperial Army and Navy forces to cease hostilities.

On August 18, Colonel G. H. Moriarty, chief of the USAAF Technical Service Command Resources Control Section at Wright Field began rescinding approval recommendations for additional projects across the country that were planned or had been under consideration. For Boeing, only one infrastructure project, warehouse construction (3G-4), was underway when the war ended, and it was canceled. At around the same time, The USAAF canceled production of 1,483 B-29s, 218 B-29As, and 5,000 B-29Cs.

On October 4, 1945, Lieutenant General Raymond Albert Wheeler became Chief Engineer of the US Army Corps and promptly put his office's newly formed Disposal Division to work shedding infrastructure throughout the United States. Throughout October, this office, as well as the Air Materiel Command's Industrial Facilities Section, set about declaring various government-owned properties as "surplus to the needs of the War Department."

Meanwhile, Congress had passed the Surplus Property Act of 1944, which established the executive branch Surplus Property Board (SPB) to share in the task of selling off infrastructure and materiel that had been built with great urgency only a matter of months earlier.

In the case of the Seattle infrastructure, "Part of the facilities not required for AAF production was to either be disposed of or leased to Boeing for commercial production." Boeing also had an option to purchase the facilities under provisions of its contracts.

On November 14, Brigadier General Edwin Rawlings, the chief of the Procurement Division of the Air Technical Service Command, categorized the government-owned property at Boeing Field and Plant 2 into two classifications. Class I included buildings, building installations, land improvements, and leasehold improvements that had originally cost the government $1,611,314,85. Class III included equipment, machinery, mechanical installations, and laboratories, which had cost the government $3,372,874.75. It was estimated that the Class I property would cost about $400,000 to prepare for sale, and that the Class II property "could not be sold on the open market."

Therefore, Rawlings recommended that the Class I and Class II property be sold to Boeing for $1,519,386.35 "in return for the release of Government liability for restoration of the premises." Boeing kept everything thus offered except the bus depot and entered into a lease arrangement for the Engineering Annex Building and the parking lot.

Meanwhile, an open secret was revealed. All those rooftop villages in Seattle and Southern California that had been constructed in 1942 as a camouflage measure were clearly visible, but they had remained unheralded in the media until the summer of 1945 because no one was sup-

In this wide-angle view of the nose section of a restored B-17G-85-DL, we see the well-worn navigator's table on the left and the two .50-caliber M2 cheek guns in staggered positions left and right. The bombardier's station is in the center with the handlebar controller for the chin turret tipped to the right. Note that in this photo, unlike vintage images, the Norden Bombsight is not shrouded for reasons of secrecy. (Photo by Bill Yenne)

posed to talk about them. Shortly after photographs of them finally made it into the papers, they were quickly and completely torn down. From Seattle to Southern California, these amazing villages disappeared virtually overnight, vanishing like mirages, but they would continue to live on as an iconic element within the collective memory of the American Home Front of World War II.

The Last Factories Fade Away

In Burbank and Long Beach, the factories that built the Flying Fortresses were a mere addendum to the sprawling operations of Lockheed and Douglas, and they were for a time incorporated into the postwar work of those companies. Both companies had sizable military contracts and a robust commercial airliner business. The latter activities lasted until 1984 for Lockheed and into the 1990s for Douglas, which merged with McDonnell in 1967 to form McDonnell Douglas—which was in turn acquired by Boeing in 1997.

In Long Beach, Buildings 12 and 13, where the Flying Fortresses were built, were demolished and are today a business park known as Douglas Park. The other facilities of Lockheed and Douglas were razed, gradually repurposed for other uses, or became parts of the Burbank and Long Beach airports.

As the last B-17Gs departed from Seattle's Boeing Field in 1945, the huge Buildings 2-40 and 2-41 at Plant 2, where 6,981 Flying Fortresses had been built, remained. Although B-29 production had moved to Renton, the Boeing Model 367, a military transport based on the B-29, was already being built at Plant 2. The USAAF (US Air Force after 1947) acquired 888 of these under the designation C-97, of which most were KC-97 aerial refueling tankers. These were all built at Plant 2, as were 56 Model 377 Stratocruisers, the four-engine, transoceanic propliners based on the Model 367. When the Air Force moved into jet bombers, Boeing built two XB-47 Stratojet prototypes as well as the XB-52 and YB-52 Stratofortress prototype at Plant 2. The latter were followed at Plant 2 by 275 production series Stratofortresses from B-52A through B-52F.

In nearby Renton, B-29 Superfortress production also came to an end, and an order for 5,000 B-29Cs was canceled. However, Contract W535 ac-13013, calling for B-29D aircraft, was fulfilled. These aircraft were delivered from Renton after 1947 under the designation B-50-BN. Like the B-29s,

Some of the last of 4,035 B-17Gs that were to pass through Boeing's Plant 2 take shape on the factory floor.

This line of B-17Gs that have spilled from the big doors at Boeing's Plant 2 on the left is about to be towed across East Marginal Way South to Boeing Field for delivery flights. As many as 300 aircraft a month or more made this journey. The faux village camouflage atop the roof of Building 2-40 can be seen on the left.

they carried the Boeing model number 345, but they were larger and more advanced. Boeing eventually built 346 B-50s at Renton, most of which were ordered after 1948. Renton later became the production location for Boeing's Model 707, 727, and 757 jetliners. Model 737 production, ongoing since 1966, still takes place at Renton.

The last aircraft to be built at Plant 2 were three Model 737 jetliner prototypes in 1967. Thereafter, the complex was used for non-aircraft programs, such as research work until being largely abandoned by the 21st century. Beginning in 2010, the buildings of the Plant 2 complex were gradually demolished. The last part of Building 2-40 was taken down on September 24, 2011, and the area was replaced by an aircraft parking lot. As this book was being produced, the parking area was filled with undelivered 737MAX jetliners that were being stored there pending a resolution of the 2019 FAA order that grounded this aircraft type.

The B-17H was not a newly produced variant. The designation was retroactively applied to a number of lifeboat-carrying search-and-rescue conversions of B-17Gs. They were redesignated as SB-17G in 1948. Seen here in 1950 is one that was assigned to the 5th Rescue Squadron. (Photo Courtesy USAF)

The former site of Boeing's Plant 2 in Seattle is shown with the bank of the Duwamish River in the foreground. When this photo was taken in 2019, the area was being used to park undelivered 737 MAX aircraft. (Photo Courtesy Sounder Bruce, licensed under Creative Commons)

DIAGRAMS AND CUTAWAY DRAWINGS

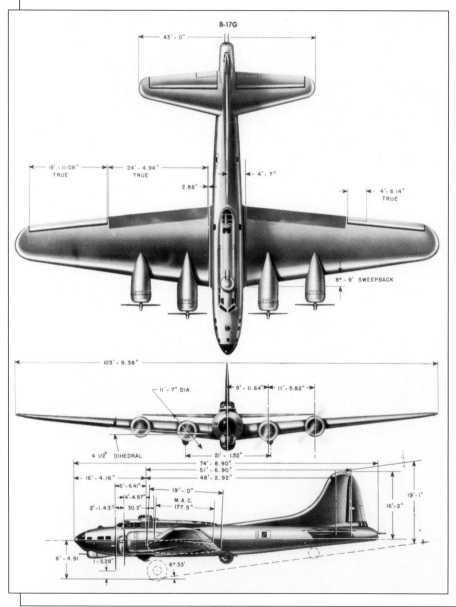

Three-View Drawing of a B-17G Flying Fortress. With very minor variations, these dimensions are also applicable to the B-17E and B-17F variants, accounting for 99 percent of all Flying Fortresses that were built.

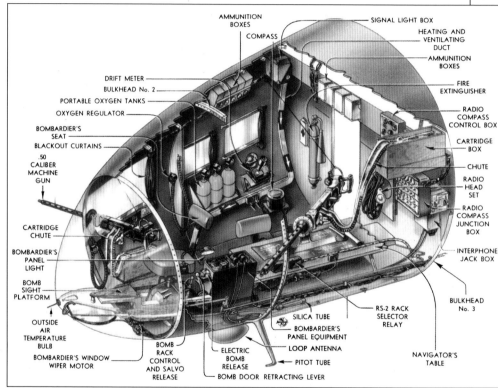

The Bombardier's and Navigator's Compartment in the nose of a B-17F. With some variations, the interior layout is like that of the B-17E. The most noticeable difference is the single-piece blown Plexiglas nose in the B-17F, whereas the B-17E had a faceted Plexiglas nose like that of the B-17C and B-17D. In all B-17Gs, this section differed in the addition of the Bendix Chin Turret. In later B-17Gs, the perpendicular-mounted side guns were replaced by cheek guns in protruding enclosures that permitted forward aiming from the sides of the nose.

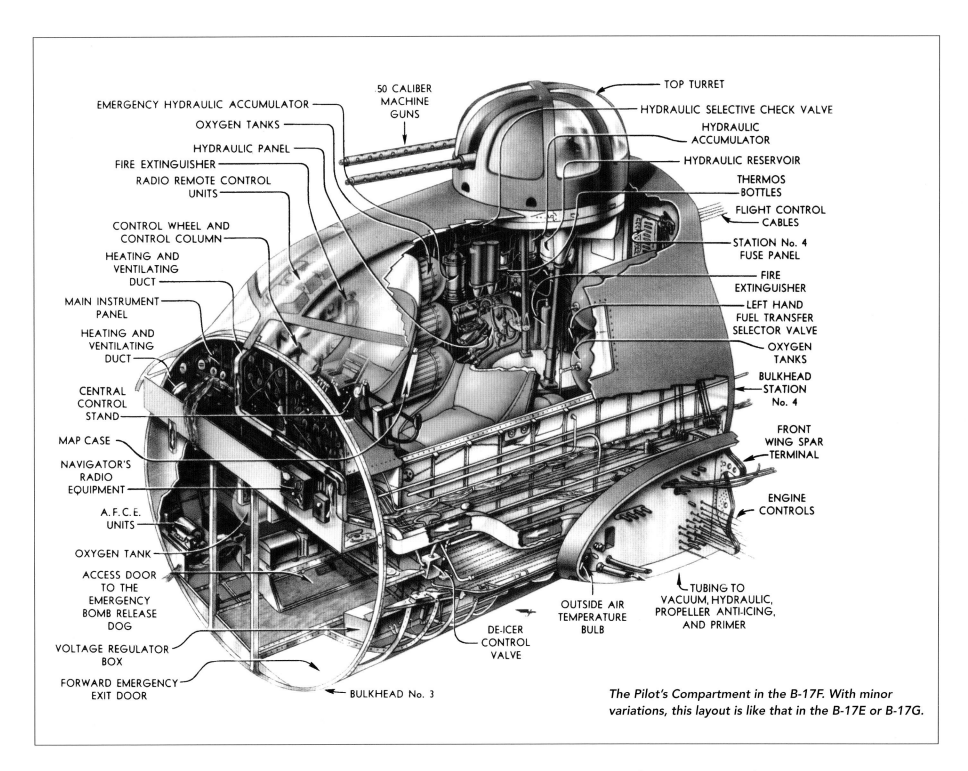

EMERGENCY HYDRAULIC ACCUMULATOR

OXYGEN TANKS

HYDRAULIC PANEL

FIRE EXTINGUISHER

RADIO REMOTE CONTROL UNITS

CONTROL WHEEL AND CONTROL COLUMN

HEATING AND VENTILATING DUCT

MAIN INSTRUMENT PANEL

HEATING AND VENTILATING DUCT

CENTRAL CONTROL STAND

MAP CASE

NAVIGATOR'S RADIO EQUIPMENT

A.F.C.E. UNITS

OXYGEN TANK

ACCESS DOOR TO THE EMERGENCY BOMB RELEASE DOG

VOLTAGE REGULATOR BOX

FORWARD EMERGENCY EXIT DOOR

BULKHEAD No. 3

.50 CALIBER MACHINE GUNS

TOP TURRET

HYDRAULIC SELECTIVE CHECK VALVE

HYDRAULIC ACCUMULATOR

HYDRAULIC RESERVOIR

THERMOS BOTTLES

FLIGHT CONTROL CABLES

STATION No. 4 FUSE PANEL

FIRE EXTINGUISHER

LEFT HAND FUEL TRANSFER SELECTOR VALVE

OXYGEN TANKS

BULKHEAD STATION No. 4

FRONT WING SPAR TERMINAL

ENGINE CONTROLS

TUBING TO VACUUM, HYDRAULIC, PROPELLER ANTI-ICING, AND PRIMER

OUTSIDE AIR TEMPERATURE BULB

DE-ICER CONTROL VALVE

The Pilot's Compartment in the B-17F. With minor variations, this layout is like that in the B-17E or B-17G.

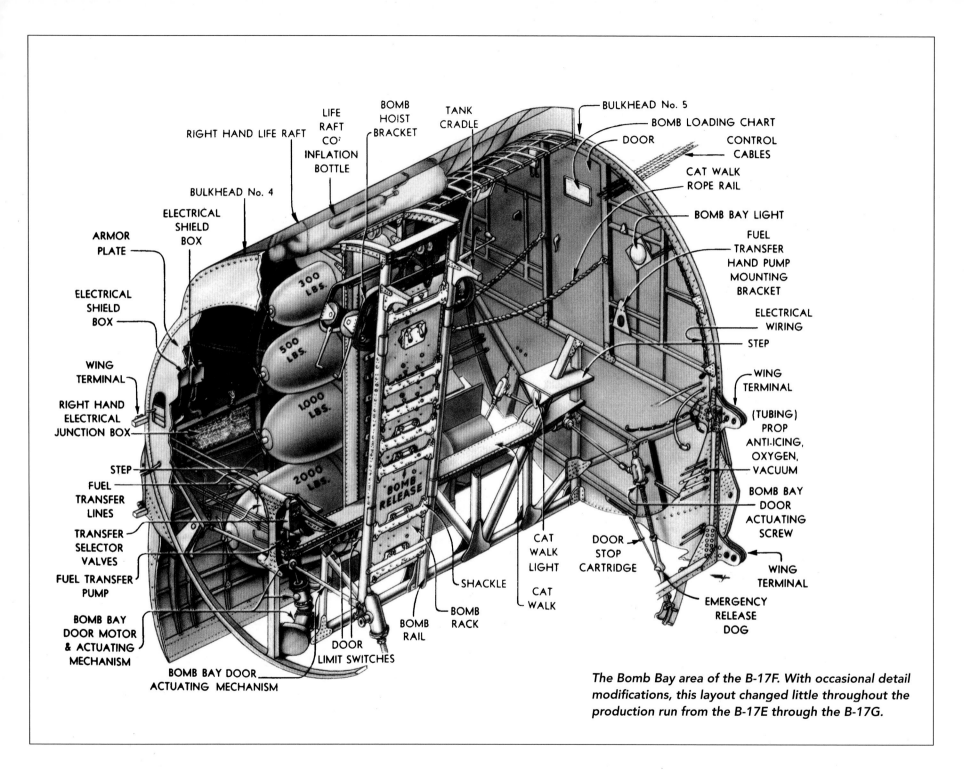

RIGHT HAND LIFE RAFT

LIFE RAFT CO² INFLATION BOTTLE

BOMB HOIST BRACKET

TANK CRADLE

BULKHEAD No. 5

BOMB LOADING CHART

DOOR

CONTROL CABLES

CAT WALK ROPE RAIL

BULKHEAD No. 4

BOMB BAY LIGHT

ELECTRICAL SHIELD BOX

FUEL TRANSFER HAND PUMP MOUNTING BRACKET

ARMOR PLATE

ELECTRICAL SHIELD BOX

300 LBS.

ELECTRICAL WIRING

STEP

WING TERMINAL

500 LBS.

WING TERMINAL

RIGHT HAND ELECTRICAL JUNCTION BOX

1,000 LBS.

(TUBING) PROP ANTI-ICING, OXYGEN, VACUUM

STEP

FUEL TRANSFER LINES

2000 LBS.

BOMB RELEASE

BOMB BAY DOOR ACTUATING SCREW

TRANSFER SELECTOR VALVES

CAT WALK LIGHT

DOOR STOP CARTRIDGE

WING TERMINAL

FUEL TRANSFER PUMP

SHACKLE

CAT WALK

BOMB BAY DOOR MOTOR & ACTUATING MECHANISM

BOMB RAIL

BOMB RACK

EMERGENCY RELEASE DOG

BOMB BAY DOOR ACTUATING MECHANISM

DOOR LIMIT SWITCHES

The Bomb Bay area of the B-17F. With occasional detail modifications, this layout changed little throughout the production run from the B-17E through the B-17G.

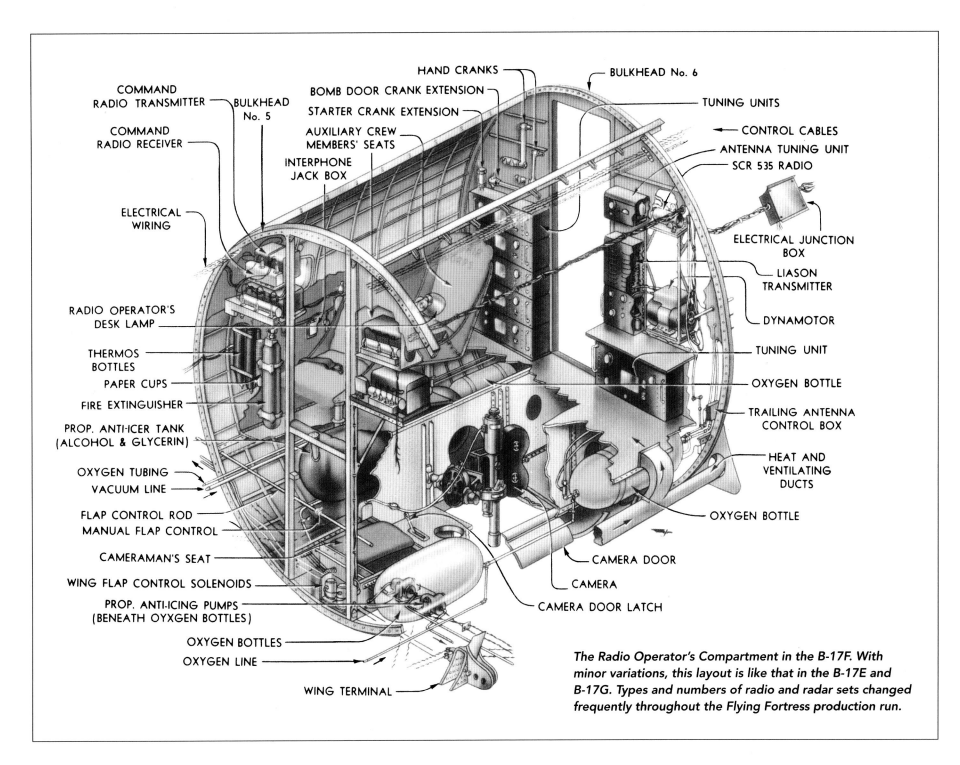

COMMAND RADIO TRANSMITTER
COMMAND RADIO RECEIVER
ELECTRICAL WIRING
BULKHEAD No. 5
INTERPHONE JACK BOX
AUXILIARY CREW MEMBERS' SEATS
STARTER CRANK EXTENSION
BOMB DOOR CRANK EXTENSION
HAND CRANKS
BULKHEAD No. 6
TUNING UNITS
CONTROL CABLES
ANTENNA TUNING UNIT
SCR 535 RADIO
ELECTRICAL JUNCTION BOX
LIASON TRANSMITTER
DYNAMOTOR
TUNING UNIT
OXYGEN BOTTLE
TRAILING ANTENNA CONTROL BOX
HEAT AND VENTILATING DUCTS
OXYGEN BOTTLE
CAMERA DOOR
CAMERA
CAMERA DOOR LATCH
RADIO OPERATOR'S DESK LAMP
THERMOS BOTTLES
PAPER CUPS
FIRE EXTINGUISHER
PROP. ANTI-ICER TANK (ALCOHOL & GLYCERIN)
OXYGEN TUBING
VACUUM LINE
FLAP CONTROL ROD
MANUAL FLAP CONTROL
CAMERAMAN'S SEAT
WING FLAP CONTROL SOLENOIDS
PROP. ANTI-ICING PUMPS (BENEATH OYXGEN BOTTLES)
OXYGEN BOTTLES
OXYGEN LINE
WING TERMINAL

The Radio Operator's Compartment in the B-17F. With minor variations, this layout is like that in the B-17E and B-17G. Types and numbers of radio and radar sets changed frequently throughout the Flying Fortress production run.

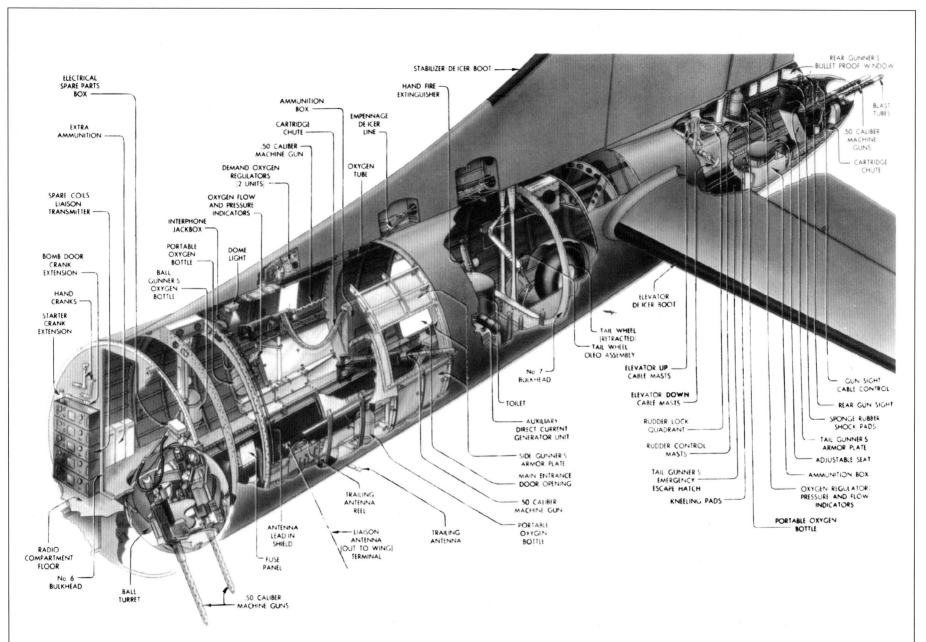

ELECTRICAL
SPARE PARTS
BOX

EXTRA
AMMUNITION

SPARE COILS
LIAISON
TRANSMITTER

BOMB DOOR
CRANK
EXTENSION

HAND
CRANKS

STARTER
CRANK
EXTENSION

RADIO
COMPARTMENT
FLOOR

No 6
BULKHEAD

BALL
TURRET

.50 CALIBER
MACHINE GUNS

FUSE
PANEL

ANTENNA
LEAD IN
SHIELD

LIAISON
ANTENNA
(OUT TO WING)
TERMINAL

TRAILING
ANTENNA
REEL

ANTENNA

TRAILING
ANTENNA

INTERPHONE
JACKBOX

PORTABLE
OXYGEN
BOTTLE

BALL
GUNNER'S
OXYGEN
BOTTLE

DOME
LIGHT

OXYGEN FLOW
AND PRESSURE
INDICATORS

DEMAND OXYGEN
REGULATORS
(2 UNITS)

.50 CALIBER
MACHINE GUN

CARTRIDGE
CHUTE

AMMUNITION
BOX

OXYGEN
TUBE

EMPENNAGE
DE ICER
LINE

HAND FIRE
EXTINGUISHER

STABILIZER DE ICER BOOT

REAR GUNNER'S
BULLET PROOF WINDOW

BLAST
TUBES

.50 CALIBER
MACHINE
GUNS

CARTRIDGE
CHUTE

ELEVATOR
DE ICER BOOT

TAIL WHEEL
(RETRACTED)

TAIL WHEEL
OLEO ASSEMBLY

No 7
BULKHEAD

TOILET

AUXILIARY
DIRECT CURRENT
GENERATOR UNIT

SIDE GUNNER'S
ARMOR PLATE

MAIN ENTRANCE
DOOR OPENING

.50 CALIBER
MACHINE GUN

PORTABLE
OXYGEN
BOTTLE

ELEVATOR UP
CABLE MASTS

ELEVATOR DOWN
CABLE MASTS

RUDDER LOCK
QUADRANT

RUDDER CONTROL
MASTS

TAIL GUNNER'S
EMERGENCY
ESCAPE HATCH

KNEELING PADS

GUN SIGHT
CABLE CONTROL

REAR GUN SIGHT

SPONGE RUBBER
SHOCK PADS

TAIL GUNNER'S
ARMOR PLATE

ADJUSTABLE SEAT

AMMUNITION BOX

OXYGEN REGULATOR:
PRESSURE AND FLOW
INDICATORS

PORTABLE OXYGEN
BOTTLE

Inside the Rear Fuselage Section of the B-17F. With minor variations, this layout is like that in the B-17E and early B-17Gs. Beginning in early 1944, though, the waist guns on the B-17G were staggered. The one on the left was moved rearward so that the gunners were not working back to back. Beginning in June 1944, the standard Stinger Tail Turret in many B-17Gs (seen here) was replaced by the larger Cheyenne Tail Turret.

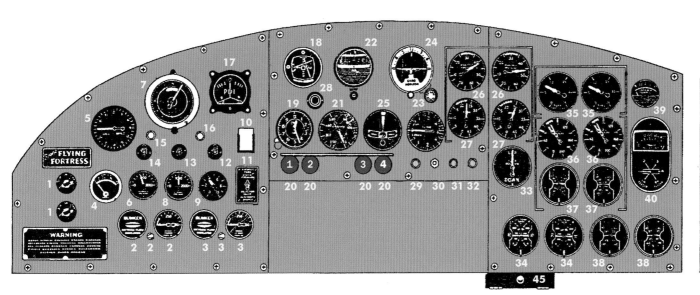
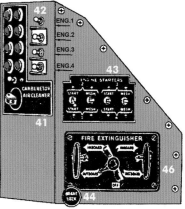

The basic layout of the main control panel for the B-17F and B-17G is seen here. There were numerous variations throughout the 12,085 aircraft produced of those two Flying Fortress variants, but they all generally followed this pattern. (Author artwork based on a USAAF manual)

1. Fluorescent light switches
2. Pilot's oxygen flow indicator, warning light, and pressure gauge
3. Copilot's oxygen flow indicator, warning light, and pressure gauge
4. Voltmeter (AC)
5. Radio compass
6. Emergency oil pressure gauge (B-17F only)
7. Flux gate compass
8. Hydraulic oil pressure gauge
9. Suction gauge
10. Altimeter correction card
11. Airspeed alternate source switch
12. Vacuum warning light
13. Main system hydraulic oil warning light
14. Emergency system hydraulic oil warning light (B-17F only)
15. Bomb door position light (B-17F only)
16. Bomb release light
17. Pilot's directional indicator
18. Pilot's localizer indicator
19. Altimeter
20. Propeller feathering switches
21. Airspeed indicator
22. Directional gyro
23. Rate-of-climb indicator
24. Flight indicator
25. Turn-and-bank indicator
26. Manifold pressure gauges
27. Tachometers
28. Marker beacon light
29. Globe test button
30. Bomber call light
31. Landing gear warning light
32. Tailwheel lock light
33. Flap position indicator
34. Cylinder-head temperature gauges
35. Fuel pressure gauges
36. Oil pressure gauges
37. Oil temperature gauges
38. Carburetor air temperature gauges
39. Free air temperature gauge
40. Fuel quantity gauge
41. Carburetor air filter switch
42. Oil dilution switches
43. Starting switches
44. Parking brake control
45. Spare fuse box
46. Engine fire extinguisher controls (on some aircraft)

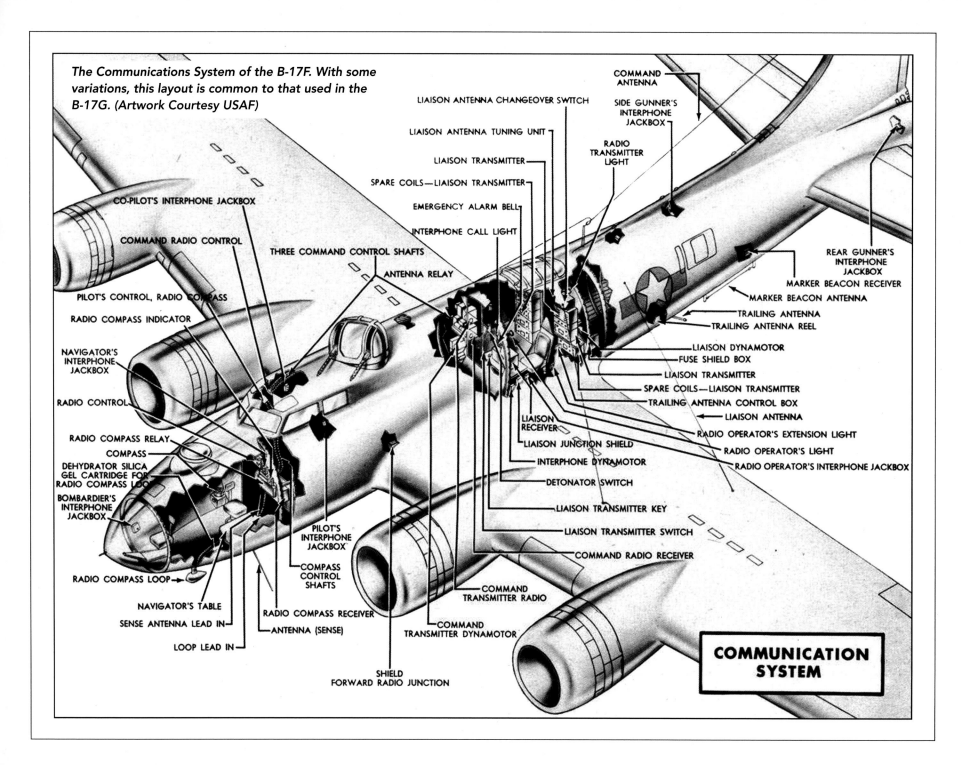

The Communications System of the B-17F. With some variations, this layout is common to that used in the B-17G. (Artwork Courtesy USAF)

COMMAND ANTENNA

LIAISON ANTENNA CHANGEOVER SWITCH

SIDE GUNNER'S INTERPHONE JACKBOX

LIAISON ANTENNA TUNING UNIT

RADIO TRANSMITTER LIGHT

LIAISON TRANSMITTER

SPARE COILS—LIAISON TRANSMITTER

EMERGENCY ALARM BELL

INTERPHONE CALL LIGHT

CO-PILOT'S INTERPHONE JACKBOX

COMMAND RADIO CONTROL

THREE COMMAND CONTROL SHAFTS

ANTENNA RELAY

REAR GUNNER'S INTERPHONE JACKBOX

MARKER BEACON RECEIVER

MARKER BEACON ANTENNA

PILOT'S CONTROL, RADIO COMPASS

RADIO COMPASS INDICATOR

TRAILING ANTENNA

TRAILING ANTENNA REEL

LIAISON DYNAMOTOR

FUSE SHIELD BOX

LIAISON TRANSMITTER

NAVIGATOR'S INTERPHONE JACKBOX

SPARE COILS—LIAISON TRANSMITTER

TRAILING ANTENNA CONTROL BOX

RADIO CONTROL

LIAISON ANTENNA

LIAISON RECEIVER

RADIO OPERATOR'S EXTENSION LIGHT

RADIO COMPASS RELAY

LIAISON JUNCTION SHIELD

RADIO OPERATOR'S LIGHT

COMPASS

INTERPHONE DYNAMOTOR

RADIO OPERATOR'S INTERPHONE JACKBOX

DEHYDRATOR SILICA GEL CARTRIDGE FOR RADIO COMPASS LOOP

DETONATOR SWITCH

BOMBARDIER'S INTERPHONE JACKBOX

LIAISON TRANSMITTER KEY

PILOT'S INTERPHONE JACKBOX

LIAISON TRANSMITTER SWITCH

COMMAND RADIO RECEIVER

RADIO COMPASS LOOP

COMPASS CONTROL SHAFTS

NAVIGATOR'S TABLE

SENSE ANTENNA LEAD IN

RADIO COMPASS RECEIVER

COMMAND TRANSMITTER RADIO

LOOP LEAD IN

ANTENNA (SENSE)

COMMAND TRANSMITTER DYNAMOTOR

SHIELD FORWARD RADIO JUNCTION

COMMUNICATION SYSTEM

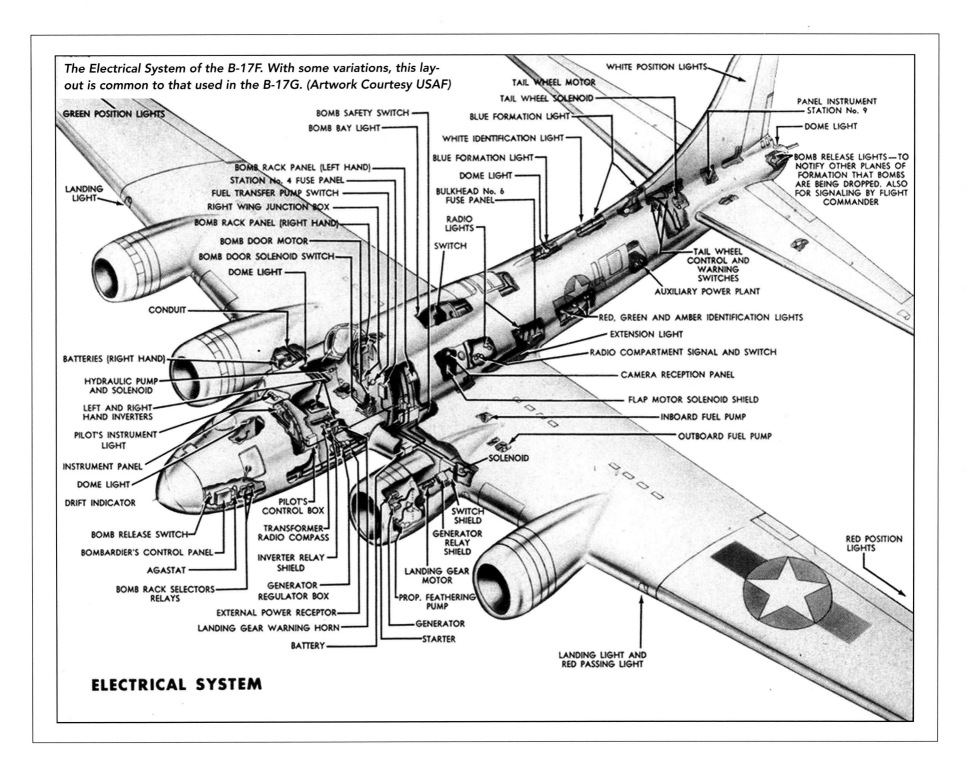

The Electrical System of the B-17F. With some variations, this layout is common to that used in the B-17G. (Artwork Courtesy USAF)

GREEN POSITION LIGHTS

LANDING LIGHT

BOMB RACK PANEL (LEFT HAND)
STATION No. 4 FUSE PANEL
FUEL TRANSFER PUMP SWITCH
RIGHT WING JUNCTION BOX
BOMB RACK PANEL (RIGHT HAND)
BOMB DOOR MOTOR
BOMB DOOR SOLENOID SWITCH
DOME LIGHT

CONDUIT

BATTERIES (RIGHT HAND)
HYDRAULIC PUMP AND SOLENOID
LEFT AND RIGHT HAND INVERTERS
PILOT'S INSTRUMENT LIGHT
INSTRUMENT PANEL
DOME LIGHT
DRIFT INDICATOR

BOMB RELEASE SWITCH
BOMBARDIER'S CONTROL PANEL
AGASTAT
BOMB RACK SELECTORS RELAYS

PILOT'S CONTROL BOX
TRANSFORMER-RADIO COMPASS
INVERTER RELAY SHIELD
GENERATOR REGULATOR BOX
EXTERNAL POWER RECEPTOR
LANDING GEAR WARNING HORN
BATTERY

BOMB SAFETY SWITCH
BOMB BAY LIGHT

WHITE IDENTIFICATION LIGHT
BLUE FORMATION LIGHT
DOME LIGHT
BULKHEAD No. 6 FUSE PANEL
RADIO LIGHTS
SWITCH

SOLENOID

SWITCH SHIELD
GENERATOR RELAY SHIELD
LANDING GEAR MOTOR
PROP. FEATHERING PUMP
GENERATOR
STARTER

TAIL WHEEL MOTOR
TAIL WHEEL SOLENOID
BLUE FORMATION LIGHT

WHITE POSITION LIGHTS

PANEL INSTRUMENT STATION No. 9
DOME LIGHT
BOMB RELEASE LIGHTS—TO NOTIFY OTHER PLANES OF FORMATION THAT BOMBS ARE BEING DROPPED. ALSO FOR SIGNALING BY FLIGHT COMMANDER

TAIL WHEEL CONTROL AND WARNING SWITCHES
AUXILIARY POWER PLANT
RED, GREEN AND AMBER IDENTIFICATION LIGHTS
EXTENSION LIGHT
RADIO COMPARTMENT SIGNAL AND SWITCH
CAMERA RECEPTION PANEL
FLAP MOTOR SOLENOID SHIELD
INBOARD FUEL PUMP
OUTBOARD FUEL PUMP

RED POSITION LIGHTS

LANDING LIGHT AND RED PASSING LIGHT

ELECTRICAL SYSTEM

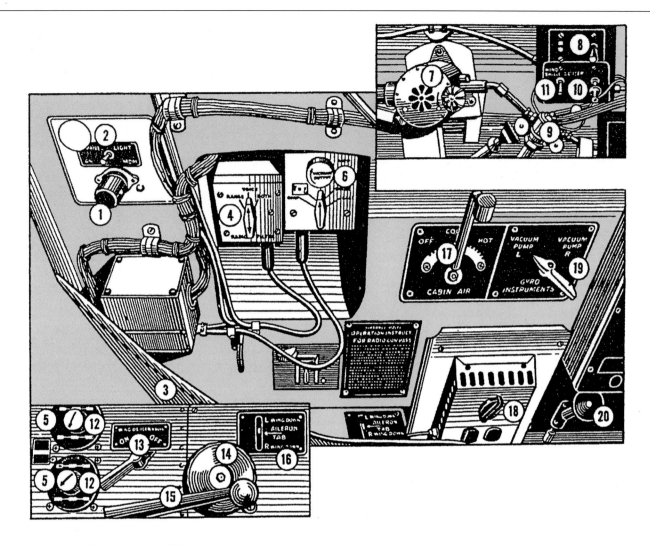

The basic layout of the side controls to the left of the pilot's position in the B-17F and B-17G is seen here. There were numerous variations throughout the production run of those two Flying Fortress variants, but they all generally followed this pattern. (Artwork Courtesy USAF)

1. Panel light
2. Panel light switch
3. Pilot's seat
4. Filter selector switch
5. Propeller anti-icer switch
6. Interphone jackbox
7. Oxygen regulator

8. Windshield wiper controls
9. Portable oxygen unit recharger
10 Windshield anti-icer switch
11. Windshield anti-icer flow control
12. Propeller anti-icer rheostats
13. Surface deicer control
14. Aileron trim tab control

15. Pilot's seat adjustment lever
16. Aileron trim tab indicator
17. Cabin air control
18. Pilot's flight suit heater outlet
19. Vacuum selector valve
20. Emergency bomb release

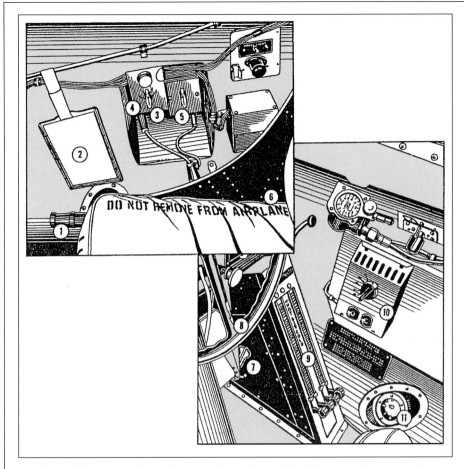

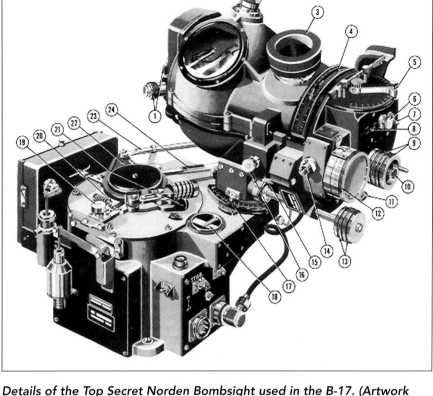

Details of the Top Secret Norden Bombsight used in the B-17. (Artwork Courtesy USAF)

The basic layout of the side controls to the right of the copilot's position in the B-17F and B-17G is seen here. There were numerous variations throughout the production run of those two Flying Fortress variants, but they all generally followed this pattern. (Artwork Courtesy USAF)

1. Hydraulic hand pump
2. Checklist
3. Interphone selector switch
4. Interphone jackbox
5. Filter selector switch
6. Copilot's seat
7. Rudder pedal adjustment.
8. Copilot's control wheel
9. Intercooler controls
10. Copilot's flight suit heater outlet
11. Engine primer

1. Leveling knobs
2. Caging knob
3. Eyepiece
4. Index window
5. Trail arm and trail plate
6. Extended vision knob
7. Rate motor switch
8. Disc speed gear shift
9. Rate and displacement knobs
10. Mirror drive clutch
11. Search knob
12. Disc speed drum
13. Turn and drift knobs
14. Tachometer adapter
15. Release lever
16. Crosshair rheostat
17. Drift scale
18. PDI brush and coil
19. Autopilot clutch engaging knob
20. Autopilot clutch
21. Bombsight clutch engaging lever
22. Bombsight clutch
23. Bombsight connecting rod
24. Autopilot connecting rod

AN/APT-5 RADAR JAMMER

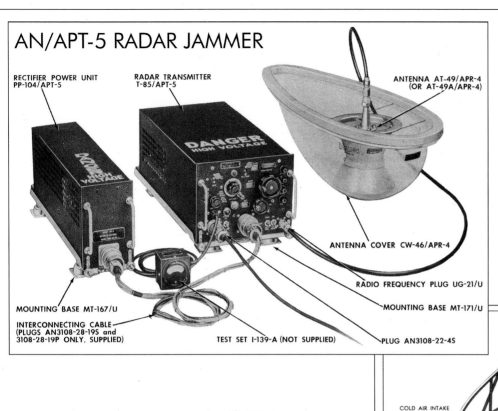

RECTIFIER POWER UNIT
PP-104/APT-5

RADAR TRANSMITTER
T-85/APT-5

DANGER
HIGH VOLTAGE

ANTENNA AT-49/APR-4
(OR AT-49A/APR-4)

ANTENNA COVER CW-46/APR-4

RADIO FREQUENCY PLUG UG-21/U

MOUNTING BASE MT-171/U

MOUNTING BASE MT-167/U

INTERCONNECTING CABLE
(PLUGS AN3108-28-19S and
3108-28-19P ONLY, SUPPLIED)

TEST SET I-139-A (NOT SUPPLIED)

PLUG AN3108-22-4S

The AN/APT-5 Carpet IV was a 350- to 1,200-MHz L-Band semibarrage jamming radar transmitter. It was manufactured by Delco as well as by Aircraft Accessories Corporation (later Aireon Manufacturing). The AN/APT-5 was used in both the B-17 and B-24 during the war but was still a component of the electronics suite in the B-47A, B-47B, and RB-47K jet bomber family through the 1950s. (Photo Courtesy USAF)

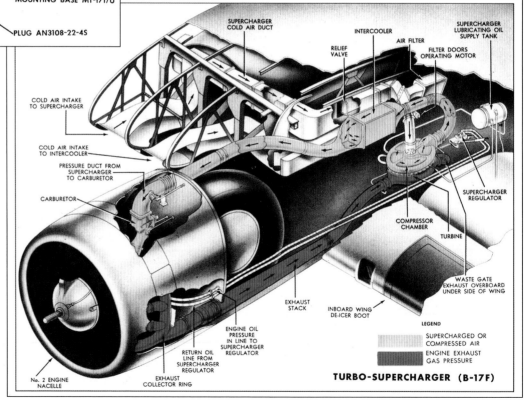

SUPERCHARGER
COLD AIR DUCT

INTERCOOLER

SUPERCHARGER
LUBRICATING OIL
SUPPLY TANK

RELIEF
VALVE

AIR FILTER

FILTER DOORS
OPERATING MOTOR

COLD AIR INTAKE
TO SUPERCHARGER

COLD AIR INTAKE
TO INTERCOOLER

PRESSURE DUCT FROM
SUPERCHARGER
TO CARBURETOR

SUPERCHARGER
REGULATOR

CARBURETOR

COMPRESSOR
CHAMBER

TURBINE

WASTE GATE
EXHAUST OVERBOARD
UNDER SIDE OF WING

EXHAUST
STACK

INBOARD WING
DE-ICER BOOT

LEGEND

ENGINE OIL
PRESSURE
IN LINE TO
SUPERCHARGER
REGULATOR

SUPERCHARGED OR
COMPRESSED AIR

RETURN OIL
LINE FROM
SUPERCHARGER
REGULATOR

ENGINE EXHAUST
GAS PRESSURE

No. 2 ENGINE
NACELLE

EXHAUST
COLLECTOR RING

TURBO-SUPERCHARGER (B-17F)

The Turbosupercharger System for the B-17F. With some minor variations, this layout is common to that used in the B-17G. (Artwork Courtesy USAF)

ALL FLYING FORTRESSES BY VARIANT AND BLOCK

Early Boeing B-17 Aircraft

Designations	Air Corps Serials	Maker Serials
XB-17	X-13372 (Civilian)	1963
Y1B-17	36-149 through 161	1973 through 1985
Y1B-17A	37-269	1987
B-17B	38-211 through 223	2004 through 2016
B-17B	38-258 through 270	2017 through 2029
B-17B	38-583 through 584	2030 through 2031
B-17B	38-610	2032
B-17B	39-01 through 39-10	2033 through 2042
B-17C	40-2042 through 2079	2042 through 2075
B-17D	40-3059 through 3100	2087 through 2128

Boeing B-17F Aircraft

Designations	USAAF Serials	Maker Serials
B-17E	41-2393 through 41-2669	2204 through 2480
B-17E	41-9011 through 41-9245	2483 through 2717

Boeing B-17F Aircraft

Designations	USAAF Serials	Maker Serials
B-17F-1-BO	41-24340 through 24389	3025 through 3074
B-17F-5-BO	41-24390 through 24439	3075 through 3124
B-17F-10-BO	41-24440 through 24489	3125 through 3174
B-17F-15-BO	41-24490 through 24503	3175 through 3188
B-17F-20-BO	41-24504 through 24539	3189 through 3224
B-17F-25-BO	41-24540 through 24584	3225 through 3269
B-17F-27-BO	41-24585 through 24639	3270 through 3324
B-17F-30-BO	42-5050 through 5078	3589 through 3617
B-17F-35-BO	42-5079 through 5149	3618 through 3688
B-17F-40-BO	42-5150 through 5249	3689 through 3788
B-17F-45-BO	42-5250 through 5349	3789 through 3888
B-17F-50-BO	42-5350 through 5484	3889 through 4023
B-17F-55-BO	42-29467 through 29531	4581 through 4645
B-17F-60-BO	42-29532 through 29631	4646 through 4745
B-17F-65-BO	42-29632 through 29731	4746 through 4845
B-17F-70-BO	42-29732 through 29831	4846 through 4945
B-17F-75-BO	42-29882 through 29931	4946 through 5045
B-17F-80-BO	42-29932 through 30031	5046 through 5145

Boeing B-17F Aircraft

Designations	USAAF Serials	Maker Serials
B-17F-85-BO	42-30032 through 30131	5146 through 5245
B-17F-90-BO	42-30132 through 30231	5246 through 5345
B-17F-95-BO	42-30232 through 30331	5346 through 5445
B-17F-100-BO	42-30332 through 30431	5446 through 5545
B-17F-105-BO	42-30432 through 30531	5546 through 5645
B-17F-110-BO	42-30532 through 30616	5646 through 5730
B-17F-115-BO	42-30617 through 30731	5731 through 5845
B-17F-120-BO	42-30732 through 30831	5846 through 5945
B-17F-125-BO	42-30832 through 30931	5946 through 6045
B-17F-130-BO	42-30932 through 31031	6046 through 6145

Douglas B-17F Aircraft

Designations	USAAF Serials	Maker Serials
B-17F-1-DL	42-2964 through 2966	7900 through 7903
B-17F-5-DL	42-2967 through 2978	7903 through 7914
B-17F-10-DL	42-2979 through 3003	7915 through 7939
B-17F-15-DL	42-3004 through 3038	7940 through 7974
B-17F-20-DL	42-3039 through 3073	7975 through 8009
B-17F-25-DL	42-3074 through 3148	8010 through 8084
B-17F-30-DL	42-3149 through 3188	8085 through 8124
B-17F-35-DL	42-3189 through 3228	8125 through 8164
B-17F-40-DL	42-3229 through 3283	8165 through 8219
B-17F-45-DL	42-3284 through 3338	8220 through 8274
B-17F-50-DL	42-3339 through 3393	8275 through 8329
B-17F-55-DL	42-3394 through 3422	8330 through 8358
B-17F-60-DL	42-3423 through 3448	8359 through 8384
B-17F-65-DL	42-3449 through 3482	8385 through 8418
B-17F-70-DL	42-3483 through 3503	8419 through 8439
B-17F-75-DL	42-3504 through 3562	8440 through 8498
B-17F-80-DL	42-37714 through 37715	8500 through 8501
B-17F-85-DL	42-37717 through 37720	8503 through 8506

Vega B-17F Aircraft

Designations	USAAF Serials	Maker Serials
B-17F-1-VE	42-5705 through 5709	6001 through 6005
B-17F-5-VE	42-5710 through 5724	6006 through 6020

B-17F-10-VE	42-5725 through 5744	6021 through 6040
B-17F-15-VE	42-5745 through 5764	6041 through 6060
B-17F-20-VE	42-5765 through 5804	6061 through 6100
B-17F-25-VE	42-5805 through 5854	6101 through 6150
B-17F-30-VE	42-5855 through 5904	6151 through 6200
B-17F-35-VE	42-5905 through 5954	6201 through 6250
B-17F-40-VE	42-5955 through 6029	6251 through 6325
B-17F-45-VE	42-6030 through 6104	6326 through 6400
B-17F-50-VE	42-6105 through 6204	6401 through 6500

Boeing B-17G Aircraft

Designations	USAAF Serials	Maker Serials
B-17G-1-BO	42-31032 through 31131	6146 through 6245
B-17G-5-BO	42-31132 through 31231	6246 through 6345
B-17G-10-BO	42-31232 through 31331	6346 through 6445
B-17G-15-BO	42-31332 through 31431	6446 through 6545
B-17G-20-BO	42-31432 through 31631	6546 through 6745
B-17G-25-BO	42-31632 through 31731	6746 through 6845
B-17G-30-BO	42-31732 through 31931	6846 through 7045
B-17G-35-BO	42-31932 through 32116	7046 through 7230
B-17G-40-BO	42-97058 through 97172	7531 through 7645
B-17G-45-BO	42-97173 through 97407	7646 through 7880
B-17G-50-BO	42-102379 through 102543	7881 through 8045
B-17G-55-BO	42-102544 through 102743	8046 through 8245
B-17G-60-BO	42-102744 through 102978	8246 through 8480
B-17G-65-BO	43-37509 through 37673	8487 through 8651
B-17G-70-BO	43-37674 through 37873	8652 through 8851
B-17G-75-BO	43-37874 through 38073	8852 through 9051
B-17G-80-BO	43-38074 through 38273	9052 through 9251
B-17G-85-BO	43-38274 through 38473	9252 through 9451
B-17G-90-BO	43-38474 through 38673	9452 through 9651
B-17G-95-BO	43-38674 through 38873	9652 through 9841
B-17G-100-BO	43-38874 through 39073	9852 through 10051
B-17G-105-BO	43-39074 through 39273	10052 through 10251
B-17G-110-BO	43-39274 through 39508	10252 through 10486

Douglas B-17G Aircraft		
Designations	USAAF Serials	Maker Serials
B-17G-5-DL	42-3569	8499
B-17G-10-DL	42-37716	8502
B-17G-10-DL	42-37721 through 37803	8507 through 8589
B-17G-15-DL	42-37804 through 37893	8590 through 8679
B-17G-20-DL	42-37894 through 37988	8680 through 8774
B-17G-25-DL	42-37989 through 38083	8775 through 8869
B-17G-30-DL	42-38084 through 38213	8875 through 8999
B-17G-35-DL	42-106984 through 107233	21899 through 22148
B-17G-40-DL	44-6001 through 6125	22224 through 22348
B-17G-45-DL	44-6126 through 6250	22349 through 22473
B-17G-50-DL	44-6251 through 6500	22474 through 22723
B-17G-55-DL	44-6501 through 6625	22724 through 22848
B-17G-60-DL	44-6626 through 6750	22849 through 22973
B-17G-65-DL	44-6751 through 6875	22974 through 23098
B-17G-70-DL	44-6876 through 7000	23099 through 23223
B-17G-75-DL	44-83236 through 83360	31877 through 32001
B-17G-80-DL	44-83361 through 83485	32002 through 32126
B-17G-85-DL	44-83486 through 83585	32127 through 32226
B-17G-90-DL	44-83586 through 83685	32227 through 32326
B-17G-95-DL	44-83686 through 83854	32327 through 32495
B-17G-97-DL	44-83855	32496
B-17G-95-DL	44-83856	32497
B-17G-97-DL	44-83857 through 83859	32498 through 32500
B-17G-95-DL	44-83860 through 83885	32501 through 52526

Vega B-17G Aircraft		
Designations	USSAF Serials	Maker Serials
B-17G-1-VE	42-39758 through 39857	6501 through 6600
B-17G-5-VE	42-39858 through 39957	6601 through 6700
B-17G-10-VE	42-39958 through 40057	6701 through 6800
B-17G-15-VE	42-97436 through 97535	6801 through 6900
B-17G-20-VE	42-97536 through 97635	6901 through 7000
B-17G-25-VE	42-97636 through 97735	7001 through 7100
B-17G-30-VE	42-97736 through 97835	7101 through 7200
B-17G-35-VE	42-97836 through 97935	7201 through 7300
B-17G-40-VE	42-97936 through 98035	7301 through 7400
B-17G-45-VE	44-8001 through 8100	7401 through 7500
B-17G-50-VE	44-8101 through 8200	7501 through 7600
B-17G-55-VE	44-8201 through 8300	7601 through 7700
B-17G-60-VE	44-8301 through 8400	7701 through 7800
B-17G-65-VE	44-8401 through 8500	7801 through 7900
B-17G-70-VE	44-8501 through 8600	7901 through 8000
B-17G-75-VE	44-8601 through 8700	8001 through 8100
B-17G-80-VE	44-8701 through 8800	8101 through 8200
B-17G-85-VE	44-8801 through 8900	8201 through 8300
B-17G-90-VE	44-8901 through 9000	8301 through 8400
B-17G-95-VE	44-85492 through 85591	8401 through 8500
B-17G-100-VE	44-85593 through 85691	8501 through 8600
B-17G-105-VE	44-85692 through 85791	8601 through 8700
B-17G-110-VE	44-85792 through 85841	8701 through 8750